The Age of Dis-Consent

Also by Christopher G. Moore

Novels in the Vincent Calvino crime fiction series

Spirit House o *Asia Hand* o *Zero Hour in Phnom Penh*
Comfort Zone o *The Big Weird* o *Cold Hit*
Minor Wife o *Pattaya 24/7* o *The Risk of Infidelity Index*
Paying Back Jack o *The Corruptionist* o *9 Gold Bullets*
Missing in Rangoon o *The Marriage Tree* o *Crackdown*

Other novels

A Killing Smile o *A Bewitching Smile* o *A Haunting Smile*
His Lordship's Arsenal o *Tokyo Joe* o *Red Sky Falling*
God of Darkness o *Chairs* o *Waiting for the Lady*
Gambling on Magic o *The Wisdom of Beer*

Non-fiction

Heart Talk o *The Vincent Calvino Reader's Guide*
The Cultural Detective o *Faking It in Bangkok*
Fear and Loathing in Bangkok

Anthologies

Bangkok Noir o *Phnom Penh Noir*
The Orwell Brigade

The Age of Dis-Consent

CHRISTOPHER G. MOORE

Heaven Lake Press

Distributed in Thailand by:
Asia Document Bureau Ltd.
P.O. Box 1029
Nana Post Office
Bangkok 10112 Thailand
Fax: (662) 260-4578
Web site: http://www.heavenlakepress.com
email: editorial@heavenlakepress.com

First published in Thailand
by Heaven Lake Press, an imprint
of Asia Document Bureau Ltd.
Printed in Thailand

Jacket design: K. Jiamsomboon
Author's photograph: Ralf Tooten © 2012

ISBN 978-616-7503-31-8

To the memory of Charlie Hebdo staff:
Stéphane Charbonnier (Charb), Jean Cabut (Cabu),
Georges Wolinski, Bernard Verlhac (Tignous),
Philippe Honoré, Elsa Cayat, Mustapha Ourad,
and Bernard Maris.

Contents

PART I
Thailand in the Age of Dis-Consent

1 Ordinary Shareholders and Thailand's Political Buffet
3

2 The Age of Dis-Consent 10

3 Hearts and Minds 19

4 Bangkok's Rabbit Hole 24

5 Neutrality as a Remedy for Political Stalemate in Thailand
32

6 Silence 41

PART II
Thai Law Enforcement and Cultural Mindset

7 Baby Factory Dad: The Coming of the First Super
Baby-Maker Dad Singularity 47

8 The High Cost of Badly Paid Cops 56

9 Guarding the Gold in Thailand 63

10 No Broken Windows 70

11 Impulse Control and Crime 78

12 Judging the Judges: Distrust and the Rise of Violence
against Courts 83

13 Personalized Swat Teams for The Filthy Rich 92

PART III
Evolution of Violence & the Borderless World

14 Violence: The Next Big Leap   105

15 The Boundary Lines of Your Life   114

16 Existential Fear in a Secular Age   123

17 Updating Madness   128

18 Grooming 150 friends   133

PART IV
Crime Investigation in a Changing World

19 Digital Tracking of Corruption   145

20 Citizen Detectives: An Online World of Investigations   152

21 Online Commercial Sex: The Digital Age of Victimless Crimes   160

22 The Online Sleuths and the Cold Case   167

23 "Taser-Like" Cuffs for the Twenty-first Century   173

24 Chimeras in the Forensic Lab   177

25 Forensic Trends to Watch   181

26 Predicting Future Crime with Big Data   185

PART V
Space, Time, Technology & Cultural Gravity

27 Disruptions   193

28 Discontinuity   199

29 Duration   211

PART VI
Information and Theory of Mind

30 Where Do You Get Your Information?   221

31 The Global Language of Bias: What Do We Use
   Language For?   225

32 The Illusion of Understanding   232

33 Spotlights and Flashlights   242

34 The Twilight of Prophecy Cultures   251

35 Crunching Big Numbers, Understanding Short Lists
   261

PART VII
On Writing and Authors

36 The Graying of Word Weavers   275

37 Beagle Sailing Lessons for Writing   279

38 Fictional Character Migration into the Digital World
   288

39 An Orwellian Look at Henry Miller   297

40 Kafka the Grand Master of Noir: A Lesson for
   Thailand   304

41 Man With a Scarf   309

Part I

Thailand in the Age of Dis-Consent

Ordinary Shareholders and Thailand's Political Buffet

I like this quote:

> "The poor have sometimes objected to being governed badly; the rich have always objected to being governed at all."—G.K. Chesterton

When I posted it on Twitter this week (in early December 2013), a lot of other people liked and retweeted it. The reason these words by G.K. Chesterton resonate today in Thailand and many other countries is that they sum up the dissatisfaction with government in both classes.

Let's face it. Government is a necessary evil we need in order to find a way to live with each other. Anarchy as an alternative creates a dystopia more bleak, dark, and dangerous than just about any political system (unless you have the misfortune to live in North Korea or Somalia). Most other systems are in various degrees of crisis, revolution, or civil war. Government is a tough racket to keep from running into the ditch.

In Thailand, on the political front, no one is happy with the current impasse. Two polarized sides blame each other for every failure, problem, or mistake over the last dozen years. Now it has all come to a head. The last couple of weeks saw an increase in strong emotions on both sides, and since that happened, finding a way to lower the temperature inside the political cauldron has proved elusive.

Over the last few weeks the traditional elites and their middle-class allies in Bangkok have taken to the streets. Their initial action was in the best democratic tradition, in which people march and voice their objections to government policy and decisions. The right to demonstrate is healthy for a democracy. Like freedom of expression, protest demonstrations are an essential part of the democratic process.

The initial goal of the most recent round of demonstrations was to pressure the government to drop an amnesty bill that would have cleared criminal and civil actions against former prime minister Thaksin Shinawatra, and that goal was achieved. Success didn't stop the protest but embolded it to move on to pressuring the government to accept the validity of a questionable decision by the Constitutional Court that effectively bars the government from amending the constitution.

The controversial constitutional amendment passed by the government would have turned the partially elected senate back into the wholly elected body it was before the 2006 coup. And finally the protest demanded that the prime minister and cabinet resign and a caretaker government be appointed. A house dissolution and election were insufficient. The protesters demanded a "people's council" to take over governing. But who elects the people's council?

There lies the rub. Elections. Thailand's Bangkok elites, who mainly support the Democrat Party, have failed to outvote their upcountry cousins in the North and Northeast, who consistently walk away with an electoral majority for the Pheu Thai Party, headed (at the time of writing) by Prime Minister Yingluck Shinawatra, little sister of the ousted Mr. Thaksin. The last time the Democrat Party formed a government, they had the assistance of the military to lever them into the driver's seat. Following the 2006 coup that tore up the 1997 constitution and removed Mr. Thaksin's administration, the Democrats replaced the previous government, which had won an election mandate to govern, with their own.

The demonstration leadership, under ex-Democrat MP and ex-deputy prime minister Suthep Thaugsuban, having tasted success and having the government on the run, saw an opening to implement its plans to radically alter the existing constitutional and political system and install a wholly new system. The anti-government demonstration was a strange bird: part-coup, part-revolution, part-rock concert—with portable toilets, tents, bamboo matts and a well-stocked mobile kitchen. It turned out the real complaint was not just the elected government but the political system enshrined—irony alert—in the 2007 constitution written under the careful eye of the military. How can we put it— the military-inspired constitution proved too much on the side of a liberal democracy for the Bangkok elites.

Despite the polarized political divide in Thailand, both sides are pro-business, pro-capitalist. No one is arguing that the free-market economic system in Thailand (where there is full employment) needs to be destroyed and replaced with a different economic model. It's not that kind of revolution.

The political issue arises because of a fundamental disagreement over who should be in charge of economic and political systems. As with a large company, Thailand's resources are spread over a large number of people. Let's call them shareholders. In a company, the dividend paid out depends on the earnings, and the board of directors determines the amount of the distribution to the shareholders. Also, the members of a company's board of directors stand for election, and the shareholders vote. In a parliamentary system, the government acts as the board of directors. Citizens, like shareholders, choose with their votes among those competing for positions of authority and power.

Political systems also distribute dividends, and that is why elections are so important and the stakes are so high. This is where the food metaphor kicks in. To add another layer to the metaphorical cake, think of a buffet. Everyone demands both a big share of the buffet and for someone else to pick up the check at the end of the meal. The buffet isn't unlimited. As the number of chairs around the table expands, the original diners view the newer ones as threatening to eat them out of their Bangkok condos and holiday homes.

The problem for the pro-establishment in Thailand is that the new diners feel they have had enough of the Bangkok elites, who traditionally have offered them crumbs and leftovers. They started *demanding* their fair share of the main course—and the pie, cigars, and brandy too. In such circumstances competition comes into play. As in the corporate world, in the political world those who have a monopoly see no reason to give it up. What we witness in this drama is a page out of the human nature newsreel as people fight over a place at the table, one of the chairs, the food, and the bill. Greed rears its head, talons and fangs appear, and fat cats and skinny cats circle each other around the table. Voters choose candidates for all kinds of reasons, but an important one is the hope that they will fairly distribute the buffet's offerings to them. Another way of looking at populism is that the buffet line becomes much longer.

To return to the idea of a political system behaving like a corporate governance system, it is important to understand the purpose of a stock market, which is to raise capital. Capital formation depends on convincing shareholders to invest in shares. The democratic political process operates on a similar idea. Politicians need to raise political capital and are willing to pay hard cash to do so, meaning that political capital is more than an ego trip. A company raises capital on the financial markets by persuading investors to part with their money. Politicians raise political capital by promising voters benefits so they will vote for them. And in Thailand that can often involve a cash transaction (and no side has clean hands in vote buying). A political system also needs to raise political capital. We judge the legitimacy of a political system by the ways it sets the rules governing how politicians are required to raise political capital sufficient to send them to parliament. Once that candidate is elected, many of those promises may be compromised or forgotten, but a politician knows that sooner or later he or she is answerable for an accounting at the ballot box.

Protest leader Suthep Thaugsuban has a plan to restructure the political process that would result in eliminating a citizen's right to vote. Viewed from a company standpoint, the effect is to replace the ordinary shareholders with the preferred shareholders. Only these preferred shareholders, presented as "good people," are entrusted with the right to vote, and they will vote for the board of directors of the "good people." In other words, the minority calls the shots, and there is no mechanism for voting the minority out of office. Flipping back to the food metaphor, the buffet line is closed. No chairs may be added at the table. Newcomers are shown the door.

This maneuver looks suspiciously like a backdoor, hostile privatization of a public company. It is more like an old-fashioned nationalization of shares without compensation for the loss to the ordinary shareholder. In the capitalist world, throwing shareholders out of the buffet room is viewed with suspicion. Drones were built for that eventuality. Without some palpable threat, no ordinary shareholder is going to accept the excuse that their interests are better served by the preferred shareholders.

In the case of Thailand, should a trial balloon to suspend the next election become a reality, and should the appointment of a self-governing people's council come about, the effect would be to annul general elections, and perhaps that could be the spark for considerable violence. Inside the newly privatized political process, the preferred shareholders would call all of the shots, including the suspension of "populist" policy tricks that anti-democracy proponents believe are the heart of the problem.

At this moment there are many unanswered political questions being raised in Thailand. Voters, like ordinary shareholders, like the buffet spread that Thaksin Shinawatra's political parties have delivered to them. Taking away their plates, spoons, and forks and chasing them from the table won't be an easy task. What price will the preferred shareholders, the Bangkok elite, pure capitalists in their hearts, be prepared to pay to take back the buffet room for themselves? The answer is unclear.

What is more clear is that many anti-democratic protesters unite around the idea that political capital is only raised from the "good people," and ordinary shareholders aren't clever or educated enough to be considered "good" and are therefore excluded from direct involvement in the political process. That idea underestimates them. Once people have been to a good buffet, no one can take away that memory. To be tossed out the door not because you've lost an election but because an elite thinks you're stupid is the kind of argument that won't win a lot of friends.

However, the opposition's argument isn't about winning friends; it's about defeating an enemy. Ultimately, a basic complaint by conservative forces is that liberal democracy helps "bad" people obtain political power over the "good" ones. The assumption is that ordinary people should be happy that the good people, the preferred people, are committed to running the system according to old values, traditions, and customs for running the "company" and the "buffet."

But you other lot, they seem to say, you go back to your bowl of sticky rice, fish sauce and *som tum*. And this is your karma; actually it is your own fault we are protesting. You, the ordinary shareholders, with your upcountry snout in our Bangkok buffet, are enablers of an evil, corrupt family that abuses political power. Besides, you are trying to sit in my chair and eat off my plate!

It is doubtful that members of this group of anti-democratic elites would ever go to the capital market to raise funds for one of their companies with such a policy statement set out in their prospectus. But when it comes to the political buffet, in Thailand people on the streets are debating when the "good people" will once again have the authority to decide the menu and who gets to stay at the head table and go for second helpings.

The Age of Dis-Consent

Consent, or the absence of consent—as I wrote as events in Bangkok unfolded quickly in early January, 2014—is a crucial concept that runs like an operating system inside political, criminal justice and social systems. In a democratic system, consent of the governed allows for a co-operative basis for the co-ordination of the administration and distribution of governmental services. Only dictatorship can ignore the consent of those it rules; instead of consent, the population is managed with weapons, prisons, and gulags to process those who demand consent.

Consent is important. So what does it mean in a political and social context?

There is a minimum age before a person can "consent" to having sex, to becoming contractually bound, to marrying, and to being governed. Below a certain age the person's consent is irrelevant. The theory is that such a "young" person lacks the capacity to form consent—the assumption being that until a person reaches a certain age, he or she can't judge matters of importance for himself or herself. The concept of a young person under the age of consent is void in a number of areas, including voting. The age for each of these categories shifts across cultures. How we structure consent is a cultural construct that is shared by people who are born and raised and live inside that culture.

Our idea of consent also applies to which groups are included in (or excluded from) the political process. Requirements for participation aren't limited to age. For example, blacks in South Africa, regardless of age, were excluded from voting in South Africa under apartheid. Criminals and the insane are commonly excluded from voting in modern democracies. So are non-citizens such as immigrants. Such a category exclusion is significant. An immigrant physicist or heart surgeon can't vote, while a citizen with no education, no job, and low mental ability can vote. Deciding who is in the electorate and who is out is itself a political decision, one that every country makes.

If your consent is embedded in the political process, you have a channel to shape and influence the officials who make and enforce the laws that affect the lives of citizens. Consent in a democracy is egalitarian. Consent in a non-democracy could mean that many citizens have no more political status to influence government than an illegal immigrant.

The current political impasse in Thailand, in my view, is largely an argument about who gives consent, how consensus is formed, and the extent to which dissenting views of a government's legitimacy are tolerated as it makes public policy, allocates funds for such policies, and creates the institutions of government through legal frameworks. A battle over an expansion of consent can be found in a recent ruling by the NACC (National Anti-Corruption Commission), an independent agency, which found a prima facie case against 308 MPs who voted to amend the constitution to make the senate a wholly elected body. At present under the constitution, it is half-elected and half-appointed. As a result, the 308 MPs may be banned from politics.

The decision should be put in context. Under the 1997 constitution, the Thai senate was wholly elected. The selection process was changed to a half-elected body in the constitution that followed a military coup that toppled a popularly elected government in 2006.

The traditional cultural system in Thailand is based on patronage and a hierarchy of ranks and statuses. Consent of the larger population is not part of such a system. Patronage was never designed as an egalitarian system or based on any ideal of equality. A patron will take care of those who rely upon his position and authority even if it means abuse of power. Benefits and privileges in a patronage system are not allocated in a transparent, public way. Large, mass-based consent is not how the patronage system works. But Thailand is also a fledgling democracy overlaying the more ancient patronage system. The problem has been that the two systems work off different playbooks. The democratic system pulls to an expansion of consent as the basis of legitimacy, and that means winning elections. The patronage system rests on notions of loyalty, unity, authority, status, and rank that provide an alternative to consent obtained by an election. A patronage system has its own internal checks and balances to monitor cheating and deception, and a patron who is too greedy will suffer from lack of loyalty.

Each political system has a founding myth and set of metaphors. The metaphor that describes a patronage system is the family. The father (patriarch), mother (matriarch), children and extended family make decisions based on their status and authority. Children don't have the right to withhold their consent to go to school, for instance, or to do their homework. The father's decision is the law, but as he's benevolent and loves his family, consent isn't (in his mindset) needed as he's always motivated to be fair, just, kind, and decent; he ensures that the family's needs are met.

When this metaphor is scaled up to run a modern nation state, problems emerge. There is an uneasy tension between the forces of domination and those on the receiving end of rules, regulations, and restrictions, who demand a voice. Absolute political domination is the unrestricted power to use education, threats, censorship, imprisonment, exile, or force to dominate the lives of others without the consent of the dominated. In the West, at various times in the past, whole classes of people had no way to offer or withhold their consent to political domination. Non-whites, women, and non-property owners lacked the right to vote. Their opinions, interests, desires, and needs might have had indirect influence, but without consent their political expression was faint and easily ignored. The expansion of political consent has been a slow process over hundreds of years in advanced democracies such as the United Kingdom and the United States. Over a long time the population granted political consent gradually expanded to replace the simple idea of the family unit as the model for decision-making.

What makes democracy an unusual political system is that it is premised on the consent of all citizens. Other systems of government hoard consent for a few: the elite, the "good people," or those inside a networked, narrowly defined ruling system. It is often said democracies don't declare wars on each other; they trade with each other and have economic interests that would be harmed by warfare. Another reason is that a democracy with a draft ensures that everyone's sons and daughters would be at risk in wartime, and consent for sending them to into harm's way is a restriction on the military's decision to go to war. War is a political decision. Going to war requires, at least in a democracy, the consent of the majority of the citizens. It is their children, parents, and spouses who will be killed and injured, and they think twice when it's their own kin who are ordered to patrol inside a killing zone.

The idea of consensus comes from a commonly shared consent to a course of action, a policy decision, an investment, or an expansion or contraction of programs. Forming consensus is a rocky, unpaved road, and conflict is the norm. Agreement by all whose interests are involved is unusual. Only in a utopia is there no conflict. In the political sphere democracy allows these conflicts to be worked out with concessions until a consensus is reached. That is why democracy has the reputation of being messy; finding consensus amongst millions of people is a messy process.

Dissent is the withholding of consent, or it might take the form of contesting that the authorities making a new policy, implementing an old policy, or distributing benefits have acted without consent. In a democracy there is an acceptance that dissent is part of the deal. Not everyone will agree to the consensus position on an issue. Those in the minority are left to register their dissent in a number of ways. Demonstrations, protests, boycotts, public petitions, referendums, recalls, and social media campaigns are common examples as those in the minority seek to undermine the consensus and substitute a new consensus in its place. Dissent is difficult to accept in a system that demands unity and conformity. Dissent can also be the response to dictatorial governments that either ignore or minimize the group of citizens that consent is extended to. Criminal defamation law and other laws work to keep dissent within defined boundaries and to punish those who venture beyond them.

In the heat of the current political turmoil, much has been written about corruption. In a patronage system it is no surprise that nepotism and cronyism are widespread. Such a system is, after all, little more than a scaling up of arrangements made inside a family. Of course, members of the family help out each other and their friends. When the family is nearly 70 million people, there are limits to the feasibility of the scaling, particularly when the family comprises different regions, ethnic backgrounds, and local customs, in a nation ever more aware of its diversity.

That gift of cash to the family friend who helped little Lek get into a highly competitive elite school isn't seen as corruption in a patronage system. It is how the system is designed to work. As power is in a few hands, the common consensus is that such things as appointing friends and relatives to official positions, or helping a friend to avoid arrest and imprisonment for a criminal offense, or colluding in distributing payments under the table, are all just lubrication of the patron–client relationship. Such activities are not flaws in the system but a feature of it; they account for how and why the system works and remains stable. Personality cults arise from the patronage system, and the powerful design laws as if they were weaponized ordnance to defeat opponents who challenge the patriarch. As with killer drones, the enforcement of laws isn't about justice but efficiently eliminating challengers who threaten the system.

In a democracy inevitably there will be corruption, but it is kept at the margins, being more difficult to conceal and justify. If voters are promised universal health care, some might say that is "corrupt" as the candidate and ruling party are "buying" votes and a bought vote doesn't represent "true" consent. A bought vote is not counted because a "genuine" vote requires true consent. The government's legitimacy, in this way of thinking, means that the motives of those giving consent must be examined as well as the political intentions of those who receive the consent from the voters.

The nature of voting is for a political party to promise voters that electing them to office will return a range of policies serving their interests. Cynics argue that most policy decisions are too complex for ordinary voters to understand, and they are easily manipulated by sleek political advertisement campaigns that appeal to emotions.

At the same time, when a patron acts to advance or protect the interest of those who shelter under his power umbrella, it begins to look like a prototype of vote buying. A patron who can't protect his charges will find his power and standing diminished. In a face culture the patron is aware that if he fails to protect, his reputation is tarnished. Patrons (in theory) fight hard to protect their *luk nong* (the Thai expression for those under the charge of the patron). Unexpected switching of roles can and does happen. In the recent case of a Thai beer empire heiress, the daughter was requested by the father to lower her public profile in participating in street demonstrations to limit voting rights. She refused. There is irony in the refusal by one in the younger generation who demonstrated alongside others in the streets of Bangkok to, among other things, impose limits on the voting system, to keep the old system.

The problem for the old system in Thailand is that once the idea of consent is expanded, it creates a widespread expectation that voters can influence policy and reward politicians who exercise power under a regime of consent, and at that point withdrawing consent is difficult. Once the Americans freed the slaves, what if a majority of American voters had voted to reintroduce slavery? Would this have been a legitimate expression of majority consent? Or what if the majority voted to withdraw the right of women to participate in elections?

The reality is that once political participation through consent has been enshrined, there may (and likely will be) a fringe of people who will work to undo that decision. Another reality is that taking away consent, once given, is going to be a bloody event. A reversal of this kind would be viewed as an enslavement by default, and a return to a purely patronage system, where relationships to power are based on concepts that devalue consent as the measuring stick for legitimacy.

On January 7, 2014, an educated middle-class Bangkok Thai man held up a handwritten sign that said "Respect My Vote" at an event organized by the Democrat Party under the title "Eradicate Corruption, Committed in Reforms." When former prime minister and Democrat Party leader Abhisit Vejjajiva suggested from the stage that the man had been sent by a rival, the protester replied, "I am not your rival. I am the people"—a reply that echoed the ancient cry, "I am Spartacus." The words "Respect My Vote" had cropped up on T-shirts and posters during the American presidential election in 2012. And now "Respect My Vote" has gone viral on Thai social media.

Thailand is stuck in the transition between patronage and democracy. The difference distills to a sound-bite-size distinction between Respect My Authority and Respect My Vote. And it won't be resolved until the idea of consent can be reconciled with the governing system and mutual respect based on equality gains acceptance by all parties.

In Thailand the scope, nature, and power of consent as the way to judge legitimacy is at the heart of the current political storm. The thing to remember: this storm never blows over. There are never clear skies politically or economically. The old generation and the rich cling to what they have and resist changes that threaten their position. They don't consent to change. The patronage system has worked for them. But a new generation and the poor have come to see giving their consent by voting as normal. Taking that right away or diminishing it with a thousand tiny cuts will not be the solution going forward.

Parents don't let go of their children easily. And children, once they've left home, aren't happy to be forced back into living under their father's house rules. As a civilian observer in the 1980s, riding with the NYPD in the early hours, I learned firsthand from the police a couple of lessons. First, both sides in a domestic argument believe that right is on their side. They become highly emotional. Kitchens are full of knives and other possible weapons. People are drunk. They are enraged. They are armed. And that's why cops everywhere, not just in New York, hate taking a domestic violence call. Because they know from experience there is a high chance someone is going to get hurt. The equivalent of police dispatchers in Thailand are calling in a domestic dispute that is just about to get out of hand.

Hearts and Minds

February 14, 2014. Valentine's Day. On this day for winning hearts, protesters remain in the streets of Bangkok. There has been another push from protest leaders to call the masses into the streets to support their anti-government demonstrations.

In war, politics, and love, winning "hearts and minds" separates the victors from the vanquished. I find significance in the traditional word ordering of this phrase. Start with the heart, and the mind will follow. The idea is straight from Hume and every modern psychologist led by Daniel Kahneman. If you can emotionally involve another person, the hard battle is won. The mind simply fills in the justification for the heart's decision.

The hearts and minds drama is being played out in the streets of Bangkok. It also has a psych ops pattern worth exploring. If one were clever and devious enough, the best line of attack would be to undermine the populist programs of the government by turning the recipients of these programs against the government.

Let's talk about Thailand's rice farmers. Any psych op that would win the hearts of rice farmers might represent a political turning point. This is an interesting story. The vast bulk of rice farmers live in the Northeast and North of

Thailand. Many of them are known as the Redshirts and are loyal supporters of the government. The Red movement is committed to representative democracy and elections. Since the election of Thaksin Shinawattra in 2001, rice farmers have voted in super majorities for members of his political party.

The current political turmoil finds his sister, Prime Minister Yingluck Shinawattra, who led the Pheu Thai Party to the polls on February 2, dealing with months of unrest led by ex-MPs of the rival Democrat Party, who resigned and took to the streets to bring down her government. The protesters have used various means in their struggle—blocking roads, cutting electricity and water to government offices, blocking polling stations, "arresting" and beating up people, even threatening kidnapping the prime minister's son. Thus far ten people have been killed and hundreds injured in violent incidents related to the anti-government protests.

The protest leaders have shifted their reason for attacking the government from an ill-conceived amnesty bill, an allegedly illegal attempt to amend the constitution (the government wanted a fully elected as opposed to a half-elected, half-appointed senate) and to the usual standby: corruption. The protest leaders have had their bank accounts frozen by a government agency. They have marched around Bangkok gathering "donations" to support their protest.

So far the protesters, looking at the dwindling numbers in the streets (sometimes a handful) are not winning the hearts and minds of their fellow Thais. But they have a new idea. The authority of the caretaker government having been effectively reduced, it isn't surprising problems are arising, such as payments which are now owing to rice farmers under a controversial rice subsidy scheme that by all accounts is riddled with problems, drawing allegations of mismanagement and corruption. The protesters, having closed down the ability of the government to pay the farmers, now blame the government for failing to deliver the payments. The protesters have powerful allies. The National Anti-Corruption Commission (NACC) is expected to bring formal charges against the caretaker prime minister for her role in the rice-pledging scheme.

The message is being spread that this heartless government you voted for is letting you down. They created a bad program. The local English-language newspapers, which are heavily anti-government, run stories of rice farmers committing suicide over money worries. They show five hundred rice farmers who have come to Bangkok to complain to the government.

The protesters have a new message that goes something like this:

> Democracy isn't your friend. Your friends pay you. This government is a false friend. Voting and democracy are unreliable. They cheat you.
>
> If your heart is in democracy, you will only be disappointed.
>
> Join us. Sing with us. Come to our picnics and nightly concerts. Happy Valentine's Day, rice farmers! We love you! Wait for the new T-shirts we've ordered.
>
> Even though we called you water buffalo and said you were stupid last month, that was last month. Forget about that. This month we are your friend and your savior.

In fact, the objective appears to be an old-fashioned psych ops plan to sow the seeds of discontent and doubt in the hearts of rice farmers. It is a cynical ploy (but brilliant at the same time), and given the track record of Bangkok's elite caring about the "hearts" of rice farmers, the odds are high that it won't work.

Still, the pitch is being made that if the rice farmers would only return to traditional Thai values, their betters in Bangkok would take care of them, just as they always have. People in Bangkok have given 10 or 20 million baht in cash handouts to the protest leader, who in turn, playing the role of "big-faced man," is to give it to grateful rice farmers. That's a photo that anyone connected with this psych op will want to frame and put on his wall.

There are several problems with this approach. It assumes that rice farmers can't see through the offer to its underlying purpose, which is to discredit populist programs and the government that sponsors them. At the core of this Valentine from the street is the message that the protesters and their allies are the ones with true hearts. Given that the outstanding amount owed under the rice subsidy scheme is in the billions, the donations in Bangkok handed to a protest leader are the equivalent of a rounding off error in the larger scheme of this mountain of debt, but that doesn't matter.

What does matter in this coded message, sent over the heads of the democratically elected government to their main rural constituency, which continues to return them to office no matter how many times the elites ban their party and leaders, is that democracy lacks the traditional Thai heart. Walk away from democracy, this Valentine is saying, as you would walk away from an abusive lover. That true Thai heart is found in the ancient concept of the *kreng jai* system, where the good people aren't elected (a concept that can go so very wrong) but are known by their rank, position, name, and status. They decide what is right, moral, fair, and just. Trust them. Trust their heart—their *nam jai*, "water heart." They have shown their good intentions by collecting donations for the rice farmers. Has the government done that?

Here's their story in a nutshell: Heartless government. Overflowing heart of protesters.

The battle for the hearts and minds of Thailand's rural voters will continue. The idea is that these donations to rice farmers will pay several dividends. The rice farmers will return a respectful *wai* of gratitude for the handout and, more importantly, will turn their backs on the unreliable government and democracy. It remains to be seen whether this will happen. I suspect that very few people who labour in the rice fields of the North or Northeast are betting their farm on the protesters looking after their long-term interests. The seeds of democracy have been planted and have yielded too many good crops for the supporters to return to the days of waiting for a coin to be dropped in their rice bowl.

Happy Valentine's Day.

Bangkok's Rabbit Hole

"Off with their heads!"—Lewis Carroll, *Alice's Adventures in Wonderland*

Power. Grab it. Earn it. Put it to a vote. The tango between power and violence is the stuff of literature. Steven Pinker's *The Better Angels of Our Nature: Why Violence Has Declined* illustrates a dramatic decrease of violence over the centuries. But the world I live in today (February 28, 2014) seems extremely violent, making such a statement appear counterintuitive. Facts are facts. And which way you ought to go, as the Cheshire Cat told Alice, "depends a good deal on where you want to get to."

In part, the thirty-fold decrease in violence means we are historically far less likely to be a victim of homicide than our ancestors. But homicide, like the future (to use William Gibson's clever observation) is unevenly distributed across countries and cultures. Richard Florida in "What the Most Violent Nations in the World Have in Common" cites three factors that explain why there are elevated homicide rates in some cultures and not others: (1) social and economic inequality, (2) gender inequality, and (3) the macho index, based on levels of masculinity, testosterone, and aggression. Florida's article focuses on private acts of violence that result in death. The question is whether these factors may also explain why some states are more ready to use violence against their citizens or why protesters in these places resort to violence against the state and its security forces.

It is public violence by state authorities and those challenging state authorities that is a common thread in the political struggles in Ukraine, Egypt, Syria, Venezuela, and Thailand. Violence of this kind has escalated in Thailand since January 2014. What is the cause of this surge in political violence in Thailand? There is no simple answer, though Richard Florida's three factors are a guide to following the precursors of violence. We had bombings and shootings. Twenty-two victims are dead. Hundreds have been injured. Four children are dead from bombings and shootings.

What emerges when you drop down the rabbit hole is that the world inside offers up a wide variety of possible sources to explain these deaths. It is one thing to describe violence. It is another to explain it. Pundits make lots of explanations of causality that are convincing and plausible. But don't be fooled. Plausibility and truth are two different matters.

What appears to fuel the current Thai power struggle is a controversy over who has the legitimate right to exercise power. At the heart of the political turmoil is a perplexing issue: on what basis does the caretaker government support its claim to govern in Thailand? Owning power, through an electoral mandate, tribal tradition, military coup, or a strongman, can be traced like bullet wounds in the corpse of empires and nations recounted in political history. Long before *The Lord of the Rings* was written, Abraham Lincoln said, "Nearly all men can stand adversity, but if you want to test a man's character, give him power."

Power means that A can compel B to do or not do an act that B wouldn't otherwise wish to do. For example, obtain a driver's license before driving, pay taxes, or refrain from drinking and driving. You don't have the option of refusal. You can be compelled with the threat of violence to do something you don't wish to. Objects of power are taught a script to perform, and the best script makers don't need guns to enforce their power over the actors. The actors patrol themselves for accuracy, which means loyalty.

Power, at its best, safeguards the larger interests of a community, and individuals sacrifice a degree of freedom they would otherwise have to accommodate such interests. Power is a river with many streams. Elections are one way power is conferred as a communal agreement; the elected power holder has legitimacy in forcing others, within legal means, to comply with new policies and laws. Power also has other rivers that flow from the barrel of a gun, a family name, a reputation for brutality, or cultural custom.

Power also means claiming privileges and immunities. Absolute power means the laws of the land do not apply to the empowered person. He or she can bury alive hundreds of public ministers or court officials on a whim. Chinese history has a number of such examples to illustrate the dangers of concentrated power. Less dramatic but still substantial is the power that comes with vast wealth, through cartels and monopolies, through the accumulation of data about your private life, or through the power to indoctrinate children with the ideology to support the powerful. True power has the capacity to make us fearful or grateful, or to silence us. There's also the power to use networks to defeat opponents.

Political power needs to be monitored and checked, and for good reason. Over time, despite the best intentions, the power holder will exhibit arrogant behavior. His privileges become entitlements. The attitude spreads like an epidemic, infecting the whole ruling class with hubris. Once the unrestrained power virus spreads through agencies, courts, armies, and civil servants, the capacity for empathy with the governed is destroyed.

The monopoly on violence is fragile. The state in many places is losing control over violence. The danger is that power and violence are being privatized, like shares sold in a state enterprise in one of those rigged auctions.

People with power are wary of those who would challenge their power, compete for it, or question it. Freedom of expression is the first defense that ordinary non-powerful people seek; it exists as a peaceful way to limit the powerful. Free speech allows us to voice our suspicion of power abuses and make the powerful accountable. The two most hated ideas of the powerful are accountability and transparency. It means you can't just shoot whoever you want without some due process preceding the firing of the bullet.

Criminalizing speech is one way the powerful push back to control their challengers. You can read a great deal about the allocation of power arrangements in a country from the degree of freedom or repression in the exercise of political speech. The more free the speech, the more accountable power holders are in the exercise of power. The powerful rarely attack the ideal of free speech. The really powerful aren't quite that stupid. They have another argument up their sleeve. As Christopher Hitchens wrote, "What better way for a ruling class to claim and hold power than to pose as the defenders of the nation?" Thus political speech is restricted to prevent "enemies" from attacking the institutions of the state and those who are the face of such institutions. The powerful need enemies, real or imagined, to give them a mandate. There has been much discussion over the nature and cause of power, including by novelists such as Tolstoy.

"What is the cause of historical events? Power. What is power? Power is the sum total of wills transferred to one person. On what condition are the wills of the masses transferred to one person? On condition that the person express the will of the whole people. That is, power is power. That is, power is a word the meaning of which we do not understand. "—Leo Tolstoy, *War and Peace*

Sometimes the messy battle to merge democratic and non-democratic power centers spills over into violence. Power now stays stable because the aspirations, economic realities, and technology are constantly shifting, often faster than traditional institutions can adapt. This leads modern political forces to undermine the authority and status of existing power holders. These forces respond by abandoning the legislative assembly and taking to the streets. Once they are in the streets, sooner or later violence surfaces. Violence is a weapon to recover lost power.

The purpose of a modern political process is to provide a mechanism to resolve conflict over the exercise of power within democratic institutions. Democracy is a peacekeeping patrol to keep the powerful forces in society from slitting each other's throats. The worry is that one faction will get the upper hand and use that position to put the knife in.

In every political system people have grievances. Never is everyone happy. What is sometimes ignored are the grievances of those who once exercised unquestioned power until losing power in an election. When power is stripped away as a result of an election, such people are left feeling vulnerable and unprotected, that their interests are being unjustly ignored. Anger and hatred, threats and intimidation, and breakdown of law and order follow. They plot to recover what has been lost. George Orwell in *1984* wrote, "We know that no one ever seizes power with the intention of relinquishing it."

It is in the struggle for power that a culture defines itself and the identity of its people is formed.

The never-ending struggle for power is something children need to learn about early on. Some of the best books that children read prepare them to understand the nature of power, its dangers, seductions, violations, and corruptions. *The Lord of the Rings* is a classic for children and adults, and the ring of power becomes a symbol for power's corrupting influence, as well as the greed and excesses surrounding power struggles. Plato wrote, "The measure of a man is what he does with power." If we measure the probabilities of what people will do with power if left to their own devices, it is clear that checks and balances are essential to prevent tyranny.

What literary influences have shaped your opinion about power and violence? And what books would you recommend to a child to learn about power? The books I'd recommend are *Alice in Wonderland*, Golding's *Lord of the Flies*, Philip Pullman's *His Dark Materials* trilogy, and George Orwell's *Animal Farm*. Readers can add their own favourites to this short-list.

Here's a brief reason for each selection:

Alice in Wonderland is a descent into the madness, capriciousness, and arbitrariness of power. There is no better book to illustrate how whim coupled with absolute power creates selfish, dangerous monsters. Once you slide down that rabbit hole, you enter an alien world of Mad Hatters.

Lord of the Flies illustrates the tribal nature of power, the symbolic nature of power attached to an object, and the abuses that lead to horrible acts of violence and murder. Stranded on an island, boys revert to a feral state where seizing power over others turns into deadly games.

The *His Dark Materials* trilogy (*The Golden Compass, The Subtle Knife,* and *The Amber Spyglass*) is a portal into the corruption of mystical beliefs and ideology by the powerful to enforce conformity and to destroy freedom.

Animal Farm is a parable of power, violence, dictatorship, repression, hatred, and injustice.

The best foundation for the writer of crime fiction, or any genre of writing, can be found in children's literature. You don't need to be a writer to take in the profound insights that will guide your own way through a lifetime of political power plays and public violence. The saddest thing about arriving at adulthood is that so many of these classics are tucked away, spine out, in a forgotten part of our personal library, gathering dust.

I would like to walk you through the maze of the political power struggle in Thailand. Unfortunately, although I set out with a compass and map, a few steps along the path I get hopelessly lost. So I go back and read *Alice in Wonderland* and ask how she did what she did. I am curious to know just how far the rabbit hole goes and what I will find at the other end.

Along my Thai journey of twenty-five years I have uncovered some clues. What I call clues are the things I stop to pay attention to. Do you ever wonder why you pay attention to some things and ignore others? Have you ever thought that just maybe people who live in different rabbit holes, with a different culture and language from yours, might stop to look at different things? That's what I seek to do in my books and essays—examine those different things.

I invite you on a journey of discovery of power and violence. To start, I ask how and why people pay attention to one thing and not another. We share many similarities on this journey, but at the same time it is a winding, twisty road, and sometimes we find that others stop and look at things we'd rush right past. I ask how all of us manage love and hate, fear and hope, lying and truth, justice and injustice. When we all put our noses against the window pane and seek a glimpse of those who control our lives and our freedom and liberty, we have to wonder if they see us as people like them. Or are we invisible?

What happens when we see each other through the pane that separates us? How does it happen that we are on one side and they are on the other? How can I see and understand what people of a different language and different culture see? Do I know to what deep passages inside their rabbit hole their language leads them? I try to follow, but I discover it is hard work understanding life deep under this surface. I try the best way that I can and know that what I witness, describe, and shape into words is a rough approximation of the reality.

I look around Bangkok, where I live, and I feel the pain of the Thais. I see the sadness and worry in their faces. I have witnessed their rage and frustrations. We all started in the same way as those four children killed in the past week. Children want to be loved and to be not just free but care-free. They want crayons and coloring books. Even a child's level of Thai fluency opens an expat's heart to the suffering all of us experience each day.

The bombs and guns, the hate, and the threats are on a page we should turn. Make it go away, a natural child's request. One that I wish was in my power to grant. But it's not. Instead we must face the violence as not some remote event, out of our sight, but as something touching our lives. Only then can we deal with it, and deal with ourselves.

Neutrality as a Remedy
for Political Stalemate in Thailand

No one wants to get in the middle of a fight between opponents who wish to knock each other out. Everyone has a theory of how to stop a fight once it gets started. A neutral party intervenes and tries to separate them. If the emotions are running high, the chances are the combatants will turn their anger on the intervenor.

As I write this (on March 28, 2014), there has been a great deal of public discussion about the merits of an appointed "neutral" prime minister to end the current political impasse in Thailand. There is a public discussion going on about a list of men (no women's names appear on it) who might qualify as a candidate for "neutral PM" by the anti-government side. As expected, this discussion has generated heat and political controversy. The Thai word for "neutral" is *pen klang*, which literally translates to "being in the middle," making it synonymous with "nonpartisan." Whether that middle is defined as geographic, ethical, psychological or ideological raises a number of complex questions.

The news reports tend to orbit around speculations and rumors focused on personalities. Discussions on social media have begun to examine the idea of what it means to be a "neutral" person appointed to high political office to resolve a constitutional crisis in a representative democracy. An examination of neutrality as a political fix in circumstances such as those we find ourselves in, in a climate where the possibility of civil war is openly discussed, may help shed light on whether this is a way out or a dead end.

Howard Zinn, an American historian, had grave doubts about the possibility of being neutral in the midst of a struggle over the political forces to be entrusted with the allocation and exercise of power and the writing and implementing of policy priorities. In *Declarations of Independence: Cross-Examining American Ideology*, Zinn wrote:

> Why should we cherish "objectivity", as if ideas were innocent, as if they don't serve one interest or another? Surely, we want to be objective if that means telling the truth as we see it, not concealing information that may be embarrassing to our point of view. But we don't want to be objective if it means pretending that ideas don't play a part in the social struggles of our time, that we don't take sides in those struggles.
>
> Indeed, it is impossible to be neutral. In a world already moving in certain directions, where wealth and power are already distributed in certain ways, neutrality means accepting the way things are now. It is a world of clashing interests—war against peace, nationalism against internationalism, equality against greed, and democracy against elitism—and it seems to me both impossible and undesirable to be neutral in those conflicts.

Zinn's skepticism about neutrality is shared by Nobel Prize winner Elie Wiesel, who said in his Nobel acceptance speech, later included in *The Night Trilogy: Night/Dawn/The Accident*:

> We must take sides. Neutrality helps the oppressor,
> never the victim. Silence encourages the
> tormentor, never the tormented. Sometimes we
> must interfere. When human lives are endangered,
> when human dignity is in jeopardy, national
> borders and sensitivities become irrelevant.
> Wherever men and women are persecuted
> because of their race, religion, or political views,
> that place must—at that moment—become the
> center of the universe.

On a more basic level Laurell K. Hamilton writes in
Narcissus in Chains: "Personally, I think neutral is just another
way of saving your own ass at the expense of someone
else's."

Neutrality means a country, a leader, or a person of
influence does not take sides in a dispute, conflict, war, or
disagreement between parties waging battle. That battle
may be armed conflict or ideological battles that spill over
from social media, TV, and the press to demonstrators and
protesters in the streets. Such a person is seen by both sides
as having no affiliation with the other party, group, tribe, or
faction to the dispute. Neutrality means no shared ideology
that prefers one side's principles and political values to those
of the other side.

A problem in some quarters in the Thai political debate
is that "neutral" is conflated with "savior." That is an
unreasonable expectation to pin on neutrality. The idea of
a savior takes us back to the core problem of personality-
centered politics. One person's prophet is another's
heretic.

Neutrality can be a distraction from a central problem,
and one such problem shared by countries in this region
(including Burma, Cambodia, Indonesia, the Philippines,

and Vietnam) is the weakness of the rule of law and the corresponding strength of a culture of impunity. To possess true power translates into an immunity that rolls through the system from human rights violations, corruption, "disappearances," and extra-judicial killings to the imprisonment or forced exile of critics. That makes the struggle for power an existential one. The winner and his friends, family, and associates are elevated to life above the rule-of-law line that catches the rest of us. The loser slinks off to exile or prison, assets taken, disgraced.

In a culture of impunity, heretics are dealt with severely. Neutrality is difficult to sow in the thin soil of a culture with a strong tradition of granting the powerful immunity for their actions.

It is one thing for a country to declare neutrality in a war between two other countries, and quite another for a neutral person to emerge from a highly divisive domestic political ground where emotions are high, battle lines are drawn, and consensus is lacking amongst partisans as to whom they believe fits the bill of being neutral.

The appointment of "neutral" persons to lead conflicting parties toward resolution of their differences is a general challenge that runs through all political systems. When it comes to issues like abortion or teaching creationism in public schools, Sarah Palin and the Tea Party's definition of neutrality would differ greatly from Al Gore's, for instance. Which raises another question: can one be neutral on issues like these?

Beyond these "social issues" there are genuine disagreements over the allocation of resources among transport, social security, health, schools, and public safety. If one decodes the anti-government side, the neutrality argument is an alternative to democracy. If a neutral person can be found—someone fair, just, honorable, wise, and compassionate—what reason can justify the cost of an election, when there is a high risk of people being elected whom powerful people distrust? Elections in most places including Thailand choose a politician who isn't neutral, who has never pretended to be neutral, and who has run on a party platform that promised benefits weighted toward the interests of those living in his riding. The purpose of an election isn't to test the neutrality of a candidate. It is to test whether his or her views and opinions appeal more to the voters than the opponent's.

The central purpose of representative democracy is to resolve disagreements through a parliamentary process that represents the majority view of voters. Voting is not a neutral act. It is a partisan choice. People are voting, in theory, out of their own self-interest as well as the larger interests of the country.

This analysis, you may rightly say, is well and fine in a functioning democracy, but what happens when the parliamentary system comes to a standstill? There are a couple of answers. The most obvious one is that democratic systems are chaotic, messy, and uncertain, but that isn't a bad thing. It means a politician who takes a position on an issue must persuade others that his or her policy or plan is rational and timely, and that, if implemented, it will advance the interests of the people. It is utopian to believe any policy could coincide with the interests of 100 percent of the people.

Also, if the parliamentary system is paralyzed and becomes dysfunctional through actions launched by opposition forces seeking to remove an elected government, a larger issue is raised as to the nature and scope of democratic principles accepted in the system. If there is a systemic issue with the nature and process of governance, it is difficult to see how a neutral person can be chosen, and by whom, and if chosen, how such a person can proceed in resolving such a deep, structural issue.

Neutrality is another way to express ideas such as evenhandedness, fair-mindedness, impartiality, and nonpartisanship. Neutral is the opposite of biased, one-sided, partial, prejudiced, or affiliated with a partisan side in a dispute. Power has a public face, but there is also a deep power, hidden from view like dark matter, that shapes and channels the flow of government activity.

Successful headhunting of such an individual to fill the role of so-called neutral prime minister is difficult if not impossible. Who chooses such a person, and who sets the terms of reference for neutrality? Who judges what records, private and public, are relevant to an assessment of neutrality? If that were easy, then those judging the neutrality issue would be neutral themselves, and that doesn't seem like an outcome anyone would be happy with.

What person with sufficient stature to break a deadlock between mortal enemies rises to that position without leaving record of public service, writings, or speeches that connect him or her with the deep power? It is quite natural that even the most respected people have signaled their preferences about process or policy. Anyone distinguished enough to have the necessary gravitas will have taken a position or made a commitment that takes one side or another in an earlier policy debate. The point of democracy is to take a side and defend a policy position and seek to attract public support for that position.

Ultimately politics is about making choices. Who makes the hard decisions? And how transparent is the decision-making process, and how accountable are the decision makers for bad decisions? How do we get rid of leaders who make bad decisions? That is a question that is resolved by ballots or bullets. Neutrality is not a means of conflict resolution. It is a way of avoiding conflict, and rallying cries for the neutral savior rise to the surface when people are seduced by the prospect of an easy way to kick the can down the road.

One of the recurring ideas one hears in Thailand is that Thais seek a middle path to resolve problems. To take that metaphor in another direction, if those in conflict are playing a game of chicken, each on a collision path, neither willing to blink or give way, the neutral person is unlikely to persuade both sides to park their ideological vehicles and shake hands and put their conflict behind them. There will ultimately be a way out of the current crisis in Thailand. It is unlikely, though, to be through the appointment of a "neutral" prime minister.

The public democratic process must be re-engaged, minority rights must be secured against oppression, and government actions must be subject to restraint and accountability. And there needs to be an open discussion on how the tradition of impunity has thwarted democratic development, and what needs to be done to end that tradition. A recent article in *Prachatai* is an excellent examination of Thailand's long record of extra-judicial killings, "disappearances" of lawyers and activists, mistreatment of minority groups, shakedowns, and corruption. No constitution to date has reigned in these abuses, and no neutral person has been able to stop them from happening again.

The architecture of all institutions in a democracy must be designed not just to work in good times but to be resilient through turbulence, when the geology of political expectations and power start to shift. If the institutions are weakened or break down, and the parties refuse to talk to one another, one of the first casualties is the rule of law. Violence accelerates as the rule of law recedes, and this loop further undermines institutions until instability becomes evident for all to witness.

There is no shortcut to a constitution that establishes institutions that can govern, co-ordinate their powers, and check and restrain one another. David Streckfuss, in a *Bangkok Post* opinion piece titled "Risky Road Ahead in Avoiding Civil War," recommended a referendum to ask voters whether they wish to revert to the 1997 constitution (annulled by the 2006 coup), with reforms leading to amendments, or stick with the 2007 constitution. The problem is that an opposition that obstructs and blocks elections would likely see a referendum as another kind of existential threat to its view of the "correct" or "righteous" political path for Thailand. Just as, in theory, an election should be the mechanism to resolve a political impasse, a referendum offers a similar resolution. At this dark time it is unlikely that the traditional mechanism will function to contain the conflict.

Sooner or later, the way forward likely will be leaders who are forced by circumstances to address the issue of what process is appropriate for constitutional change and the substantive nature of such change. Stripping the powerful of their unofficial immunity won't be an easy task. Both sides want immunity and the ability to act with impunity for their interests while denying that right to opponents. Not surprisingly, given what is at stake, there has been a drastic polarization of political forces in Thailand. Meanwhile, one can expect political strife to intensify.

If there is to be a new constitutional framework, it will need widespread consensus among the powerful and the restive electorate caught in the middle of a power struggle. How that constitutional framework will deal with the culture of impunity remains unclear.

Neutrality as a Remedy for Political Stalemate in Thailand

Political conflict at this stage is fueled by fear, anger, and hatred, and that is no climate in which to write a constitution. The architects of the new legal structure will need to wean the players from their addiction to high emotions and easy slogans. They should also learn an important lesson in designing a political system: the new legal structure will require the installation of shock absorbers to enable it to survive future political earthquakes. The political geology of our times promises to deliver substantial seismic activity ahead. And sometimes the health of a system is established when a powerful person isn't able to subvert the course of justice with money and influence but must bear the full weight of the law like an ordinary citizen. Such a turn of events is not going to flow from the words of a new constitution. When this does happen, something will have first changed in the mindset and culture. We are a long way from reaching that point, not just in Thailand but elsewhere in the region and large parts of the world. Meanwhile, we remain hostages to personalities who will never be expected to pay for their crimes.

Silence

"Silence is the ultimate weapon of power."
—Charles de Gaulle

There are two silences that concern me and should concern you.

You'll recognize this statement from the world of American TV and film: "You have the right to remain silent." What usually follows is: "Whatever you say may be used against you in a court of law." This right to be silent is enshrined in the fifth amendment to the United States constitution. Like many constitutional rights, the right to remain silent has been chipped away, sculpted into an object that continues to have similar traits but is a different species. In principle, the right to maintain silence against the vast power of an oppressive state is a symbol of resistance to tyranny.

The right not to speak when questioned by the state is a radical right. The right is your shield against forced self-incrimination. It is why torture and beating are so repulsive and threatening to freedom. In the face of overwhelming power, all citizens, even those we despise and hate, need protection from authorities. One man can stop a column of tanks through sheer defiance. But how long can he stand there before being run over? It's for our own sake that we protect our right to silence. To exempt one is to exempt everyone. The onus is on the authorities to make a case of wrongdoing without torturing the suspect into a confession.

But confessions are popular in many places. Confessions have an enormous advantage: they cut through the tedium of dead-end investigations, paperwork, false leads and trails, and the search for incriminating evidence and witnesses.

The second category of silence is connected to the truth. Freedom of expression is the truth-telling process. Of all the rights spelled out in the American constitution, this is the number one right of a citizen. As George Orwell wrote, "In a time of deceit telling the truth is a revolutionary act." He also wrote, "Political language is designed to make lies sound truthful and murder respectable, and to give an appearance of solidity to pure wind."

Silence is not just a right. It is a condition that can be imposed. Silence can be commanded on political grounds. In this case, not remaining silent becomes a crime. It can be seen as a provocation to those in authority. Under tyranny, both speaking and non-speaking must pass the test of loyalty. There is no other feature in such a system by which silence can be judged.

Silence is one of the aims of repression as it mutes critics, those with the awkward questions, those who wish someone to explain a contradiction, a paradox for which there is no good answer. Silence never embarrasses the authorities; it comforts them.

Illustrating or describing silence in words is difficult. The act of writing breaks the silence. This state of being quiet is both an internal mental process we aren't privileged to witness in others, and an external signal of the silent process. When I am silent, you may guess that something is going on inside my mind, but it remains a guess until I reveal my thoughts.

I can illustrate silence by describing an exterior event. An empty dining room table with a woman reading. A bedroom with an elderly man staring at the ceiling as death approaches. A crime scene with yellow tape draped across a doorway, with a woman in a bloodied blouse staring into space. Silence envelops each, expressing a different range of possibilities for why words are absent.

There is another kind of silence that writers throughout the ages have faced. Not a tyrant seeking to incriminate the writer for a crime he didn't commit, but the tyrant who uses power to stop a writer from voicing criticism, challenging dogma, or pointing out errors, mistakes, flaws, or deceit. Silence in this case is the tyrant's friend and ally. The weight of occupation is the enforced silence the occupiers impose. As with torture or beatings, the command to shut up and obey causes suffering.

Silence in the interrogation room is prohibited. But silence inside the marketplace of ideas may be required. Power has this contradictory relationship with silence. You have to say the state's position on silence depends on the context.

Writers such as George Orwell have been curious about the meaning of silence. Most people are not by nature silent. In a silent room, look for the censor. Ask him the score. He won't be able to tell you more than I've told you: either remain silent or join in praise of the leader. "You see," he says, "we give the same choice to all people. The good people and the bad people are known by their choice."

We have a natural impulse to explain, to discuss, to debate. We test, challenge, and contest theories, beliefs, and principles. But in a time of repression, the spontaneous discussions grind to a dead halt. It is a time for thinking, in silence.

You have a choice. You can be defined by the censor's edict or you step forward in front of a tank. Until this week (this article was first published on May 30, 2014, eight days after the last military coup in Thailand), I never emotionally felt how brave that man at Tiananmen Square was, and how he gives me hope in a world where words bend to the iron will and tanks of rulers. That is our history. What our ancestors experienced. They understood the lesson repeated generation after generation, that to break the official silence is a crime. The truth card won't get you out of jail, and it may well be your one-way ticket to a prison cell.

Here are some thoughts from writers about the nature of silence, truth, and censorship.

"It's a beautiful thing, the destruction of words."
—George Orwell, *1984*

"When truth is replaced by silence, the silence is a lie." —Yevgeny Yevtushenko

"I said nothing for a time, just ran my fingertips along the edge of the human-shaped emptiness that had been left inside me." —Haruki Murakami, *Blind Willow, Sleeping Woman*

"If people cannot write well, they cannot think well, and if they cannot think well, others will do their thinking for them."—George Orwell

"Silence is the ultimate weapon of power."
—Charles de Gaulle

"Orthodoxy means not thinking—not needing to think. Orthodoxy is unconsciousness."
—George Orwell, *1984*

Part II

Thai Law Enforcement and Cultural Mindset

Baby Factory Dad: The Coming of the First Super Baby-Maker Dad Singularity

Twenty-four-year-old Japanese national Mitsutoki Shigeta, who hired multiple surrogate mothers in Thailand, has been a leading news item in the Thai press, both Thai-language and English-language, for a couple of weeks. As I write this on August 22, 2014, there is no sign that the news desk or pundits (or their readers) are growing tired of feeding the public a diet of speculation, outrage, moralizing, finger pointing, and official statements. Mitsutoki Shigeta has ignited social media from Twitter to Facebook. He is becoming one of the most famous Japanese personalities ever. And there are several reasons that the story of this baby factory dad demands a second look.

The Daily Mail has demonstrated that there is a large appetite for scandal, gossip, and conjecture about the famous. When sex is added to the mix, even the non-famous suddenly appear day after day in news accounts. The shambolic local Thai press reports on all of it, and op ed pieces show a remarkable ability to rearrange the facts faster than a cop caught with a car full of drugs. This is a caveat to bear in mind as you read through the "facts" below. The point is, no one has personally interviewed Mitsutoki Shigeta to get his side of the story, his motives, or his future plans, or to ask the biggest question of all, what happened to him at age twenty-one to make him determined to embark on a personal repopulation program?

Shigeta over the past two years has traveled to Thailand approximately sixty times (the press hasn't settled on a precise figure, but the reported range is sixty to sixty-five times). He has, if reports are accurate, Japanese, Hong Kong, Chinese, and Cambodian passports. Big money buys lots of airfares, passports, and, as we shall soon see, children. Apparently he didn't come here to sit on the beach and sip those tall tropical drinks with little bamboo umbrellas. He hired a local lawyer. That's always a sign that someone is either very careful or up to no good, or both. He also hired the services of several clinics that specialized in surrogacy. Shigeta managed in twenty-four months to use surrogates to give birth to fifteen children. Allegedly a number of these children have been moved from Thailand and have been reported to be with nannies in Cambodia.

From his base in Tokyo Shigeta has submitted DNA samples to prove that he is the father. The eggs came from women whose identity has yet to be determined. Local Thai women were paid a fee (up to $10,000) to carry the babies to term. All expenses were paid, including hospital, medical, housing, food, and the services of a nanny when the children were born.

The press has speculated without the slightest shred of evidence that Shigeta wanted the children for: 1) trafficking purposes; 2) selling organs; or 3) other dark, evil purposes they imagined must lurk behind the decision to produce so many babies over a relatively short period of time. The clinics offering surrogacy services are under investigation. A bill that has been knocking around parliament for ten years is suddenly being pushed through by the junta-led regime. The politicians, the press, polite society, the gangsters, the farmers, the workers—all of them are united in the opinion that Shigeta has done something wrong. Broken some law. They can't be certain what law, but they want him to return to Bangkok and tell the police why he wanted so many children.

I have a theory that may or may not be true for Shigeta's case. Rather than Shigeta, of whom we know little at this stage, let's examine a hypothetical Super Baby-Maker Dad. Shigeta's case raises a larger issue—a world where there is no law against a wealthy young male fathering a small town of offspring. The possibility demolishes one of our most cherished and widely agreed-upon social constructs: that people live in family units of a certain dimension. The family niche is "typically" occupied by one mother, one father, and one to six children. Of course in reality families are much more diverse. We know some couples have more than six children. There are also single-parent households and LGBT households. And some men of wealth maintain more than one family. The hypocrisy and secrecy surrounding these variations from the norm are the stuff of legend, film, books, and reality TV. Some men may have two or three wives, and two or three children by each one. A high achiever male might sire nine or a dozen children by various women, or, at a stretch, a couple of dozen. At some threshold eyebrows are raised. These high achievers' stories come to us through papers like the *Daily Mail*, whose reporters are dispatched to gather the lurid details.

From the little we know, it appears that Shigeta has scaled biological fatherhood beyond what the average philanderer could have imagined possible. It is as if the starting gun was fired in the intergalactic population race and Shigeta was determined to go for the gold. The rest of us are simply running in a very different race, with new ground rules modeled after Moore's law, combined with Darwinism and Ayn Rand's version of capitalism. With these rules in place, the finish line starts to look very different.

A fair number of Thais and foreigners expressed outrage over the number of babies Shigeta had fathered, especially in light of the narrow window of time in which they had been born (two years). This raised all kinds of suspicions. The Thai police apparently have requested that Shigeta return to Thailand and explain his behavior. Shigeta is in Tokyo and has not shown signs of wishing to come in and have a chat over his philosophy of fatherhood. There is a Mexican standoff.

The burst of outrage, the demands of officials, and the hurry for legislation are signals to which we should pay close attention. It is evidence that an important social construct that shapes our identity is being threatened. There is nothing in nature that says a man can't have as many children as he can find women who agree to bear his children. No one up to now has thought there should be a limit on the number of children a man can father. The social constructs of fatherhood and motherhood are, with minor variations, so similar that the subject rarely comes up. What Shigeta has done is to reengineer the meaning of "father" and "mother." Having children through a surrogate removes the "mother" from the normal sexual reproduction cycle. How does that work? The father acquires (presumably through donation or purchase) suitable egg cells from a female. This is a medical procedure. The woman who has been selected goes to a clinic or hospital, and some of her eggs are removed. The cells are stored and transported to a clinic that offers surrogacy.

At this juncture one woman has provided the eggs and another woman has provided the womb for the fertile egg to be implanted in. The father is not treating either of the women as mothers but rather as his employees. Once the surrogate mother has delivered the baby, she's contract bound to "give up" the baby to other employees. These post-birth surrogates—nannies—act as the primary caregivers. Reproduction is starting to resemble Henry Ford's first auto assembly line. Ford hired employees. For his baby project Mitsutoki Shigeta also appears to have hired employees. Assembly-line babies, assembly-line cars—it all makes sense in a world where unrestrained, unregulated capitalism is allowed to produce a more "efficient" exploitation of resources.

Shigeta comes from an ultra-wealthy Japanese family (billionaires) that has extensive economic interests in Japan, China, Hong Kong, Cambodia, and Thailand. Japan is also a country where the demographic future appears especially bleak. Let's add the insular Japanese perspective that believes, at the extreme, that Japanese culture, values, and blood are superior to others. If your country is no longer producing the next generation, how will you maintain the "Japanese" identity of your empire in the future? You will be forced to recruit from the locals throughout your empire, but your personal socialization causes you to look down on these locals as inferior.

Since we don't know the specifics of the Mitsutoki Shigeta case, let's imagine that a Super Baby-Maker Dad appears on the scene with the necessary resources to organize, recruit, and sustain over time a breeding program. What might his reason be for siring all of these children? Let's say he wishes to staff future upper management positions across a vast business empire. If he had a thousand children over twenty-years (at the rate of fifty children a year) and could organize their education, instill his system of values in them, and shape their attitudes to reflect his heritage, that might allow him to plan for perpetuating his customs, traditions, values, language, and biases and act as an invisible hand to ensure his way of doing things continues through the end of the century. While his competitors are putting all of their eggs in a basket, he has gathered eggs of a different order of magnitude, giving Super Baby-Maker Dad an edge in business over his rivals.

Any man in the top 0.1 percent would have sufficient resources to sire, support, and educate a thousand children. This is a good case to illustrate the power of a social construct— one reinforced by religion, ethics, and morality—that programs our beliefs about family, parenthood, fatherhood, and motherhood. No law of nature is violated in all of this mass-production of babies. But we feel somehow violated on a personal level as the idea challenges our values, attitudes, and perceptions, which we must admit have been running on automatic pilot. Suddenly we are hit by a typhoon, and only now do we realize that it is our culture that chooses for us. These beliefs circulate like the air we breathe. We are drilled in them at every turn, and we defend them as "right," "ethical," and "moral" and condemn and wish for punishment to be inflicted on violators.

Any current look at intergenerational conflict, whether in Thailand or elsewhere is inevitably bounded by the comparative ratio over time between older and younger people. The two generations co-exist while younger people wait for their elders to retire and die off. As the seniors and juniors overlap, they inevitably clash over values, priorities, policies, and the allocation of benefits. It has always been so. Once a mega-corp-family comes of age, it is hard to foresee what kind of new conflicts will emerge as one thousand siblings compete for the attention and favor of one father. How will such conflict spill over and destabilize the larger community? No one knows. Also intra-generational conflict might spawn alliances and factions as the half-brothers and half-sisters compete for power against each other. Such families will likely be structured more along the lines of a corporation, with the siblings as shareholders, rather than a traditional family enjoying a holiday in Spain.

Once the taboo is breached, others with extreme wealth may decide that they have no choice but to enter this baby production race. Bill Gates has created a charitable foundation, which does good work with a reach around the world. But the Gates Foundation, one day, will be run by blood strangers. Bill's vast wealth will be in the hands of other people who have no DNA connection to him. By contrast Super Baby-Maker Dad, with a city-sized population who share his DNA (all of whom are half-brothers and half-sisters with a father in common), has the human power to control the future not available to his peers. Super Baby-Maker Dad's children will have the opportunity to continue the family business in a way that maintains genetic and cultural connections into the distant future. As a cohesive unit, they would have leverage that other families would lack to exploit future opportunities in information, data mining, bio-medical technology, and nano-technology by being able to educate and staff multiple labs, offices, and other facilities. And herein lies the difference between East and West. In the East a dynasty is family based and is central to controlling the family fortune. In the West business has traditionally been built (in theory) around an ideal of merit, which results in the best and brightest being recruited to run the business. In the West the corporation relies on strangers; the founders lack sufficient family members to run a big, diverse business empire.

In fifty years, when super-intelligent AI runs the day-to-day operations of government, business, medicine, entertainment, and travel, Super Baby-Maker Dad may be viewed as a visionary, who saw that in the future, those with the most off-spring would have the best chance in this Brave

New World of machines to survive, prosper, reproduce, and defeat human and machine rivals. Meanwhile, the Thai press will continue to follow the Shigeta story and that of the surrogate mothers in Thailand. They will struggle to make sense of what the story means.

How do journalists prepare the public to understand the implications that arise when one of the founding social constructs is questioned? We stare dumbfounded into that wreckage and try to come to terms with the meaning of a young heir to a fortune, who has a missionary zeal to spread his message across time. We seek to understand the game that is being played. A man of immense fortune has hedged his bets in outsourcing reproduction; he has hired "employees" in developing countries to act as human incubators for a breeding program designed to mass-produce hundreds of children, who one day will carry his gospel to the masses.

In the hypothetical case of Super Baby-Maker Dad, run the numbers for five generations, with each of offspring each producing fifty children, and his grandchildren, great-grandchildren, and so on following the family tradition, and soon the numbers balloon. While Generation 1 has one thousand babies from Super Baby-Maker Dad, by Generation 4 his descendants have increased to 125 million. This comes close to what might be described as a biological singularity.

Technological change has accelerated. What Mitsutoki Shigeta's saga indicates is that future shocks in the area of human reproduction are likely. Once a lab can create an artificial womb, the employees in the birth cycle can be eliminated, and all the laws on surrogacy will become redundant, and politicians will scramble to regulate such labs. Even with legal controls, there will always be someplace in the world that allows activities that others find reprehensible. Sooner or later, how we regulate reproduction, and particularly how we prevent the 0.1 percent from using their vast wealth to increase their DNA legacy, will require a new consensus of what it means to have children. Meanwhile, expect conflict, tears, and teeth-gnashing, and accept that the very, very rich will always find a means to disperse their wealth.

A thousand children would be the ultimate immortality-vanity project. When you are that rich, you likely get bored with the old game. Super Baby-Maker Dad is a new diversification game for the elite club to explore. If something can be done, ultimately it will be done. Whoever is Ground Zero in the Super Baby-Maker Dad explosion won't be looking to the stars to make his mark; he will be looking at this planet and beholding the potential after four generations of leaving a legacy population of genetically related people who will shape the political, social, economic, and demographic fate of more than one country.

The High Cost of Badly Paid Cops

To understand a police force in any meaningful way requires information about the culture in which the police are recruited, educated, paid, promoted, and disciplined. In a *Bangkok Post* article published last week (on July 25, 2014) that highlighted the suicide statistics among Thai police officers, it was noted:

> At present, the force is divided into two distinct classes—the bosses who graduated from the Police Cadet Academy and junior officers from schools for corporals. The classes operate in an oppressively feudal and closed society where subordinates have no say whatsoever. Due to their low pay, the police tend to get involved in all sorts of underground businesses.

There are the bosses and then there is the vast underclass whose members carry out the bosses' commands. The division is officially designated as between commissioned and non-commissioned officers (source: www.aseanapol. org/information/royal-thai-police). The national police force is a quasi-military organization that comes under the Ministry of Interior (see Wikipedia, Royal Thai Police).

Senior appointments by the government have been routinely controversial. For years there have been many studies, commissions, and reports delegated with a mandate to recommend reforms. The members of these study groups and commissions have recommended a variety of reforms to the structure and culture of the Thai police force. But no substantial reform program has been implemented from these recommendations.

The size of the police force in Thailand exceeds more than 230,000 officers, according to Wikipedia. To compare with countries with the same or larger populations: the United Kingdom has 167,318; the Philippines has 149,535; Myanmar has 93,000; and France has 220,000. In other words, in Thailand, the number of police relative to population size is large by international standards. In 1987 Thailand had 110,000 members in the Royal Thai Police Force. It would be interesting to analyze the political processes that resulted in more than a doubling of the police force over a quarter of a century.

The statistics and brief background fail to convey the day-to-day reality of the non-commissioned rank-and-file police officer. Who is this man or woman behind the uniform in Thailand? What story can we tell about the "self" behind the uniform?

> We are also the story we construct about ourselves, our personal narrative that interprets and assigns meaning to the things we do remember and the things other people tell us about ourselves. Research by the Northwestern University psychologist Dan McAdams, author of *The Redemptive Self* (2005), suggests that these narratives guide our behaviour and help chart our

path into the future. (Source: http://aeon.co/
magazine/being-human/where-do-childrens-
earliest-memories-go.)

Police training and police culture are materials out of
which that self is constructed. Another block of "self-worth"
and "self-image" emerges from the economic conditions in
which a person lives, works, and interacts with others. In
Thailand a police officer's sense of self also takes a battering
because many people view the police with mistrust and
suspicion. This likely causes the police to withdraw further
into their own subculture for emotional and psychological
support, widening the gap between "us" and "them."

Inequalities of wealth are experienced by police
officers like anyone else. Unlike the rest of us, the police
are authorized to carry guns and to use them inside such
societies. And where there are businesses that operate at the
margins of the law and those outside the law that are hugely
profitable, policing by cops who don't have a living wage
can be compromised with cash payments.

A chart showing the pay scale for Thai police was recently
published by Police BD 51 Online (www.policebd51online.
com/salary.html). The first three columns indicate the salaries
of non-commissioned officers, and the other columns are for
commissioned officers, with the last two columns reserved
for officers of the highest rank.

What the chart shows is that unless you are a non-
commissioned, column-1 Thai cop who entered the police
department with a high school education, you are paid after
four years on the job (assuming no additional step increase
beyond the usual annual increase) a salary of 5,580 baht
($177.42) a month. That works out to 183 baht or just under
six bucks a day. I don't know about you, but I'd pay for any
travel guidebook that reliably promised accommodation,

food, and transportation plus sidearm, uniform, haircuts, and entertainment in Thailand on a budget of six dollars a day. The minimum wage in Thailand is three hundred baht a day, which is closer to ten dollars a day. While officers can exploit possibilities to supplement their meager pay packets with per diems and overtime, the overall monthly amounts paid to police are, as the chart demonstrates, small.

If officers are appointed to a position such as inspector or chief inspector in suppression or forensic units, they receive an additional 3,000 to 5,700 baht. If they are investigation officers (regular to expert), they receive an additional 12,000 to 30,000 baht. Executive positions bring 5,600 to 21,000 baht and special expert/teaching positions, 3,500 to 15,000 baht, increasing with rank. As is evident, the chance for supplemental pay is limited to the higher ranks, whose officers have received specialized education or training. Typically a university graduate would start as an officer with a higher pay.

How could there not be corruption in a police force when the pay scale for non-commissioned officers condemns them to poverty? A man or a woman faced with a spouse and children he or she doesn't have the money to feed can easily cross ethical and legal lines on a routine basis. If you were in that position, what would your conscience tell you to do: fail to feed your family or ask for a hundred baht from a driver who made a turn out of the wrong lane? It might be assumed (and it is impossible to prove with solid evidence) that the division of spoils falls mainly to the benefit of the high-ranking officers. Such a lopsided division would be consistent with how money flows between the ranks inside any feudal organization. No one has ever suggested that egalitarian principles feature large in such a mindset. In a feudal structure most of the workforce, among the police and elsewhere, can be thought of as extras in the larger drama, and there is room on the marquee for only a few big names. The lion's share of rank, status, and money is, in the main, set aside for the stars.

There are also psychological and social consequences arising from a police force modeled on a feudal structure. Most of these issues have not received serious attention from any of the many recent governments. One is the suicide rate among the rank and file police. The *Bangkok Post* article mentioned above told a story about such an officer:

> On Wednesday, 24-year-old Police Lance Corporal Nitikorn Kulawilas shot himself in the head with a pistol and died at the Phaya Thai police station. The young traffic policeman was the fifth officer to take his own life since January.
>
> If the average police suicide rate per year is anything to go by, 25 more families may lose their beloved son or daughter this year.
>
> According to the Police Department, the number of officers taking their own life is steadily on the rise. The annual average number of suicides over the past five years is 29.17. Last year, it rose to 31.

In the general population suicide rates have been in decline in Thailand since the peak rate of 8.4 per 100,000 in 1999. Hanging is the most common method to end one's life and is ten times more prevalent than a handgun. The police officers' rate of suicide works out to be about double that of the population as a whole.

What is it about being a cop that increases the odds of suicide? The superiors of the dead officer in the story explained that his suicide was caused by work stress and family problems. In other words, the suicide had nothing to do with low pay and the culture in which he worked. This is the kind of denial that isn't restricted to the attitude of a few superiors. The explanation is based on a widespread perception that when an officer is caught stealing or aiding and abetting a crime, or kills himself, that is wholly the individual responsibility of the officer.

It is this consensus that explains, despite all of the recommendations for reform, how the current system, which hugely benefits a select few, continues. The argument goes that we should consider the collateral damage that drives officers to crime and suicide as incidental, personal, and particular to the man or woman who felt they had no other choice.

What mental health screening and counseling is done for police officers? I can't find any answer to that question. I suspect that silence is significant. Suicide rates are only one small sampling of those with mental health problems. Rates of depression should be examined and the results made public. The rates of divorce, domestic violence, alcoholism, and drug abuse are additional indicators of personal stability that are probably worth exploring.

The suicide rates of police officers have been analyzed in the United States. The American police officer is statistically more likely to kill himself (or herself) than a Thai police officer (Police One.com). There is no, and likely never will be any, clear, unbiased, and unambiguous set of statistics to support the premise that low pay is the cause of suicide among police officers in Thailand. One needs to accept that some of these suicides may have occurred no matter what job the person worked at, and analysis needs to take into account mental problems such as depression, assignment to high-anxiety areas such as the South of Thailand, family or domestic violence, and separation or divorce.

The *Bangkok Post* article hammered home a point that has been made periodically over the years, but the political will to change the culture of the police has failed. "[An] honest and efficient arm of the law," it suggests, "is not possible if low pay, poor welfare, and a lack of unaccountability [sic] and meritocracy remain the norm."

The correlation between low pay and the hidden economy is difficult to establish as the data are largely inaccessible and must be drawn from stories in the press. All that can be said from a common-sense point of view, with no set of viable statistics to back it up, is that the low salaries paid to many police (I know there are honest, incorruptible Thai police as I've met some of them) are likely subsidized by other opportunities that are only available to a man or woman in uniform who carries a gun. The question is whether there is the political will to change the salary and policing culture in Thailand.

Guarding the Gold in Thailand

It is difficult to find a reliable figure for the number of gold shops in Thailand or specifically in Bangkok. As I write this in late August 2014, one source (Fun Trivia.com) puts the number of gold shops in Thailand at six thousand. I'd venture a guess that there are at least a couple of thousand gold shops scattered throughout Thailand's capital. And the Chinatown along Yaowarat Road is a gold shop mecca. For a point of comparison, there are 2,170 bank branches in Bangkok according to the Bank of Thailand (www2.bot.or.th) and 405 sub-branches.

The above statistics show how Bangkok dominates the banking industry by centralizing banking activity in Bangkok. But that is another story. This essay is about robbers.

An American bank robber named Willie Sutton is alleged to have said, in reply to a question about why he robbed banks, "That's where the money is." Thai robbers also know that gold shops are as good as gold when it comes to robbery. Gold shops, like banks, are natural targets for criminal activity. This makes it natural to ask a few questions:

1) Is there a serious problem in Bangkok of robberies at gold shops and banks?

2) What security precautions do gold shop owners and bank branches use to protect their staff and inventory against robbery?

3) What role does new technology play in improving security?

4) Have traditional security jobs been disrupted by the new technology?

Is there a problem?

According to one report in the *Bangkok Post* (which gives no statistics to support the claim), gold shops have become a high-profile target, and the thieves are running off with gold worth in excess of one million baht annually. The police, it is reported, have made little headway in solving these robberies. This information is alarming on the face of it—until you read the lead story in the same edition stating that between August 2013 and July 2014 a total of five gold shop robberies took place (four banks were robbed during the same period). I don't know about you, but to me the hold-ups of five gold shops annually out of several thousand and four banks out of thousands of branches qualifies as a rounding-off error.

It amounts to a low probability that any one gold shop or bank will be robbed over the course of a year. Of course, if it is your gold shop or bank, the robbery is hardly insignificant. Like lightning, when it strikes, it can cause considerable damage, and that is why landowners buy insurance. It's also why gold shop owners buy insurance. Someone in the insurance industry can set me straight, if necessary, but I'm willing to bet that the premiums paid for robbery and theft insurance were increased based on those five gold store and four bank robberies reported during the one-year period. Only one arrest was recorded for each category: one gold shop robber and one bank robber.

That's 20 percent and 25 percent caseload clearance, respectively. In the other 80 percent and 75 percent cases, the police, one presumes, are still looking for clues. With a total of nine robberies in one year, an observer might conclude this falls below the threshold of a crime spree. The low investigation success rate supports the *Bangkok Post* theory that these are well-planned heists, unlike the convenience store robberies committed by drunken teenagers who live in the neighborhood and act on an impulse. Robbing a neighbor when you are drunk is bound to cut down on your odds of getting away with the crime.

A senior police officer was quoted in the article as saying gold shops are the hardest nuts for criminals to crack. Certainly compared with a convenience store robbery, which is a nut with a very soft shell.

We can conclude that, in the scheme of things, gold shop and bank robberies are a minor part of the crime industry operating in Bangkok and elsewhere in Thailand.

What security arrangements are used by gold shop owners?

I've written above about the poor pay of the police in Thailand. Many rank and file Thai cops work a second job to make ends meet. One of the popular moonlighting gigs is working as a security guard in a gold shop. For many years you could walk past a gold shop in the main shopping areas along roads such as Yaowarat, Silom, or Sukhumvit and spot a uniformed Thai police officer through the window. He (I never saw a female cop working in a gold shop) would be inside the shop, usually seated on a chair, looking bored.

The use of regular police officers rests on two premises: 1) the presence in a gold shop or bank of a uniformed cop, a gun strapped to his hip, means only the most hardened and determined criminal can be expected to rob the place; and

2) there is a ready supply of police officers willing to act as security guards as they are underpaid in their official jobs. With enough of the security moonlighting jobs for lowly paid cops, it takes the heat off the politicians to increase police pay. The authorities can factor in the second-job income received from the security detail and conclude that overall the average cop is able to get by. In the traditional system everyone benefited. The shop owner from enhanced security, and the government in its ability to get away with underpaying the police.

What role has new technology played in disrupting the old arrangements?

In recent years two game-changing technologies have appeared: closed-circuit television (CCTV) cameras and the Internet. CCTV cameras became cheap and reliable, and robbers, except for the total morons among them, know that gold shops and banks have cameras recording everyone coming in and out. The thing with CCTV cameras is that although they work 24/7, they never get tired or bored or read newspapers. They aren't fitted out with guns (wait five years for that development), which deter robbers but may also terrify some customers. A terrified customer is less in the mood to buy gold.

Point the finger in the direction of the Internet. The trail of disruptions mostly leads back to new technology and the use of the Internet. CCTV cameras can be linked directly to police stations. Why continue to employ human security guards when CCTV cameras can do the job cheaper and better?

The disruption of the security job sector in gold shops and banks

Most employment sectors are bleeding jobs. It started with ATMs, an easy way to do banking without joining a queue. For bank employees this trend line will only become worse over time. Computers and robots can simply do the work cheaper, longer, better, and without expecting a bonus at New Year's. Gold shops and banks are in the business of keeping costs low, revenues increasing, and profit margins high. In the cold-blooded, rational world, security guards are an expense to be measured against the costs of alternative methods of providing security. If the costs of new technology plus the insurance premium paid to insure against theft and robbery are lower than the wages and benefits paid to an off-duty police officer, the capitalist mind easily draws its conclusion—no more security guards. Money is saved. Profits go up. Shareholders are rewarded with higher dividends.

If the premiums on the insurance are low, then the cost to the bank for a robbery is not the money stolen but the premium paid. It's like health insurance; you have a heart attack, and the insurance company pays your costs. But if you are in good health, the probability is you won't have one, and the premium is low. That's why insurance companies become rich. We overestimate the probability of something bad happening because we read about someone who died of a heart attack, or we read about a plane crash or a bank robbery. We suddenly feel vulnerable. It's irrational. And business is there to take money from irrational people who want protection.

This didn't stop a senior Thai police official from telling the *Bangkok Post* that Kasikorn Bank's robbery record (it is not clear how many of the four bank robberies occurred at a Kasikorn branch) is attributable to the bank's failure to hire security guards. As the police are mainly the ones hired as security guards, one would expect a senior cop to take that position. He's looking after the welfare of his men and packaging it as the welfare of the bank. That sleight of hand is normal in such circumstances.

A senior vice president of Kasikorn Bank who was quoted in the article agreed with this official assessment. It seems that the bank hadn't employed security guards at its branches because it feared clashes between the guards, thieves, and customers. That's the sort of thing that makes an interesting scene in a movie: a shootout in a bank as guards and thieves and customers all trade gunfire. There is no evidence, though, that this has happened in a Thai bank or gold shop in the immediate past. Still, it makes you understand how fear drives corporate policy when it comes to security, so that worst-case scenarios are used to justify an expense.

The possibility of a shootout, however improbable, raises another point in the disrupted banking employment world. It's not just that security guards are no longer needed; most bank employees are in the cross hairs of their HR department's firing squad. It's called Internet banking. Which of course raises another issue: in the past customers had no choice but to go in person to a branch to transact business, but with online banking most transactions can be conducted.

What has the bank decided? To hire security guards for its one thousand branches (this number isn't consistent with the Bank of Thailand figure, but that is likely a mistake in the report or another story). That's good news for the moonlighting police. It's also good news for the Thai taxpayers who won't worry the officials in charge will seek a tax hike to pay higher salaries to the police. Instead that money comes out of dividends paid to the shareholders of the bank. I am certain the shareholders will be happy to subsidize police salaries. When it comes time to lay off tellers, it will be interesting to revisit this issue and find out, as compensation is fought over amongst the dwindling staff, whether robbery is the least of the problems faced by an industry in the midst of major disruption.

No Broken Windows

It's official. No Broken Windows has been adopted as policing policy to be taught in a senior police training course offered by the Central Investigation Bureau in Bangkok.

In April 2014 the *Bangkok Post* reported on the adoption of this policy: "The Central Investigation Bureau has sent its senior police back to school in order to learn about what it calls 'sustainable' crime reduction."

It seems, to judge from the press report, that the No Broken Windows training program for senior cops, as explained to the press by the police, means pretty much whatever the police say it means, whether it's stopping three or more people from riding a single motorcycle, apprehending pedestrians not using zebra crossings, or of course taking broken windows more seriously.

As the senior brass go back to school to learn about No Broken Windows, I have a few suggestions for extra reading on the theory.

The No Broken Windows theory overlooks the reality that in Thailand the routine violation of minor traffic laws (not to mention murder, kidnapping, assault with a deadly weapon, trafficking) by the rich is a significant law enforcement issue. Ever notice those luxury cars speeding up as they approach a zebra crossing? Getting people to use a zebra crossing as a means to deter crime is indeed a challenge for several reasons, the most important of which is that a zebra crossing doesn't carry the same message for Thai motorists and pedestrians. To assume that using a zebra crossing in Thailand is the same as in England can be a death sentence.

Nothing quite highlights cultural and historical differences more than a policy borrowed from another culture. New York City conceived a policing policy under the same name—No Broken Windows. For whatever reason Bangkok is scheduled to adopt this policy. Let's take a stroll together and talk about what this means, how it's supposed to work, and whether it does work.

The No Broken Windows theory emerged from a 1982 article written by social scientists James Q. Wilson and George L. Kelling. Here is the basic idea:

> Consider a building with a few broken windows. If the windows are not repaired, the tendency is for vandals to break a few more windows. Eventually, they may even break into the building, and if it's unoccupied, perhaps become squatters or light fires inside.
>
> Or consider a pavement. Some litter accumulates. Soon, more litter accumulates. Eventually, people even start leaving bags of refuse from take-out restaurants there or even break into cars.

When Rudy Giuliani was elected mayor of New York City in 1993, he hired a police commissioner to implement a no-tolerance policy. Under the umbrella of that policy, NYPD began a strict enforcement program, targeting those engaged in subway fare evasion, public drinking, public urination, graffiti, and unwanted squeegeeing of car windshields. The theory was also used to support the New York Police Department's policy of "stop, question, and frisk."

Having lived both in New York City in the mid- to late 1980s and in Bangkok since 1988, I have observed law enforcement efforts in both places. There are significant differences between the two urban environments—for example, the absence of an equivalent of the vast slums of Klong Toey curled up in the heart of Manhattan. The typically windowless Klong Toey slum is situated right next to the richest part of Bangkok, the Sukhumvit area, sometimes called the Green Zone.

In the mid-1980s New York streets at night had few people on them. Bangkok streets overflow with hawkers and food vendors. CCTV camera coverage is widespread in Bangkok as well (although many of the cameras, as I have written elsewhere, may be dummies). The tight-knit social organization of Thai society may have less traction in Bangkok than in the provinces, but the bamboo telegraph remains operational and ensures most of the time that staying anonymous is more difficult than in New York.

The No Broken Windows theory rests on the idea that a neighborhood's general appearance can have an effect on criminal activity. If social norms tolerate a shabby and neglected appearance, No Broken Windows suggests, this is an invitation for vandals to increase the chaos. The assumption is that No Broken Windows will restore the city to an orderly and clean state and discourage minor acts of crime that would otherwise lead to more serious criminal misconduct. It also makes implicit assumptions about the scope and degree of relative poverty within an urban environment. (I like Utopia as much as the next person, but I accept that this state is an idealized fiction that never existed and never will.) The contemporary Bangkok neighborhood scene is better known among foreigners for its glitzy high-rise towers and shopping malls, but along the edges are hard-core areas of poverty that you'd be hard-pressed to find the equivalent of in New York City—not in the New York that I knew thirty years ago and certainly not now either.

Under No Broken Windows the police monitor the disorder in the environment and arrest those breaking windows, littering the streets, and painting graffiti on walls, bridges, and train cars. The idea is to reclaim the environment as a clean and well-maintained place and put the vandals on notice that they are at risk of being stopped and arrested.

The central question is whether the New York City policing experience under the No Broken Windows policy brought about a reduction of crime? The research has not uncovered solid evidence of benefit resulting from the police targeting petty crime. The causal link between the theory and the dramatic drop in crime is also questionable because crime decreased in that period across the United States, including New York but also other urban environments that had no such policing policy. Other factors such as the reduction of the number of young men between the ages of sixteen to twenty-four, the reduction of the crack epidemic, the increase of prison populations, and the fall in unemployment rates are likelier explanations for the decline in crime rates. The theory hasn't been supported by the evidence and alternative explanations.

There is another downside to the No Broken Windows policy—it allows for an inflation of policing powers. Researchers and scholars have documented the abuse arising from vesting the police with broad discretion. The main conclusion is it results in the repression of minorities within an urban community (see Steven Levitt and Stephen

Dubner's *Freakonomics: A Rogue Economist Explores the Hidden Side of Everything).*

Others have written that such a policy results in criminalizing the poor and homeless, who are mainly members of racial minorities. The policy was a way to use "science" as a basis to expand the discretionary power of police to stop, frisk, and arrest young black and Latino men. The racial divide, and the fear of ethnic minority criminals, is never far from the surface in American policing policy formulation or from the positions of those leading the resistance to gun control legislation.

The police are issued a free pass to arrest locals "for the 'crime' of being undesirable." The policy becomes a fig leaf to cover racist profiling. In the context of Bangkok, dark-skinned natives from Isan and migrant workers from Burma and Cambodia would be more vulnerable than others to arrest. Their appearance makes them a convenient target for stop-and-frisk street operations. And their arrests would have the legitimacy of the No Broken Windows theory behind them.

Joshua C. Hinkle and Sue-Ming Yang have questioned the methodology used to test the No Broken Windows theory out in the field. The perception of what is an acceptable level of disorder is not universally agreed upon, they point out. Cultural and class attitudes play a large role in what is an acceptable level of litter on the street, for instance. "That is, people with different demographic backgrounds and life experiences might react to the same environment in very different ways . . . [S]ocial disorder is a social construct, rather than a concrete phenomenon."

Precisely. Not to mention that the hiring, training, and monitoring of the police and widespread corruption make Bangkok's law enforcement issues light years away from the broken windows in New York City. The cultures of New

York and Bangkok are vastly different, and that is reflected in their street life, the slums, the nature of policing, the social hierarchy, and the prevailing *kreng jai* system, through which important people are immune from the law. Count the illegal gambling casinos operating in Bangkok; then count the ones operating in New York.

There are certain behaviors in Bangkok that after many years seem almost normal to locals but may stop outsiders in their tracks, such as a chorus line of synchronized women police officers dancing in the street. It is difficult to imagine this scene in New York. My point is that Bangkok cops march to a different drummer from the one that leads the New York band of brothers. Indeed, if the police dancing scene suddenly appeared in midtown Manhattan at lunch hour, tourists numbers would balloon, housing co-op prices would inflate, and hedge fund managers would spend more time on the street. Markets would suffer. No one would care about a broken window. A SWAT team and snipers would be dispatched to seal the area. Drones overhead. But I digress.

So how did the Thai police force, which excels in dancing around tough law enforcement issues, conclude that a thirty-year-old American policy called No Broken Windows, overloaded with baggage, was suitable for Bangkok in 2014? That is exactly the kind of question the authorities hate foreigners for asking. It might be worth asking the instructor at the police training seminar, though. Let's journey a bit down that theoretical road and stop now and again to see what we find.

New York City hired thousands of new police officers in the early to mid-1990s, and regular patrols were conducted throughout the city. As a civilian observer in the mid-1980s, I rode along with the NYPD to see firsthand how laws were enforced in tough, crime-infested neighborhoods with high-rise slums and illegal immigrants. There was a major crime problem in New York during that time. New York City has changed dramatically over the last thirty years. Can we say that the No Broken Windows policy was responsible for that change? Many experts conclude that wasn't the case.

As with most social engineering, the knot of complex features working in one environment at a particular time and in a certain culture yield a result. But one cannot discount that complexity, believing that one policy alone will produce the same result in a radically different environment, culture, and time frame.

Judging from the local English press reports in Bangkok, I can see no indication that new resources will be allocated to the Bangkok version of No Broken Windows. An expansive and subjective interpretation of that theory as a kind of social control of behavior—such as encouraging the use of zebra crossings (but don't expect the person behind the wheel to stop)—does fit the Thai cultural inclination to favor the vague over the concrete. It also speaks to a certain mindset that underwrites senior police training programs.

Part of Bangkok's charm has long been the crowded, broken pavements, motorcycles driving on the pavement or the wrong way on the street, the pure chaos of food vendors with bottles of gas cooking up pad thai to order as dogs beg at tables for scraps of food. *Klongs* (the canals) in most parts of the city are laced with an evil brew of refuse and sewage. Taxi drivers routinely stop along the road to relieve themselves against a wall or a bush. Broken windows? You've got to be joking, if you think that's the way to solve the crime problem in Bangkok.

No one can deny the big cultural differences between Bangkok and New York City. During Songkran white powder paste is traditionally used as a kind of graffiti to vandalize people's faces, including those of the police.

Instead of replying with Tasers, the Thai police reply with a smile. Bangkok police officers have been seen standing and smiling, their faces covered with white powder, behind a banner that reads: "No powder play on Songkran holiday. Violators may be found guilty. With best wishes from the Police Department." Songkran is a special holiday where nearly everyone extends tolerance to total strangers who insist on throwing water on them and using their faces as canvases.Given that difference, how did a two-decade-old, heavily criticized New York City policy end up in Bangkok? It is as if Doctor Who arrived in his time-traveling TARDIS and convinced the top brass he had a solution to their law enforcement problems. Sometimes things have no explanation. They just happen and you deal with that happening in the Thai way—wait a couple of months before it is shelved and Doctor Who arrives with another foreign policy that promises to make Bangkok streets and canals look like a version of Geneva.

I wouldn't want to think what would happen to the person rubbing wet powder on the face of a member of the NYPD. I am guessing the probability is high that the cop wouldn't respond with a smile.

Meanwhile, an alert has gone out for Doctor Who to retrieve a law enforcement plan from the future, one that has gone through all the research and testing phase and produces jaw-dropping reductions in crime. But his arrival may remind us that some political ideas imported from other realities can be—well, not to put too fine a point on it—disappointing.

Impulse Control and Crime

In July 2014 in Thailand, two unrelated crime stories shared a common theme: impulsive, violent behavior. In one case a sixty-two-year-old mother confessed to the police that she had shot her daughter dead with a .38 caliber handgun. The shooting occurred in the daughter's bedroom in the family house and was caused, according to the mother, by her sudden anger over her daughter's outstanding debts, which totaled a million baht. According to Thai press reports, after shooting her daughter, the mother said that she turned the gun on herself and fired but missed.

In the second case a twenty-six-year-old katoey had gone on a surprise visit to her lover, but he wasn't at home. Soon after, still frustrated, at 5:30 a.m. she came across a paralyzed seventy-two-year-old grannie. The katoey told police she was drunk and felt an irresistible urge to have sex. The katoey's attempted rape of the grannie was interrupted when the grannie involuntarily evacuated her bowels.

The sudden impulses of the killer mother and drunk rapist katoey propelled them to commit violent criminal acts. Under questioning by the police, the killer mother attributed her actions to *a-rom chua-woop*, a sudden impulse. My Thai sources tell me this phrase appears frequently in local crime reports.

To what degree are cultural issues useful in understanding the psychological contexts of crime? The criminal justice system, whether in the West or the East, often faces offenders who claim a mental disorder. The way we control our impulses, like the way we process reality in general, has cultural foundations, at least in part. The Chinese and Thai view of gambling, for instance, will to some extent dictate the attitudes that authorities and others in those countries have toward casinos, lotteries, and slot machines. Rational choice-making can be handicapped both by mental disorders such as impulse control and by cognitive traps or illusions. In other words, we can be irrational over a range of activities, and some of those activities may involve crimes.

To start our discussion with the cognitive process, let's consider a concept from the work of Israeli-American psychologist Daniel Kahneman. In *Thinking, Fast and Slow* Kahneman divides the thinking self into two systems. The first is the one that reacts to, contemplates, or considers something that has happened. The event in question could be presented to you by a fellow human or by nature, or it could be just one of the thousand and one small decisions we make every day such as where to have lunch, whether to hit the "like" option on Facebook, or which movie to watch or book to read. This is System 1 thinking, which happens fast, perhaps in an instant.

System 1 is our automatic, auto-pilot decision-making process for matters that require little or no deliberation, such as when we see $2 + 2 = (\ )$. Leaving aside the political implication of Orwell's *1984*, we don't have to think; we "know" the answer is 4. System 2 thinking, in contrast, is deliberative, slowed-down decision-making; it is hard, taking up time and mental resources, and most people avoid it in favor of the easy-rider feeling of System 1. An example of System 2 thinking is 29 x 347 = ( ). There are people for whom this is a System 1 equation, but most of us will have to make an arithmetical calculation, or open the calculator app on an electronic device, to come up with the answer: 10,063.

Both System 1 and System 2 are normal tools we apply throughout each day. The first is unconscious decision-making, and the second is conscious, calibrated decision-making. There is another system, one that is pathological and considered a medical condition, listed in the fourth edition of the *Diagnostic and Statistical Manual of Mental Disorders*: impulse control disorder.

The lack of impulse control unleashes aggressive conduct that features in many areas of criminal behavior. Offenders of this kind either lack control over their emotions or easily lose control of them. Law enforcement officers often encounter such people when they are called to the scene of a crime to confront someone who has destroyed property or physically assaulted or killed another. Other criminal areas where this type of offender turns up are theft, gambling, and arson.

A person with such a personality is often called a "hothead" in English or *jai ron* ("hot heart") in Thai. Though the mental condition may stem from personal choices, some scientists have traced the disorder to neurological and environmental causes. Others such as A. Saha in Industrial Psychiatry Journal, are more skeptical about attempts to pin impulsive behavior on underlying causes: "It can become clinically difficult to disentangle [impulse control disorders] from one another, with the result that the impulsivity at the core of the disorders is obscured."

A person with this disorder usually blames the victim for doing something to cause the act of violence. Rarely do such offenders accept responsibility. They believe they were right in their response and feel no guilt for the suffering or harm they've caused. People with this disorder are disproportionately represented in domestic violence and rape cases. They lose control and in an irrational mental state harm others.

Criminal charges and penalties often are determined by whether the crime was planned or premeditated as opposed to impulsive or spontaneous. The difference between a hit man and a wife killer often turns on judging whether the offender had planned the murder or it was an explosive, irrational act.

We hold people who plan and use logic to commit a crime more blameworthy. These are the System 2 deliberate thinking criminals who calculate the odds of pulling off the crime, weigh the risks against the benefits, and contemplate the optimal time in which to strike. Our criminal laws reflect an assumption that people who are planners are more easily deterred by a heavy penalty. Conversely, as manslaughter counts indicate, there is an assumption that someone with an impulse control disorder wasn't in full control of himself and wouldn't have been deterred by the threat of punishment.

While the death penalty might deter the planners, it will be useless to stop those with a personality disorder, in whom logical, rational thinking is disabled. These assumptions take us into the realm of personality disorders' effects on free will and self-control. The authorities select out those whose crimes appear unplanned and spontaneous as suffering from a decreased responsibility for their acts.

There are limitations on this analysis in Asia, where culture is a factor in assessing what in the West is viewed as a matter of psychology. For example, in a 2008 study of Thai lottery gamblers (David Godot, 2010), one observed group was guided by superstitious methods such as obtaining a "lucky" number from a temple or divining a number by dripping candle wax into water; the other group didn't report using superstitious methods. The use of superstition was found to increase the probability of the "gambler's fallacy," creating an illusion of predictability and control. The study indicates that one shouldn't assume that cognitive problems and psychological disorders, as defined in the West, are applicable in places like Thailand.

The System 2 type of thinking also has a large cultural component that is reflected in the educational system. It is nurtured in schools and universities where critical thinking is valued and promoted. Rote learning is a way to reinforce System 1 automatic thinking. This isn't to suggest that System 1 translates into impulse control disorder. They are different concepts and involve different mental processes as well as different underlying causes. Where a culture promotes superstition, magical-thinking, and prophecy, people educated in that culture will have an increased probability of failing to recognize circumstances in which their beliefs have created cognitive illusions. That way of thinking colors the approach to impulsive control disorders. The way of dealing with the disorder is less based on science than on the belief that non-scientific exorcism will solve the problem.

The next time you read one of the "strange" crime stories that come your way from another country, consider why it is strange to you. The way thinking is taught, rewarded, and honored may be different in that foreign land, and the way of dealing with mental disorders may also reflect a different way of thinking. In Thailand, should you encounter someone in the throes of *a-rom chua-woop*, clear away the knives and guns, hide your daughters and grannies, and quickly run for the exit. You won't have much time.

Judging the Judges: Distrust and the Rise of Violence against Courts

Judges are expected to be impartial storytellers, weaving their narratives from the evidence presented to them, considering previous cases with similar facts, and deciding how the law applies to the findings of fact. A judge without impartiality is like a priest without faith. Religion is not an accidental metaphor. Good faith in the judicial system is underscored by a belief in its impartiality.

If you spent time in courtrooms in Canada, England, Burma, or America, you'd find the same churchlike devotion to symbolism, ritual, gowns, and reverence from those in attendance. Oaths are taken to tell the truth. Lies made under oath are punished by fines and imprisonment. Judges sit on an elevated bench looking down as from Olympus at those in the courtroom, and those below look up to them.

Judges are in a business not unlike that of a mystery author, who must tie up the loose ends that explain the story. Unlike most writers they must also be public performers in the ritual of justice. Eighteenth-century Irish statesman Edmund Burke wrote, "It is hard to say whether doctors of law or divinity have made the greater advances in the lucrative business of mystery."

A crime fiction writer may entertain, enlighten, stimulate, provoke, or expand our understanding of the psychology of criminal and victim. Judges have the heavy responsibility of knowing their finding of the "true" story has great consequences for the liberty of the people in the courtroom and the security of the society outside the courtroom. Like all storytellers, judges write decisions that can't help but reflect their own cultural and personal biases.

Is it reasonable to expect our judges to rise above the prejudices of their history, culture, class, and time? That is a burning question asked in Thailand, where (as I write this in early March 2014) there is talk of a judicial coup to oust the government. Many judicial systems, not just that in Thailand, are bending under the weight of full-scale political conflict. In those parts of the world set on fire with violence and strife, people seek answers about who is judging the authorities inside a political system and who is judging the judges.

Around the world most judges are drawn from the ranks of the ruling elites. They aren't elected. Judges are vetted and appointed by a narrow spectrum of state officials. They serve for life. During their tenure on the bench, it is fair to ask: is the main duty of judges to protect the powerful and the system that confers power on them, or is it to mediate impartially among all parties? Could it even be part of their duty to protect ordinary citizens who challenge power or conventional wisdom, including those who dissent from the mythology in which power cloaks itself for legitimacy?

"As long as you're scared you're on the plantation," African American academic and activist Cornel West has written. To which I'd add, justice cages fear while injustice opens the cage door. Judges act as the gatekeepers, opening and closing the door on the actions of others, including state officials who, left to their own devices, would gladly resort to force to generate fear among powerless people.

Unlike other storytellers, judges can send people to prison, ban them from civil rights and liberties and political office, overturn laws, regulations, and edicts, and select among competing philosophies, norms, and values the ones that become the law of the land. Judges in many systems exercise through their position considerable power over other institutions of state and over citizens. That is why their role has enhanced importance in times of great dissension and debate about the direction of society.

In the common law countries, such as the United States (where at the state level judges are often elected) Canada, Australia, and elsewhere in the Commonwealth, judges are selected and appointed from the top ranks of lawyers. These are lawyers who have proved themselves with respect to not only mastery of the law but qualities of restraint, honor, knowledge, experience, fairness, and integrity. In civil law countries such as Thailand, Japan, and most of Europe, judges enter the justice system soon after law school and work their way up the civil service ladder. The civil law system has a different tradition of recruitment, advancement, and cultural history.

In Thailand judges have been an important source of power within the context of the political turmoil that has followed the 2006 coup. A number of decisions on the constitution and laws have created controversy over the neutrality of the courts to administer justice in light of powerful forces seeking to expel the government. The Thai political system and judicial system are going through a period of credibility crisis.

Distrust of politicians is acceptable and perhaps necessary to ensure that decisions aren't made just for the benefit of politicians and their cronies but for the people. But distrust of the courts undermines the courts' position as the last resort, within the boundaries of the law, for resolving differences between state authorities and those contesting them.

The players may cheat, but the referees are there to keep the game within the rules. If a referee's calls appears to be favoring one side, the game is judged by the crowd to be rigged, and a free-for-all may follow. If a judge is seen to appear at a demonstration protesting for or against the government, then he or she has given the appearance of taking sides.

A judge's authority rests upon the appearance of neutrality. If a member of the federal court in New York had carried a placard at the Occupy Wall Street demonstrations, such an act would make it difficult for the judge to appear neutral in a hearing based on the legality of those protests and an application for an injunction against the rally organizers.

The quickest way to compromise a judicial system is for judges to become associated with one faction in a political dispute. The friend of justice is seen as being neither friend nor enemy to either side of a dispute. If that appearance of neutrality is shattered, the probability of attacks against the courts rises.

A number of recent stories reporting insurgent attacks on courts around the world suggest they are becoming routine in a number of countries. Courts and court officials are being targeted as combatants on one side or the other in political struggles. An extreme example of discontent with the court system spilling over into acts of violence happened in Pakistan on March 3, 2014 (as reported recently by the *Bangkok Post*), when a suicide bomber settled scores by blowing himself up in a courtroom, killing eleven and injuring twenty-four people. In early April 2013 the journal of the American Bar Association reported that fifty-three people were killed and ninety injured, including two judges, when suicide bombers attacked a courthouse in western Afghanistan. A few days later USA Today reported that in mid-April 2013 in Mogadishu, nine Al-Shabab Islamic extremists wearing suicide vests and firing rifles attacked Somaliaersself up in a courtr Sixteen people, including all the attackers, were killed. In February 2014 the Bangkok Post reported that an armor-piercing grenade was fired at the Criminal Court on Ratchadaphisek Road. And earlier this week, on March 3, the Bangkok Post reported that two M-61 grenades were used in an attack on the Criminal Court in Bangkok by two men on a motorcycle.

It would be a mistake to think such attacks are limited to judges and court personnel living in quasi- or non-democratic countries in the Middle East, Asia, or Latin America.

Fourteen years ago, in a report titled "Safe and Secure: Protecting Judicial Officials," Neil Alan Weiner and several others detailed violence in the American judicial system. The report illustrated the rising threats and actual violence against judges, judicial personnel, and others working in the courts. Measures such as designing a court building as a "harden target," using metal detectors and X-rays to detect weapons and installing alarms and CCTV cameras, were undertaken as responses to potential attacks.

It is one thing to survey and describe the attacks on judges and court personnel, it is quite another to explain why such attacks are occurring more frequently and with substantial casualties. One explanation is that illiberal, traditional tribal forces are taking their insurgencies to the place where captured insurgents face justice. (In Thailand some have argued that the illiberal, traditional non-democratic forces are protected by applying a double standard that is supported by the courts.) Throughout the world, violent attacks on judges and their personnel may originate from deep-seated political conflicts in a society, and judges may find themselves in the crosshairs as warring factions demand that courts favor their interpretation of justice.

Another explanation is the absence of perceived fairness and impartiality of judges. Seneca confirms that this is an ancient issue: "*Auditur et altera pars*—The other side shall be heard as well." If one side to a dispute believes their side is systematically, as a matter of policy, not being heard and perceives that judges are automatically siding with the powerful, violence may well follow.

There is, in the Western tradition, a notion that courts, like free speech, are one of the safeguards needed to secure democracy. American theologian Reinhold Niebuhr wrote, "Man's capacity for justice makes democracy possible, but man's inclination to injustice makes democracy necessary." Courts are places where people in conflict go to obtain justice. And justice lies in the quality of a court's assessment, or story, that most plausibly emerges from the competing stories told by the parties through witnesses, forensic evidence, and expert testimony.

In times of political chaos, the judges in a political system are called upon to resolve issues arising from a constitution or other laws. The problem is that what is argued as a legal issue may have a significant political dimension, and that draws the judges into the fray. Each side of a political conflict seeks to convince the judges of the merits, fairness, common sense, and justice arising from the assembly of facts, time lines, and role of actors in the political drama. What is at stake isn't often found in the ordinary civil or criminal case. State authorities often have a horse in this race. Judges are by their nature also state authorities, but the theory has been that part of their job is to keep all authorities in check and to enforce civil liberties on behalf of those challenging what may be abuses of authority.

There is considerable gallows humor about the courts that goes back many years. Judge Sturgess, eighteenth-century jurist from Fairfield Connecticut, wrote, "Justice is open to everyone in the same way as the Ritz Hotel." Raymond Chandler would have agreed, as would any noir fiction writer. Similarly, Italian author and politician Ignazio Silone said, "An earthquake achieves what the law promises but does not in practice maintain—the equality of all men."

None of this jaundice about political systems or the courts that are an essential part of them is new. As Roman senator and historian Tacitus reminded us, "The more corrupt the republic, the more numerous the laws." Tacitus hasn't been alone in this view over the centuries. The author of *The Art of War*, Lao-Tzu, wrote, "The greater the number of laws and enactments, the more thieves and robbers there will be." And our cultural view of judges may veer from admiration to suspicion as we contemplate another oft-quoted piece of wisdom (source unknown): "Good lawyers know the law; great lawyers know the judge."

When it comes to the character of judges, one finds a range of opinions, including this one by David Dudley Field, a nineteenth-century American law reformer: "Judges are but men, and are swayed like other men by vehement prejudices. This is corruption in reality, give it whatever name you please."

"Corruption"—a word currently swarming around the hive of anti-government protesters in Thailand—has more than one sting in its tail. As Horace wrote, "A corrupt judge does not carefully search for the truth." A good judge, on the other hand, will seek out the truth even if it may discredit the actions of the powerful.

These observations raise the awkward questions of what the truth is and who is to be entrusted with the task of finding it amongst disputing factions, each claiming the prize for itself. Even judges of US justice Benjamin Cardozo's standing have recognized the issue: "There is in each of us a stream of tendency ... which gives coherence and direction to thought and action. Judges cannot escape that current any more than other mortals. All their lives, forces which they do not recognize and cannot name, have been tugging at them—inherited instincts, traditional beliefs, acquired convictions; and the resultant is an outlook on life, a conception of social needs. ... In this mental background every problem finds its setting. We may try to see things as objectively as we please. None the less, we can never see them with any eyes except our own."

Each age recreates its own justice system and selects the judges and other personnel to run it. And in each age, the status, reputation, and standing of the judges is reinvented to suit the purposes of the day. In our own day much of society has been disrupted by technology, including the courts, and now America has a secret court with judges deciding on the scope of government surveillance of its citizens. Thai courts sometimes hold closed sessions in lèse-majesté cases. US judge Michael Ponsor wrote in his novel *The Hanging Judge*, "If you want the best evidence of just how strong our democracy is, come into the courtroom." That's hard to do if it meets in secret. American novelist George R.R. Martin, whose works have been adapted for *Game of Thrones*, had his own idea about the connection between judges and the justice they administer: "The man who passes the sentence should swing the sword."

History suggests that once the courts are drawn into political conflict, the seeds of doubt and suspicion are easily sown in the fertile field of doubt about government institutions. The search for truth, justice, and impartiality is difficult at the best of times; at the worst of times hard men take justice into their own hands, sometimes with the tacit approval of the courts, and sometimes for face or revenge for the suspicion of such back channel signals of approval.

In Thailand today all eyes are on the courts to deliver judgments on a host of legal cases with large social and political implications. In a judicial system where judges have the power to remove prime ministers, sack MPs, and dissolve political parties, the perception of good faith is essential.

Whether the Thai judges, through their decisions in fact-finding and legal reasoning, will clear a path that appears fair and reasonable is a question on the minds of many. Whether any court of law can be designed for making, or can recruit judges capable of making, such political decisions acceptable to most citizens is another question altogether. Go to Google and type in Thai courts and click on images. The visual montage you get will tell a story about conflict, power, justice, anger, fear, and hate, and in the midst of this narrative are the courts, seeking a legal way out.

Personalized Swat Teams for the Filthy Rich

I am also interested in how others perceive Thai crime and Thai criminals. Wikipedia, that first stop on the journey to enlightenment, opens its article on the subject with this: "Crime in Thailand is a persistent, growing, complex, internationalized, and underrecognized problem. Crime in Thailand is reported by the Royal Thai Police, however, *there is no agency which acts as a watchdog and publishes their own statistics*" (emphasis mine).

The first sentence is one of those Chinese fortune cookie pronouncements that reads as though written by a sage until you think how you could substitute a few dozen other countries for "Thailand." Or it could be the lead sentence for an article on any one of a host of unrelated subjects, for example: "Misshaped mango in Thailand is a persistent, growing, complex, internationalized, and underrecognized problem."

You get the picture. Research limited to Wikipedia has its limitations. That's why a writer, like a journalist, need his or her sources on the street, and must spend time on the street cultivating old and new contacts and experiencing life in all of its odd, strange complexity.

It is the second sentence from the Wikipedia article, the one about statistics, that is more interesting to me. In crime writing one of the first things an author needs to figure out is who runs the statistics business about crime. It is, after all, a business, and a vital one. That fact about statistics about Thailand hints at a few matters about crime that you ought to pay close attention to. If you control the statistics that reflect upon your competence and ability to do the job, you just might have a bias about how those statistics are collected, stored, analyzed (along with the policy implications they imply), and communicated. It's called a conflict of interest. Trusting the fox to count the chickens is good for the fox but not always good for others.

What Wikipedia is saying is that without independent agencies (a loaded term if there ever was one) tracking them, you have to regard the reliability and accuracy of the statistics that the police are keeping with a certain amount of caution. You don't need a fortune cookie to tell you that he who makes the cookies is the one who is telling you what your future holds. Don't let the mango growers define what is a misshaped mango unless you have an appetite for some funny business about the nature of geometry.

Crime comes in all kinds of packages. In Thailand, if Wikipedia is to be believed, we can carve up criminal activity into a few categories: drugs, rape, white collar, tourist scams, human trafficking and prostitution, prison crime, identity theft and passport racket, gender violence, and school violence—a kind of pick-and-choose your poison list. If you want to write a crime story, you'll find some bones that haven't been picked clean by the previous pack of hyenas with typing skills.

The problem with this approach is that it's so 1990s or early 2000s. If you want to know about the future, study crime statistics and trends. That is the story of criminal activities down the road and around the bend. Most crime operates as a kind of rough-and-ready redistribution of the wealth that capitalism allocates unevenly among different segments of the population.

Before looking ahead, let's look at the history of one criminal hero. Robin Hood was a legend—a gang leader, militia boss, mafia chief, and Robocop rolled into one, who also had empathy for the little people. That is why his story is mere legend; over the sweep of history real Robin Hoods don't make a dent in the wealth of the powerful, any more than they go around singing ballads in the forest with a group of merry men. Most of them end up imprisoned, exiled, or killed. You can't look only at Robin Hood without looking at the position, influence, and power of the Sheriff of Nottingham and his boss. After all, it is the sheriff who is keeping the statistics on local crime.

The Sheriff of Nottingham, who is responsible for maintaining law and order and recording any criminal activities going on inside the forest, historically has suffered from some serious credibility issues. Nothing much has changed in the Thai part of the forest, rural or urban. It is the Thai police who keep tabs on the nightspots in Bangkok and collect the statistics about crimes conducted there, including illegal gambling, prostitution, and corruption. Getting tough on crime with harsher penalties is also a way to increase revenue flows from those who violate the laws so they can stay in business. When a man's job depends on not knowing something, there is a good chance he will argue against attempts to interfere with his ignorance. He will oppose anyone who seeks the installation of some windows in the wall of authority. That kind of renovation can be dangerous.

Chaiwat Limlikitaksorn is a Thai national park chief who has been accused of involvement in murder, arson, and disappearances in a forest under his jurisdiction in northern Thailand. Though charged with serious crimes, he continues to work in his position (as of April 25, 2014, the time of writing). A man named Por Chalee Rakcharoen (nicknamed "Billy"), a young ethnic Karen environmental activist, was recently stopped in the park by Chaiwat and fined for possessing six bottles of wild honey before supposedly being sent on his way. By coincidence, Billy had been on his way to gather signatures for an appeal against the park chief's abuse of power (for torching the homes of Karen villagers, the indigenous forest dwellers who are Billy's people). Billy never arrived. No one knows where he is. Chaiwat is quoted as claiming that he has no knowledge of what happened to Billy, but he may have been the last person to see Billy alive. The case has been in the news lately, but such cases in Thailand quickly fade away as media attention is drawn elsewhere. In the real world of Thailand, political activists who challenge authority in the tradition of Robin Hood don't last long, whether on the streets of the city or the trails of the forest.

The obstacle faced by most modern criminals, who fit less in the tradition of Robin Hood and are more likely motivated by personal gain, is finding out who has the wealth, where they keep it, and how best to relieve them of some of it. The first thing you figure out, if you look into such matters, is that the identity of the real criminal class, a small segment of society kept from public view and the risk of prosecution, is a closely held secret.

Since you are reading this book, the chances are you fit somewhere way above the average of wealth on the planet. When one reviews the statistics, the question that emerges is why the poor are content in their criminal activity to take crumbs from the rich, as there are vastly more empty rice bowls in the world than overflowing ones.

Credit Suisse's 2013 Global Wealth Report observes: "Our estimates for mid-2013 indicate that once debts have been subtracted, an adult requires just USD 4,000 in assets to be in the wealthiest half of world citizens. However, a person needs at least USD 75,000 to be a member of the top 10% of global wealth holders, and USD 753,000 to belong to the top 1%. Taken together, the bottom half of the global population own less than 1% of total wealth. In sharp contrast, the richest 10% hold 86% of the world's wealth, and the top 1% alone account for 46% of global assets."

At the upper end of wealth concentration, a clearer picture emerges of the number of people who own staggering amounts of wealth: "We estimate that there are now 31.4 million HNW [high net worth] adults with wealth between USD 1 million and USD 50 million, most of whom (28.1 million) lie in the USD 1–5 million range. This year [2013], for the first time, more than two million adults are worth between USD 5 million and 10 million, and more than one million have assets in the USD 10–50 million range."

And the upper limits of wealth display the numbers of truly outstanding fortunes: "Worldwide we estimate that there are 98,700 UHNW [ultra-high net worth] individuals, defined as those whose net worth exceeds USD 50 million. Of these, 33,900 are worth at least USD 100 million and 3,100 have assets above USD 500 million. North America dominates the regional rankings, with 48,000 UHNW residents (49%), while Europe has 24,800 individuals (25%), and 14,200 (14%) reside in Asia-Pacific countries, excluding China and India."

With the proliferation of information and statistical analysis, our notions of crime, criminals, wealth, and power are undergoing a serious transformation. Thomas Piketty's *Capital in the Twenty-First Century* has installed a whole set of windows into the wall that the very rich have up to now lived behind. In the United States, where statistics are now available and from multiple sources, we find that the top 10% own 76% of the nation's wealth, and the top 1% possesses 35%. The bottom 40% of the population has a negative wealth, and that picture is quickly growing worse for the overwhelming number of Americans. I suspect somewhere there is statistical evidence showing that the top 10% of Thais (with the top 1% having a big share of that percentage) have national wealth concentration at the same level or even exceeding that of the Americans.

Historically, the way to prevent revolt by people who have nothing has been repression or justification. That's where the Sheriff of Nottingham has done his historical duty: he's the enforcer for the 1%, and he's enforcing laws that maintain the status and power of the 1%. It's a cozy arrangement. (At least it used to be, but the arrangement has come under strains even in a society like Thailand, where the rich and powerful and titled are now being challenged—unthinkable before—and the likes of Billy are fighting for their rights to even what little they have.) It makes sense that the 1% wouldn't want any more statistics about crime, especially their involvement in crime, circulating among the bottom 99% of the population, who might have a question or two about the fairness or justice of such an allocation of wealth (and income also tracks a similar ratio).

Here's a breakdown of how these percentages translate into the number of people within the population of a country:

USA population, 310 million:
1% = 3,100,000; 0.1% = 310,000; 0.01% = 31,000
Thailand population, 66 million:
1% = 660,000; 0.1% = 66,000; 0.01%= 6,600

The lion's share of increases of wealth and income since 1980, according to Piketty, have accumulated to the benefit of those at the 1% level and above. This elite group has also experienced the most rapid increase (enjoying most of the gains of wealth and income) at the expense of all other members of the population. Piketty also has found there is no noticeable difference in skills, training, and education to account for the large difference in wealth and income from individuals who occupy the bottom nine-tenths of the top 10% and those in the top tenth of that group.

That is unfortunate for the top 1% because, without a convincing story to justify a vastly larger piece of the wealth-and-income pie, their continued good fortune becomes vulnerable as the forces of political change push for a new allocation. It makes their claims to superior abilities sound like classic Dunning-Kruger effect arguments (the poorly skilled tend to overrate their ability, while the highly skilled underrate theirs). The ultra-wealthy, one would have thought, would wish to distinguish themselves from the likes of Mr. McArthur Wheeler, the American bank robber who believed rubbing lemon juice on his face made him invisible.

What the PEW research doesn't break out is how much of that pie is taken by the top 1% and the top 0.1%, and how much of total wealth has flowed to those two groups. Judging from Piketty's research, it is a safe bet that more than 50% of wealth is assigned to just 7% of the population.

Now for the future: here are some possibilities (nothing is inevitable and many factors stemming from technological changes may change everything)—the 0.1% is the real problem. This category is for people making an income of more than $1.5 million a year. The further you go up this chain, the more concentrated and vast are both wealth and income. These are the people who hire lobbyists, fund political campaigns, and use their wealth to preserve their status and power. In less developed countries there are more incidents of outright brute force and legal intimidation, as political systems with shallow roots in democracy and powerful forces behind the scenes act together to operate covert dictatorships.

What Thomas Piketty's research has done is to provide a laser-like focus on this highly elite group—where they are, what they own, and what their presence means for everyone. The initial targets will likely be the super-managers of large American companies who make $11.5 million or more a year in compensation. Until now, great wealth has successfully dodged the spotlight that follows the superstar actor, athlete, or inventor. The shadows adjacent to the spotlight are a good place to hide as at least a case can be made to justify the superstars' wealth based on a combination of skill, knowledge, and talent. But the old, inherited wealth, which remains a source of enormous power and influence, lacks that justification. It becomes more of a hard sell to the 99% to maintain that degree of inequality of wealth and income.

Future criminals will be able to get their hands on information that will afford them access to these people. Kidnappings and abductions of the ultra-rich and their family members and associates are likely to grow. Tracking down the off-the-book wealth that the extremely wealthy own will be another growing line of criminal activity; because of such efforts there is already a convergence (this is why the sheriff keeps the records) between the ultra-wealthy and high-level criminal organizations. We don't really know how much business they do together. In the future we will find out a lot more about that connection.

Leaving aside crimes of violence, crime for economic gain is largely conducted by the poor against the rich. That makes a great deal of sense as the rich write the laws to protect themselves from theft and kidnapping by the poor. So long as the wealth concentration is hidden—or if not hidden, at least justified—the imprisonment of poor people who seek illegal means of redistribution has broad-based support, as long as we consider them common criminals and not Robin Hoods.

The stories we tell about the wealthy and their riches are effective in this regard to the extent that the population holds a consensus about social justice and fairness. A large inequality gap that continues to grow undermines that consensus. If highly concentrated wealth is denied a plausible story to justify it, alternative stories will begin to question the legitimacy of the wealthiest. We are at that crisis point. Wealth is being viewed as a by-product of a profoundly unfair economic system. As a result, normative judgments about which class are the criminals and which class requires protection from predation will shift as the spotlight moves from the poor to the ultra-rich.

I will also predict a boom in online wealth locators: individuals and organizations that specialize in identifying who owns what, where it is owned, the income generated, and its current market and book value. This information lies inside the "big data" of our modern information systems, waiting to be mined. The ultra-wealthy won't much like this intrusion into their business and personal lives. In the stock market of the future, I'd invest heavily in companies with advanced surveillance technology. That sector might prove to be a winner as those seeking a means to uncover the location and nature of wealth will be in an arms race against those who want to block any windows that stare into their deepest bank vaults. We can also expect security firms and technology companies to combine. They should experience a bullish period from selling products and services such as highly trained SWAT teams, personalized armored vehicles, CCTV technology, computer security, and drones to the 0.01% for protection. SWAT teams of this kind work for a private person or family. They roam the streets of New York, Bangkok, London, or Tokyo as if they worked for heads of state, and indeed their bosses are looking more and more like those powerful figures.

We are at a crossroads where economic slowdown, technological change, and big data are changing perceptions about the concentration of wealth and income. The 0.1% have to date enjoyed a near monopoly on story telling concerning them and their interests, anointing co-operative story tellers and information gatherers along the way. It is tempting to say that that world is about to end. The reality is that extreme inequality of wealth and income has been the normal state of political, social, and economic life in almost all places and times, especially since the industrial revolution. It isn't some evil system that arose thirty years ago.

The test is whether new political institutions and legal systems will evolve policies to limit wealth and income concentrations accumulating at the 1% level. Over the next twenty years, will the world's wealth and income look more compressed, as in today's Denmark, and less like the United States or Thailand? Alternatively, as we can assume the 0.1% won't go gently into that good night, it is just as likely that the world will build on American inequality, and the Denmark of our time will become an old story like that of Robin Hood, to be told to children who are innocent enough to believe a hero could defeat the entrenched power of the Sheriff of Nottingham. What Piketty's book has done is show that if you dig hard enough into the historical record, you can find a great deal of information about the nature of wealth, how income concentrates over time, and how policies, wars, revolutions, and depressions have caused temporary shifts in the direction of equality.

Up to now we've lived in a statistical dark age when it comes to wealth. We are waking up to the reality of what gross inequalities bring. Like a dentist peering into the mouth of an elderly patient who has never owned a toothbrush, we aren't quite certain what treatment is appropriate, but we're reasonably clear there is considerable work to be done and at great expense.

Part III

Evolution of Violence & the Borderless World

Violence: The Next Big Leap

Crime authors deal in the currency of violent behavior. Every society has violent actors. Mostly they play the part of villains, except when they are portrayed as heroes. The shifting between roles is confusing.

Crime fiction is filled with guns, victims, criminals, police, prosecutors, judges, and prison guards. Flip through the pages of a crime novel and you tune in to some point in the continuum of violence. Crime fiction readers process violence through the vicarious experience of following the characters as they live the story. Books, TV, and movies deliver the planning, execution, conspiracies, corruption, and lies that propel violence.

Crime of the violent kind appeals to some desire or need that is deeply embedded in our brains. The fear of and fascination with violence are keys that unlock some of the mysteries of our true nature. Thomas Hobbes built a philosophy on this cruel feature of the human psyche. He wasn't alone. David Hume, the great Scottish philosopher, argued that there is no justice, equality, or fairness in nature. People invented social constructs like religion and tribe to organize themselves against possibility of violence by outsiders. They taught these social constructs through parables and myths, installing them at the foundations of their culture as sacred text. We cling to these ideas as a shield against violence and conspire to maintain the illusion that they are innate in all people rather than made up by people just like you and me.

Crime writers tap into a long tradition of writers and thinkers who chart the pathways of violence and the safe byways to steer clear of them. The noir writer, like Hobbes, believes in holding people's true nature hostage by nothing short of ceding authority to one powerful representative who can maintain the peace.

We are in the midst of a modern story of violence reported from many parts of the world, which shows how fragile our defenses have become. Social justice, fairness, and equality need a political structure to have meaning. Without a structure, brute central force is the substitute we are inevitably offered, ostensibly to keep the other brutes at bay.

When faith in a democratic structure loses its grip on a substantial minority of people, we lurch to non-democratic alternatives for keeping the peace. Such repression does little to prevent or contain violence. In such an environment the bonds that tie us to each other begin to fray and fall apart. Has Thailand reached that point? My answer, as of March 2014, is not yet. The fact remains that, despite the increase in violence and the instability of the political process, Thais enjoy a mostly peaceful existence in most places.

Around the world we can see cities that have collapsed, or are in the process of collapsing, into the black hole of violence, as well as countries that have fallen into the category of failed state. These are isolated events. In Thailand we are a substantial distance from a failed state. But the potential for a rapid, uncontrollable expansion of violence remains.

In general we should be worried about the early warning signs that our great experiment in domestication (another term for an internalized non-violent, co-operative code of behavior) and may ultimately fail in the context of huge, dense concentrations of people. Is the world doomed to become a massive crime scene?

Before I discuss weapons (essential instruments of the domestication process along with drills, routines, and propaganda), I want to talk about the scaling of large concentrations of people. None of our closest cousins in the great ape family, with whom we share our mental and psychological roots—chimps, bonobos, gorillas, or orangutans—scale their communities beyond small groups. There are no cities of apes (nor have there ever been), where thousands or millions live side by side. In stark contrast to our close animal cousins, billions of people now take shelter, feed and bathe themselves, play, and kill each other in cities. Given our genetics, it's amazing that there isn't more killing. It is evidence that domestication has been largely successful.

If you shoved one hundred chimps into a Skytrain (BTS) carriage in Bangkok, closed the door and ran the train from Siam station to On Nut station, when you opened the doors, you'd likely find multiple wounded or dead bodies amid clumps of hair, blood, ripped-off testicles, and severed eyes and noses. And these chimps wouldn't have been fighting over the merits of a political system. They would have had no political system or abstract ideals to fight over, but neither would they have had any process for controlling their anger and violence when clumped together in a train. They would simply have reverted to natural instinct, the lid swiftly popping off their bottled violence. We couldn't exactly say that these imaginary chimps have behaved badly. They have simply displayed their chimp-like nature, one that is very close to our own.

Civilization and modern big cities wouldn't have arisen without a number of other essential features such as fire, language, and tool making. But without a way to control our violence-prone species, scaling cities to populations like Bangkok's 12 million would have been impossible. My theory is that a pair of big bangs drove that inflation in numbers and density: the role of the sacred and the technological advance of ever-increasingly powerful weapons.

The feeling of transcendence makes it possible for a person to feel part of a much larger collective or community. The sense of awe as we regard the ineffable lifts us beyond the narrow borders of our daily lives. A long time ago religion saw the opportunity to fill this need. In close-quarter living, the goal has always been to strive for a domesticated species that believes that it is part of something larger than itself and fears exclusion from the community where this collective communion takes place.

One of our most powerful social constructs, learnt from an early age, is fueled by the strong desire to belong, to fit in—to the family, the neighborhood, the school, and the church. The sacred, through religion, provided the stories and rules for such belonging to a larger whole. That early sense of the transcendent eventually decoupled from religion and found voice through the arts: music, literature, dance, and painting. The same mechanism is at work in this new realm, run by a sprawl of sacred creators who are our unofficial, unorganized secular priesthood. Celebrities and other snake oil sellers mingle in the crowd, offering their visual and aural cathedrals.

However, no matter how widespread the sacred is, it isn't enough to stop our inclination to use violence. The incidence of violence has never been zero. The idea of zero tolerance for violence is utopian. Violence remains at the margins everywhere. When a political system halts through gridlock, an uptick in violence is one of the first things to notice.

In Bangkok in recent weeks, as the government has come under siege, scattered acts of a different kind of violence have arisen. Isolated shootings and bombings such as we have experienced here lately have quickly been absorbed into our day-to-day manner of living. In Bangkok we read daily news reports of this renewed violence. We read about it on the Internet or in the *Bangkok Post*, or watch it on TV. For most of us the sound of gunfire remains outside our direct experience, along with the sight of bullet holes in the windows of cars and houses, or of badly beaten people. Life in Bangkok goes on pretty much as usual, with trains and restaurants packed, offices filled with workers, and traffic jams along Sukhumvit Road. The general calm of the vast population indicates that violence's increase around the edges of consciousness has not panicked the population.

Domesticated animals that we are, we sense no clear and present danger as we head out the door. Violence in Bangkok remains at a level far from those found in Baghdad, Kabul, Caracas, Nairobi, Cape Town, Peshawar, Sana'a, Ciudad Juarez, or other cities on the top ten most violent list (according to India.com's *ZeeNews*).

One of the common threads running through the list of violent cities is the breakdown of domestication, especially of young, unemployed men. The ability to control violent people, armed and ready to use their weapons, isn't working in these cities. The danger is greater today because the capability for fast, cheap communication and alliance-building provided by social media can create instant communities fueled by anger and hatred. It is hard to have mass violence without those emotions infecting a significant number of people.

People are emotionally driven, and our communication breakthroughs have enabled the amplification of anger and fear over vast populations, as well as the organization and deployment of angry individuals. When we look around at the world today, we find no shortage of fronts where people attack each other or strike out against neighbors who happen to accept a different view of the sacred or come from a different tribe or ethnic group.

Another feature of widespread violence is that it points to questions of respect for the legitimacy of authority, or the lack of fear of the authorities. In the top ten most violent cities, the legitimacy of the government is openly questioned by force of arms. Those challenging the authority aren't deterred by any credible threat of state violence to stop them. A small minority can create enough chaos to make a city impossible to live in, driving refugees to flood across borders, in turn destabilizing neighboring nations and exhausting the resources of international humanitarian agencies.

In my first novel, His Lordship's Arsenal, I created a story about the invention of the Thompson submachine gun and how that weapon changed the way violence was projected and distributed in a way that revolutionized the world. The idea of weapons and their capability on the eve of World War I was based on assumptions about the relationships between soldiers, officers, and the state. Modern weapons toppled political systems in Europe, causing them to collapse like a house of cards. In my book I explored the theme of this technical/political change. The grunt with a machine gun had a weapon that could kill hundreds of the enemy, including their officers, heroes, and officials. That humble soldier's trigger finger represented more power than had ever been wielded by any previous warrior who'd gone to battle. No longer did an officer distribute rounds to his troops in the field. The troops in the field had their own supply ammo fed by belts into rapid-firing weapons. A generation of young men, well-bred and lowly-bred alike, consequently died in European trenches, felled by other young men bearing these machine guns.

One hundred years later another technological change threatens to change power arrangements between those with a monopoly over violence and the domesticated populations who bow to these overlords. Hovering above the future event horizon is another leap in weapon technology: military drones—remotely controlled spy aircraft, some of them armed. What is in store for us is beginning to take shape. There is a window for the state authorities to retake control of violence and neutralize the egalitarian nature of automatic infantry weapons. The elites equipped the infantry with such weapons and feared that such weapons could be turned on them. If one could keep the firepower with the elites, as in medieval times, this fear could be more easily managed.

Nuclear weapons and guided non-nuclear missile systems are overkill for this purpose. But a drone that can stay overhead for hours, watching, waiting for the digital command from an operational center ten thousand miles away, is another kind of weapon entirely. The new infantry sit in front of computer monitors continents away from the action, in ordinary cities, go home at night to their spouses and children, go to school plays, shop at the mall, and see the latest film at the cinema. They don't carry an automatic weapon home at night.

A recent essay in the online magazine *Quartz*, "Drones Will Cause an Upheaval of Society like We Haven't Seen in 700 Years," examines the implication of new drone-robotic weapon systems and concludes that this generation of weapons represents a game changer. Why? Because a drone means the 1% no longer need the 99% as muscle in the violence business. Owning the software and hardware does away with the need for heavy lifting by troops in the field. Weekly meetings to agree upon the kill list, expansion of surveillance to detect the violent troublemakers, and using, in essence, white-collar computer workers to pull the trigger creates a new weapons/violence paradigm. The idea is that the 1% can use drones to subdue the 99%, who are no longer essential as frontline troops. This not only reverses the equality earned through the use of automatic weapons in World War I, but it upsets the whole notion of projecting violence and re-domesticating the population with instruments to instill genuine fear.

If this premise turns out to be true, no matter how much oppression we feel from the authorities that administer the current state of weapon technology, (in a year not far down the road) it will appear that our time, in retrospect, to have been the end of the golden age of freedom and liberty enjoyed by billions of people. Policing, the administration of justice, and the process of controlling criminal conduct will all—if this future pans out—be thoroughly disrupted. Crime novels will be an oddity from the distant past and will be read by the survivors by a degree of awe and disbelief.

The struggle over violence containment has up to now inevitably sought the golden mean, the sweet spot between too much tyranny and too little. The goal has been enough control to keep our primate violence in check, so that large populations whose members are competing for scarce resources and mates can live in peace, but not so much as to allow outliers to convince the average person it is in his or her interest to risk life, limb, family, and property to turn to violence against his neighbor or combine with his neighbors to challenge the authorities.

There are other possible outcomes. As autonomous robotic systems integrate with artificial intelligence, it is likely that eventually the 1% will find the weapon systems pointed at them. The newly grouped 100% will have an overlord to ensure not the survival of the fittest humans but the survival of the most domesticated, and once again the term "drone" will apply to people rather than to smart weapons. Our social constructs will no longer be programmed by the 1%; they will be programmed by a machine world that will know our biases, our weaknesses, and our primate nature better than we do. Such knowledge drawn from big data will be more effective than codes, stories, myths, or sacredness penned by any ruler, philosopher, historian, psychologist, or the smartest person working at Facebook or Google. Our sacredness will evolve in ways we can't yet imagine. Our overlords will program our faith.

Past wars have had the collateral effect of culling the herd of angry, unemployed young men. Artificial intelligence may decide it is more efficient to cull the populations down to a historical level, one at which violence-prone primates need less managing. Realistically, we have to face the fact that an AI system might question the wisdom of feeding, housing, and controlling 7 billion people, large numbers of whom are prone to acting on violent impulse. These numbers create a big management, logistical, and environmental problem.

No country or leader has shown the resources or ability required to resolve conflict between and inside a group of 7 billion individuals, and our population shows no signs of stabilizing. At the same time we are being reminded of our human limitations. When we can't find a 250-ton plane with 239 people two weeks after it disappeared, we are learning a lesson in humility: for all of our advanced technology, we have large blind spots. It is only a matter of time before machine intelligence eliminates these blind spots and decides that a general culling of the population would restore our primate species to the destiny we broke free from on our journey out of Africa.

The Boundary Lines of Your Life

In late March 2014 I wrote an essay about violence. Now, a couple of weeks later, I have two companion ideas I'm developing: borders, boundaries, and hegemony; and the essential role of hierarchy in running a modern political, economic, or social entity. Understanding how these three threads are connected—violence, borders, and management—opens a portal into the cultural, political, social, and economic source code that computes most of the reality people experience. A great deal of what goes on around us in our daily life, from our safety and welfare to our opportunities and livelihood, depends upon the right balance between these three forces. Disruptions through the forces of instability and random chance are what makes life "interesting," often in the way the Chinese use the word—meaning chaotic and uncertain.

Passports, visas, refugees, work permits, occupation, red line, occupiers, invaders—these are among the terms that arise from the reality of boundaries, the kind that defines a recognized border, the edges measured, recorded, mapped. A world map is a visualization of these boundaries. I have a globe with lines etched in it for the frontiers of countries. What makes maps of other planets and moons in our solar system so foreign is the absence of any recognizable boundary marks. These alien landscapes go on and on with a tedious, mind-dulling, featureless repetition. It seems that what these faraway worlds lack is a life form that has evolved to defend its territory against outsiders. That life form creates and acts on a mental construct of borders as part of its evolution. Borders aren't an organic part of nature. We invent them.

I've been thinking during the past two weeks about boundaries and how they set the human dimensions of movement, affiliation, and self. What they mean, how we define them, and our connections to them. Boundaries can be a geographic term that we associate with nation-states such as Canada, Thailand, or Australia. The last of these is surrounded by ocean boundaries only. The first two share at least some land boundaries with other countries, and those boundaries have resulted in disputes. Whether the location falls on land or water, boundaries can be real and tangible or completely abstract, even romantic.

I am a realist as a writer. The use of the phrase "reality check" as part of the title of the International Crime Writers blog that I contribute to is no accident. I accept, though, that the range of writing expands beyond the boundary lines of the ancient Roman Empire, so to speak, to also encompass the mythical kingdom of Camelot, where boundaries float in the imagination. Ordinary life is boundary-contained, and writers usually orient themselves within those boundaries, reporting on the activites there. Other writers might rebel against boundaries and write about lives outside them.

I am also interested in other boundaries, such as knowledge or experience. There are limits to what we can know and limits to what we can experience. You can't experience X-ray frequency waves, for instance. You can't know the physics that existed before the Big Bang. We have boundary gaps, although we live our lives as if all information and knowledge were accessible. That is a delusion that allows us to feel in control of our lives.

You were born within a boundary. That act of birth played a role in shaping your identity. You are a Thai or a Russian, a Canadian, a Japanese, etc. What happens inside those borders becomes a version of your own personal story. Boundary stories and personal stories inside a bounded area are something we take for granted when reading a novel or watching a film or a TV drama.

All boundaries have an element of control. There is nothing in nature that corresponds to a boundary, though primates, such as our close cousins the chimpanzees, band into small groups to patrol territories. Their border patrols exist to chase away intruders, to look for weaknesses in a boundary line beyond which resources might be harvested, and to cross the line into another band's territory. That is our heritage. Boundaries run through old bloodlines that predate our species. What we've managed to do is to use technical means to create weapons and transport systems that allow us to scale a geographical space, draw its boundaries (over the objections of others living there, if need be), and install security forces to guard the borders.

The chimpanzee culture of border patrol shows the evolution of violence as a means of boundary enforcement and boundary encroachment. When those two principles collide between rival chimpanzee bands, violence is the likely outcome. Borders come at the cost of blood. The aggressors who are better equipped and organized, and who are more violent and more willing to put themselves at the risk of death or injury, will likely gain the upper hand.

Boundaries are never static for long. Online you can Google to find a digital map of Europe that shows the continent's changing political borders over a span of a thousand years. In less than three minutes you watch a millennium of borders twitching, receding, expanding, disappearing, in wave after wave of change. Chances are that if you were to trace your ancestors back through ten generations, you would discover your relatives ten generations removed were born within boundaries that no longer exist in the same way they did at the time of your birth. You have no feeling for that "place" as it was a location that existed in one time but failed to survive. Maybe it's not unsettling for most people to view their distant forebears as irrelevant to their modern life. The point is that boundaries are no more immortal now than they were for these ancestors, who also thought their boundaries possessed a permanence that time proved to be illusory.

Borders are also an underlying reason for abuse and human rights violations against minorities. A recent example in this part of the world is the Rohingya people, an ethnic group inside Burma, who have been systematically persecuted and killed, their villages burnt and women raped, as Burmese authorities consider them as not "belonging" inside their borders. But what is "Burma"? The answer lies not in nature but in the boundaries drafted by British colonial mapmakers. There are many other minority groups considered outsiders or aliens around the world, born inside the borders of countries that deny them identity or nationality. Stateless people are those not accepted by any country. With no place to be or to go, they face a dismal future.

The vast scale of migration around the world over the last twenty years, as people cross borders, is captured in the online chart (http://www.global-migration.info) prepared by researchers at Wittgenstein Centre for Demography and Global Human Capital in Vienna, reproduced here.

Your geographical connection is a leading piece of information about you. When you meet a stranger, one of the first questions that you ask is, Where are you from? Your own answer to that question supplies a database of assumptions about your education, culture, language, wealth, religion, sports, and your attitudes about guns, abortion, health care, funding for education , war, and peace. One word fills in a library of preconceived notions about what you find funny or sad and the foods you probably like.

Thais are forever asking me where I am from. Canada. Snow, ice hockey, near America, cold, Bryan Adams, Leonard Cohen—I receive responses along these lines as the listener tries to say something nice about Canadians. Foreigners will hear some Thais say that a *farang* doesn't understand how Thai people think. There is a tacit, shared feeling among a lot of the world's peoples that outsiders don't quite get how they think, so Thais aren't alone in this assumption based on geography (and race).

Of course race and boundaries have a close connection in the minds of many people. A person born in Thailand is expected to look different from someone born in Finland or Nigeria. This ignores the fact of ethnic and racial diversity within all countries. Even today people are raised to think not so much "globally" as tribally, as people coming from and belonging to a certain geographical location.

Globalization promised to liberate trade, commerce, and finance from the traditional boundaries that have long restrained them. Instead you might say that globalization has allowed powerful states the same kinds of advantages that empires exercised in the past. Our new Rome is Washington, D.C., where those in control of the forces of violence make decisions about certain activities inside the borders of other states.

When Russia decided to adjust Ukraine's borders by assuming control of Crimea, the reaction from Europe and America was condemnation. Modern states aren't supposed to invade other countries and claim them as part of their own state. That's the theory, but the record, going back to the thousand-year map, shows a long history of land grabs and border changes. The US expansion into North America's western frontier in the nineteenth century represented another example of occupying the territory of others, expelling the occupants (in this case into reservations), and confiscating their resources.

When you live in a country in which you weren't born, aren't a naturalized citizen, and haven't been granted permanent residence—which is my situation in Thailand—you receive regular reminders that you are inside the boundaries of a place that considers you an outsider. These reminders include specific duties that you must perform to remain. For ten years I made ninety-day visa runs mostly to neighboring countries, including Laos, Malaysia, Singapore, Cambodia, Vietnam, and Indonesia. I had to leave before the expiration of each ninety-day visa, get a new visa, and re-enter Thailand to start another ninety-day period. I never complained about this feature of expat life. In fact I felt the requirement worked in my favor as each ninety-day period gave me enough time to concentrate on writing a draft of a book. Each ninety-day period allowed me to work on my next draft, until after three or four visa runs I had a finished book. I was living with a ninety-day sword hanging over my neck. I didn't want it falling before I'd finished a novel. I convinced myself that this sword was actually a chance for an international holiday between book drafts; it worked like an incentive plan. I lived with that delusion. It kept me productive, focused, and aware of how much there was to explore outside the borders of Thailand.

With a minimum of forty international trips prescribed over ten years (I often made trips more frequently than every ninety days), I had a chance to spend time in places where battles over borders were still fresh in the minds of the local people. Cambodia, Laos, Burma, and Vietnam provided me with lessons about how boundary lines can define a people, and how civil wars often turn on the identity issues that divide people who share space within the same borders.

Years ago I switched to an annual visa, but I still must report my address every ninety days. That takes me back to where I started. Authorities take notice and keep track of "foreigners" within their borders. A certain suspicion about foreigners seems to linger from humanity's time spent in roving bands, when a stranger was likely to be either enslaved or killed.

Crimes such as illegal logging and fishing cross borders continually. The trafficking of people, drugs, weapons, logs, ivory, and other contraband is enticingly profitable for criminals precisely because of laws written to control the movement of people, goods, and services across international borders. Organizations like Doctors Without Borders and Reporters Without Borders are the exception that proves the general rule that borders are vigilantly patrolled and regulated.

Life inside every culture is shaped by a shared heritage of what it means to be born, schooled, and employed within a space defined by certain political boundaries. Step out of that space and "foreign" authorities and laws suddenly apply. Substantial legal differences may arise in your life, ranging from women's exclusion from the right to drive in Saudi Arabia to legalized gambling in Macau to a single-payer health care system in Canada. To cross a border requires the foreigner to be alert to the laws of that place.

In Thailand it is common to find tourists who, having left their country, act as if the new space they occupy has no laws or rules that apply to them. And every year there are sad cases of foreigners arrested, tried, and convicted for breaking Thai law (doing things that in the vast majority of cases would be just as illegal in their home country).

That sense of anything goes, of freedom from constraints, happens when our normal borders are erased through travel.

We lose our sense of perspective and comprehension once we are deprived of familiar boundary markers. It is strange to contemplate spaces without working out the boundaries that make up that space. The search for Malaysian Airlines flight 370, for instance, gives us a glimpse of failure to understand the featureless huge expanse of the area in the Indian Ocean where the search has been concentrated. Or consider how, with climate change and the melting of the northern ice caps, ship passage through the Arctic Ocean is becoming possible, and countries are starting to assert which portions of Arctic geography they can draw within their borders. Another likely disruption caused by climate change is the mass movement of hungry and thirsty people whose lives have become untenable inside established borders.

Geographical and political borders provide a sense of order, define a finite world that gives a feeling that, for all their arbitrariness and the problems they bring, we have a need for boundaries. The infinite makes us recoil. Lacking borders by definition, the infinite simply has no meaning for us, like the decimal points of pi beyond the standard 3.14. This is a universe where there is an endless roll of the dice, with no winner or loser, and with no point or meaning.

The infinite might have a sound, of sorts. A mathematician/musician created a hauntingly beautiful piece for piano using the decimal points of pi for a taste of the infinite nature of this series of digits, with its seemingly random structure. I hear the music of those pi decimals when I read about the search operation for Malaysian Airlines flight 370. It has become a substitute for the dark feelings that sometimes descend.

I am forced to concede that even though borders are phony constructs I've been taught, they have always defined who I am and how I experience the world and will continue to do so. As land and resources are finite and sometimes scarce, defending a territory defined by borders will remain a natural part of political, economic, and social life. We can't imagine a life where borders are irrelevant except in a utopian fantasy. We may listen to the music that pi writes, with its promise of infinite decimals, but without our geographical and psychological maps with the borders colored in, our sense of self disappears. That selfless state may be one definition of enlightenment. Or alternatively such a state could turn out to be a refugee prison, whose occupants write an eternal song of grief and madness.

Existential Fear in a Secular Age

hristopher Hitchens, Richard Dawkins, Sam Harris, Daniel Dennett, and John Allen Paulos have written best-selling books subjecting religion to the rigors of science, testing, evidence, and logic. The belief in the sky god was never able to withstand such a compelling analysis. The borders of faith have shrunk inside many people's lives, though those who describe themselves in surveys and polls as atheist continue to remain a minority in most Western countries. It may be that many people remain under the cloak of religion only nominally. Strip away the cloak and the reality is they have all but in name abandoned faith in the sky god. Meanwhile, the rituals of faith continue like a steam locomotive. We love the experience of ritual—the sights, the smells, and the ride with fellow passengers. We temporarily close our eyes to the fact that other forms of transportation have long ago overtaken us.

What is the evidence for this covert loss of faith in religion to supply satisfactory answers to the large existential questions about death? It is found in the rise of government as an alternative manager of fears. The second string in the violin that religion brought was the fear of being a sinner, doing wrong, angering the sky god. The old violin has lost both strings. Our existential angst goes unanswered by faith, and no one worries much about sinning. Guilt, like sin, is a word that no longer functions to keep antisocial behavior in check.

The old hierarchy of fear managers—monks, priests, rabbis, ministers—has for centuries claimed jurisdiction over ministering to our existential fears. As absolute faith in religious answers is no longer comforting to a growing mass of people, who have switched allegiance to the scientific method, a gap has opened. Our secularization has brought about a great leveraged buy-out of the fear business. The private sector has co-ventured with the government in the acquisition, data mining, storage, and analysis of the big information once controlled by religion.

The new secular clergy are organized around the language of mathematics as the church once used Latin for its elite. Mathematicians are our new cardinals. Their algorithms communicate the sacred and the secret. Outside the inner sanctum of government, a large, private group of lay novices are often ex-clergy who shuttle back and forth from public to private.

In gaining control over the fear business, governments and their private partners have found an effective way to expand and consolidate power. The medieval role of the church found that fear of the sky god's wrath was effective to control kings who ruled under its grace in Europe. History teaches an important lesson about those who claim the mantle of fear managers: power, whether religious or secular, manipulates our fear of the "other" and our fear of death to serve its own interests. As with worshippers before our secular age, the population has been excluded from the modern process of fear management. The new secular priesthood determines, in secret, what actions work best in the war against fear. Fear needs a face. Fear needs an enemy. In religious times it was the devil; in secular times it is the terrorists who have brought us to the edge of the apocalypse; these are the people who haunt us and make us fearful.

Secular governments have learnt what large religious institutions have known for centuries—the masses will abandon claims to civil liberties and rights in return for safety from the enemy, the non-believers, whether the enemy is to be found within or outside. The masses have no issue with giving a free hand to officials and private contractors waging this war against fear. Priesthoods rely on magical thinking. To defeat the enemies who cause fear, all-out war is necessary. In this worldview, there is no choice but to permit the authorities to collect metadata, mine it for threats, and pursue those threats by all available means.

Institutions that work in the fear business are not only good at data mining—math as the new Latin gives them a huge edge—but they are also adroit at understanding the psychology of the faithful. The reality is that people are highly vulnerable when it comes to fear. They want to be cleansed of it. Churches no longer offer a sanctuary to repress this destabilizing emotion. We are witness to a great shifting of the guards as religious institutions are going the way of the manual typewriter. In the digital age the amount of fear has increased at the same rate as Moore's law for computer speed. Fear has increased in tandem with our exposure to information about the dangers of the world. The uneasy anxiety of the masses demands that something be done to contain it.

In response to that demand, we are witnessing the result: a huge, burgeoning intelligence-gathering empire, one tailored to managing the globalization of fear. In America, for instance, intelligence agencies gather, store, and process metadata about millions of ordinary people's personal messages harvested from their email messages, telephone calls, and social networks, despite their never having been accused of any crime. The majority of those people have no problem with the government keeping information about their lives. They feel they've done nothing wrong. Only the kind of people who might harm them or kill them should be worried.

Don't tie the hands of the fear managers, we are told. Let them mount their steeds, draw their swords, and eliminate the bad people from our existence. In the religious realm heaven is on the side of the righteous. For the modern, secular population heaven requires mass storage facilities and algorithms to mine the huge amounts of data. This new secular church, and the vast network of lay novices, operates under the watchful eyes of hundreds of thousands of the workers with the sacred task of monitoring those who generate fear. They are our representatives of righteousness, the high priests who have been granted top-secret clearance, the vanguards to guard us against the fears that were once the preserve of the sky god and his representatives.

Our secular masters have become the new class of priests of the new digital technology, which like the sky god is everywhere and sees all. We use our new technology like prayers, believing that it will allow our secret clergy to decipher patterns and acquire knowledge about probable associations and outcomes to prevent crimes before they happen and to identify the criminals before they commit crimes. In the ancient days when religion played a central role in people's lives, we had to wait until a criminal acted before he could be investigated for evidence to catch him or have a confession extracted from him. In our secular, technological age that process, a remnant of the steam locomotive age, is no longer convenient.

We live in a new age, one in which fear propels us to allocate resources to identify people who use, or just possess the potential for, violence, aggression, and brutality. We no longer rest at night knowing the sky god keeps these transgressors' primitive impulses in check, just as we have begun to have serious doubt that the sky god is waiting on the other side of death. We face life alone as troubled, insecure, short-lived creatures, seeking shelter among our own violent species on a rocky planet and trying to get by day by day.

This new secular regime has crept up on us. We blinked. One moment it suddenly appeared. We are all part of the congregation. Dismantling the new clergy, or effectively controlling its actions, won't happen easily, and for a reason. We yearn not for freedom or liberty but for security from the terrible uncertainty of meaning in lives without the sky god, and the oblivion we confront in our death. As with all great religions, the day will arrive when one among them follows Martin Luther by challenging the authority of the digital Leviathan over our lives. We wait for that edict as it travels at the speed of light through cyberspace to offer a secular order where the clergy cedes power to the congregation it serves. Only then will there be any chance for a reformation.

Updating Madness

The publishing world recently passed a fifty-year anniversary that needs celebration. One way to mark the occasion might be to reconsider the meaning of "insanity" and related terms. Our evolving use of language in everyday conversation—in novels, movies, newspapers, TV, and on the Internet—can change the meaning of the words we use. Take the trio of "insanity," "craziness," and "madness." Those three ideas have been around since we've had language. In fact, I'm pretty sure that one day someone will find, from big data on the development of language, that one reason we acquired language was to keep tabs on people who the community thought weren't quite right in the head.

It has been more than fifty years since Ken Kesey's novel *One Flew over the Cuckoo's Nest* was released in 1962, striking a chord with the public and was much amplified by the film version that emerged thirteen years later. That makes this a good time to revisit and ask questions about how the ideas of insanity, craziness and madness remain powerful and effective tools to protect state power and authority.

Even today, McMurphy could be any of us who pushes back against authority. McMurphy, a criminal in the prison system with a relatively short sentence to serve, thinks he has cleverly gamed the system by getting himself transferred from prison to a mental hospital. He challenges the power of the head nurse. He discovers that he is inside a system that can keep him indefinitely, and no law, no institution, no authority can prevent the head nurse or her staff from using the full range of "treatments" (in the name of medical science) to break him (or from their point of view, cure him).

If you are anti-authoritarian, then you run the McMurphy risk of being labeled insane, rebellious, and troublesome. You go on a list. Nothing that you can do, as McMurphy eventually finds out, will prevent the authorities from disabling or destroying you, in McMurphy's case through a lobotomy. At the end of the story the Chief sees what they've done to McMurphy, whose unresponsive face is a testament to the power of the state to employ words like "insanity," "craziness," and "madness" with the precision of armed drones.

"Insanity" is both a legal and medical term. "Madness" and "craziness" are vernacular synonyms. Political correctness has suppressed these terms, and now discussions that would once have used them refer to "mental disorders." Science has dispatched madness and craziness to the old world of magic, herbal cures, and shamanic trances. Science has replaced the local shaman with doctors, nurses, researchers, and psychiatrists. This transition has been called progress and a victory over superstition and backwardness. However, in the fifty years since the novel was published, science hasn't been successful in changing the attitudes, emotions, and nature of mankind. In 1962 Kesey's medical workers, in the name of science, doomed the rebellious McMurphy. Science acted then, as it does now, as a good cover for those in power to legitimatize the repression of McMurphy and his kind.

It is difficult to say what is more dangerous—the old witch-doctor's non-scientific approach, or the new "scientific," medical approach. It is cruel and senseless and barbaric that a person's liberty should stand on the magical thinking of superstitious people, as science has put an end to the era of witch doctors? Many people are doubtful. The history of insanity does not correlate as one would wish with developments in science. The idea is that science brings progress, leaving the ways of superstitious people in the past. What we are discovering is that science is creating better tools for the lobotomy of critics and opponents. "Insanity," "craziness," and "madness" become mud-slinging words hurled against the rise of new ideas, philosophies, and technologies. Don't forget that at the end of *One Flew over the Cuckoo's Nest* it was Nurse Ratched who won. In 2013 we have a new cast of Nurse Ratcheds and McMurphys, and every indication that the outcome will be the same as it was a half century before.

Remember the Coke bottle thrown from the plane in the South African movie *The Gods Must Be Crazy*? Whenever a tribe comes in contact with an unknown technology, the existing system of belief and thought grows unstable and starts to list like an oil tanker that's rammed a reef. Soon the peaceful tribe of the movie is racked with high emotions such as hatred and envy, and violence follows as the hotheads arm themselves to control, own, and monopolize the novel invention. At the end of this 1980 film the hero Xi sets things right again by throwing the bottle over a cliff.

But the days when the hero could return the world to its pre-bottle ways are over. What is new is not a bottle thrown from a plane but the Big Data that is quietly culled, stored, analyzed, and applied to marketing, economic policy, and dissent suppression. That bottle won't be thrown over a cliff. It is here in the village to stay. New tools to spot and isolate (or control) "hostile disruptions" increase the reach to track and watch people who are supposedly mad, crazy, or insane—though those terms may not be the ones used. The powerful, who have a long history of of loosening scientific standards to taintmargalizing their critics by applying the stigma of insanity, have begun to copy and paste terrorism into places where they once found insanity, madness, and craziness.

The mental health issue always has risked being politicized into a campaign to reduce violence and maintain security and order. We don't have to look very far back in history before we stumble upon the inconvenient truths about state authorities using mental health as a method of repression and control. A list of the "Reasons for Admission" used by West Virginia's Trans-Allegheny Lunatic Asylum from 1864 to 1889 gives an idea of the kinds of thoughts and acts that could land you in the bunk next to McMurphy back then. These nineteenth-century reasons, describing the mental state or behavior of a person before being admitted to the asylum, included "hysteria," "immoral life," "laziness," "mental excitement," "over action of the mind," "political excitement," both "self abuse" and "suppressed masturbation," and "novel reading," among many others. To judge from *One Flew over the Cuckoo's Nest*, a case could be made that many items on the list had survived well into the twentieth century. One might even make the case that, dressed up in different terms, the list is still sufficient to catch the early twenty-first-century version of McMurphy.

"Business nerves and bad company" along with "brain fever," "sexual derangement," "dissolute habits," and "women trouble"—all on the Trans-Allegheny list—could fit about 90% of the writers I have met over the years. The reasons associated with the definition of crazy may explain why many people view writers, painters, dancers, and others under the big tent of art as crazy or insane. The point is that people who don't wish to fit into the morality and norms of their society, or are incapable of fitting into them, are by definition psychologically abnormal, and their alternative ways of living might be seen as further evidence of abnormality. Religious or ideological fanatics see non-believers as abnormal. Our technology hasn't updated the definition of craziness, only the capability of tracking people who fit one of the categories.

The clear and present danger of the concept of insanity that finally caught up with McMurphy in *One Flew over the Cuckoo's Nest* has been summarized by Wikipedia. It is a term that "may also be used as an attempt to discredit or criticise particular ideas, beliefs, principals, desires, personal feelings, attitudes, or their proponents, such as in politics and religion."

In our time would McMurphy's outcome have been any different? Have the last fifty years, with all of their advances in technology, given us better outcomes? Or are we still back at the gate of the Trans-Allegheny Lunatic Asylum, where McMurphy is put out of his misery and only the Chief escapes? But there *is* a big difference. In the 1960s escape was an option. In 2013, Nurse Ratched's forces would find the Chief, and he would end up like McMurphy.

Whether you identify with the Chief or McMurphy doesn't matter. It is Nurse Ratched's world. *One Flew over the Cuckoo's Nest* was a warning unheeded. We live in the shadow of the Reasons for Admission to the Trans-Allegheny Lunatic Asylum. As "novel reading" is one of the grounds for admission, you'll forgive me if I put on my track shoes and go looking for where the Chief has gone to ground.

Grooming 150 Friends

Everyone has lots of "friends" on social media. According to an online article in *Business Insider*, for instance, some people you've never heard of have millions of followers on Twitter. How can anyone have that many friends, you may be wondering. Obvious answer: they aren't really friends. Internet followers are a new and different category of relationships. I have under a thousand "friends" on Facebook, and I follow thirty-six people on Twitter. That's a large spread, and I'll return later in this essay to the idea of the maximum carrying weight for "friends."

We are a violence-prone species when it comes to expanding our territory in search of resources and mates. Until recently, like other primates, we lived in small groups. The size of our total population remained relatively small and stable for twelve thousand generations. It was only in the last five hundred generations that a number of events happened that allowed an inflation of population size. And in the last twenty generations the way people clustered together and organized their lives inside that cluster expanded exponentially. In terms of evolution, the human species experienced something like a Big Bang in technological evolution, even as our brains have maintained much the same wiring configuration.

We've all had moments, as we're tearing out our hair over red tape, when we'd vote for anyone who would dismantle bureaucracy. The far right wants to do something like that in America and elsewhere. Getting entangled with bureaucrats makes a revolutionary out of many. Or have you ever wondered why the monitoring of elections, demonstrations, and protests need layers of bureaucracy? Given the interconnected age of the Internet, why haven't we figured out a way to leave bureaucracy in the past?

The answer to this riddle is found in what might be called the Dunbar Number: 150. British evolutionary anthropologist Robin Dunbar, director of the Institute of Cognitive and Evolutionary Anthropology at Oxford University, discovered that 150 is the maximum number of people that our cognitive abilities can keep straight in terms of their relationships with us and each other. These are the people you know and keep in social contact with. The cognitive limitation that accounts for this phenomenon is found deep in our 250,000-year-old brain structure. It found deep in our 250,0, in other words. We evolved to live off the grid. Blogger Christopher Allen have argued that rthe optimal size for active group members for creative and technical groups—as opposed to exclusively survival-oriented groups, such as villages—hovers somewhere between 25 [and] 80, but is best around 45–50.

These numbers are linked to brain size and grooming habits. What has made our species different from other primates, according to Dunbar, is we use language as a substitute form of grooming. In language our species found a more efficient and effective grooming kit as words largely replaced the hours of picking lice and fleas from our friends' hairy bodies. In other primate social groups a significant portion of the group's time is spent on grooming as a means to maintain social cohesiveness.

Language, as it turns out, is a more effective and efficient kind of grooming. We are now in the next stage, where digital grooming has begun to replace face-to-face language exchange. Pressing the Like, Share, Retweet, Reply, or thumbs-up icon button may be thought of as grooming techniques. Many people among us do this sort of grooming of others all day on social media. Most of us have our social grooming colonies that share our personal biases online. Rather than 150 groom-mates, many people have a thousand or more, and we appear to have returned to a once-familiar environment where many spend much of their time digitally grooming their fellow primates—only we don't think of it as grooming any more than we usually think of ourselves as primates. Humans are as delusional and biased as we are inventive. We clutch onto these illusions as our reality so long as we find them useful in making our way through the jungle of everyday life.

For the sake of argument, I am using Dunbar's 150 as the upper limit on the number for the self-management of effective social relations among people that doesn't require someone from outside the group to organize resource acquisition or distribution. Inside Dunbar's world, things are done in-house. The group doesn't need a manager. It is useful to note that the upper limit is not the same as the optimal number, which hovers closer to 60 people rather than 150 people (as Eliezer Yudkowsky suggests on the Less Wrong blog).

How did we scale from small bands of fewer than 150 individuals to living in cities like Bangkok with 12 million people—all of whom, at some point, need transportation, sewers, drinking water, food, hospitals, schools, and jobs? That jump in scale required creating a "grid," and creating, refining, managing this grid in the face of the technological destruction of our history is a work in progress.

This is a massive scaling problem, and experiments with ever larger numbers living in densely concentrated areas have been going on for the last ten thousand years. But it is in the last couple of hundred years that the management of resources and people with ever better technology, systems, and logistics has permitted the co-ordination needed to feed, clothe, house, and control millions. Bureaucracy has been the backbone of the system that distributes resources and benefits. From the beginning there was a conflict of interest between those governing the allocation of benefits and the people who received those benefits. History is filled with slavery and oppression arising from the governing elites' marshaling of bureaucracy and the threat of violence to domesticate people and use them as a resource rather delivering resources to them.

Why would anyone agree to such an arrangement? Rebellion and uprisings are a constant feature in our culture. Herding large numbers of people into close quarters and demanding that they do things they'd rather not do often requires tools such as genocide, displacement, starvation, exile, and territorial expansion through wars. It also leads to rebellion.

The question is, who has the whip hand in running the vast enterprise of an entire culture, society, and economy? And how are individuals and groups under the control of the whip treated? The elite members seek to give an appearance of grooming the rest of us. Our new grooming venue within the social media suggests that appearances are no longer sufficient. People want something more akin to actual grooming. And what does that mean? It translates into demands for justice and fairness and liberties, and rights to participate in the decision-making process. They no longer like the old way of being treated like members of a herd to be managed and culled for the benefit of the rulers.

We don't groom sheep; we sheer them for their wool. Modern economic models have adapted the sheep template to humans and packaged it as grooming. A clever, sinister streak runs through our desire to dominate and to acquire resources, mates, and power.

The problem for the elites lately has been doubts about the legitimacy of the bureaucrats coercing people to do or not to do things. Once the threat of official violence underwrote their orders. The original bureaucrats, in religious or civil organizations, operated under the authority of religious leaders, kings, chiefs, warriors, or strongmen. They were sacred and objects of worship; they inspired awe and respect, tying the following of orders to loyalty, purity, and honor.

Once the social setting expanded to a level that vastly exceeds the Dunbar number, there was no going back. The new society will be organized along very different principles, and its values and ethics will evolve to reinforce authority and to punish nonconformity. Our brain-ware doesn't give us any other choice. Our neocortical architecture is our cognitive prison. The grooming prison is egalitarian, housing everyone equally despite differences in IQ, status, birth, or abilities. No one, but no one breaks out of the brain's prison holding cell.

Democracy, in the modern sense, is a very late arrival—first with the Greeks but the lift off happened only about five hundred years ago—when the sentiment shifted to asking whether the authority to devise and implement the policies that controlled the actions of the bureaucracy ought to come from the citizens. That was and remains a revolutionary idea. Almost all of history up to then had seen people either living together in small bands where everyone knew one another or, much later, forming into larger agricultural communities that had various degrees of tyranny to compel compliance with the allocation of resources according to the desire or whims of the top leader.

We live in a time when extremists seek to reinstate a council of elders, purists, who are truth believers in an ideology or faith, a strict hierarchy of authority beyond outside challenge or change. That's the Taliban model with the suicide bombers, oppression of women, and hatred for gays, infidels, or foreigners. Inside the capitalist system it is wealth that is used to terrorize and control; the wealthy co-opt the bureaucracy like ancient caliphs for their own personal benefit.

Capitalism, in the gilded age mode, has produced a kind of suicide vest destruction, leaving the people who most need bureaucracy unable to access it or, if access is allowed, a reduced range of benefits. The battles in the United States to expand bureaucracy into the field of universal health care in a way that many developed countries have done is a classic example of ideological beliefs undercutting the distribution of resources to the wider population.

The old grid our parents were born into, one based on a monopoly of "state" bureaucracy, is threatened by a new grid built by the social media. The people signal status, wealth, success, and power through a registry of "likes." A lot of companies and people pay for "likes." They use wealth to generate authority. It is an illusion that "likes" bought to artificially increase status have any meaning. But it is not an illusion that the social media are causing a reorganization of how people accumulate into groups with shared goals, values, and interests. The center of management is returning to smaller groups who define themselves by affiliations to political, economic, or social causes, charities, sports teams, or other social communities.

In the world we were born into it has been difficult not to question Winston Churchill's observation that "it is the people who control the Government, not the Government the people." But now the very wealthy are retaking the government, meaning the vast management system that runs the machinery of life for millions, and they are doing so with the intention of dismantling it.

It is utopian, as the Khmer Rouge demonstrated, to believe that millions of people living in large cities can be emptied into the countryside and coerced into a social system based on "self-sufficiency" or "self-reliance" to survive as their ancestors did. Such a time never existed, except in a romantic, idealized imagination. The disastrous Cultural Revolution in China miscalculated our capacity to form large coherent rural communities without the inevitable brutality, murder, and oppression. The scapegoat in both cases was the educated, urban person. Destroy that type and return the population to its roots was the policy. But the roots had died long before. There is no going back to where we've come; that road washed away centuries ago.

We haven't quite come to terms with the importance of having crossed a system threshold that has allowed more than 7 billion people to exist. How far can we scale before the whole system comes tumbling down? No one knows. Our cognitive abilities can't take in those numbers. We can't imagine the implications of that number on the overall population. We will continue to experience collateral fallout from the planet's large population and face the prospect of a climate change so dire that it may well cause the population to crash.

Our weakness is for the benefits of scaling population, and convincing the population that the government is working for them. As Gore Vidal wrote, "The genius of our ruling class is that it has kept a majority of the people from ever questioning the inequity of a system where most people drudge along paying heavy taxes for which they get nothing in return."

The ruling class has its own set of grooming rules. When someone within the ruling class is perceived to have violated the elite grooming protocols, there is the risk of a huge disruption such as Thailand is experiencing. Thaksin Shinawatra's problems began when he stopped grooming the "right" people and brought in a new grooming tribe. Until the elite grooming system is revised, agreed upon, and implemented, expect more violence, disruption, and instability. Nothing makes primates more irritable and insane with anger than having their grooming interfered with, especially by another member of their band.

People pay for a system that watches them, controls their lives by pandering to their biases, feeds them propaganda, and uses them for the watcher's purposes. To transcend our inability to keep track of people and their connections, we have put faith in a system of organization, logistics, and management that woke up to its own power, and that is when the nightmare started. We haven't woken up from the reality that we've been captured, harnessed, domesticated by a system that herds the population and limits their grooming rights. We had a taste of coherence—social media has created the illusion that we've busted through the 150 Dunbar number. It has made us unruly, more demanding, more suspicious of authorities outside our grooming stables.

We've gone way beyond the 150-group-member limit. Our cognitive abilities are flawed by cognitive biases and have limited carrying capacity, but we are smart enough to look around and understand that once we've handed the keys to the bus to others, they will ultimately drive us to whatever destination they have in mind. It will be a place that suits and benefits the driver. We have no choice but to go along for the ride. We are passengers riding together in one of those double-decker upcountry Thai buses at three in the morning, on a narrow road skirting 150-meter ravines, at the mercy of a driver taking another large slug of whiskey.

This is our transport. It isn't really our choice of how we'd like to travel. It's the way things turned out as the speed of change started to accelerate about ten generations ago. There is no evidence that the pressure on our cognitive resources is slowing down. More friends, more data, same meat operating system to process it.

Look out the window—look over the edge into the ravine—and ask yourself if the airbrakes will hold on the next hairpin curve. It's too late to get out and walk. That is a definition of noir to keep us awake at night and force us to flee back to our computer and log on to our grooming station, looking for "likes" and thumbs-up icons for coherence, comfort, and calm. Our ever more diligent grooming seems to be in pursuit of a Hollywood ending, one where all that social activity leads to redemption, fulfillment, and happiness. Our primate cousins made friends finding and eliminating head lice and ticks. We are trying to do something similar through our relationships with our digital friends. It makes us feel far superior and worthy—until you sit back and think about the implications.

After some thought, can I offer you, my friend, a red pill, or blue pill? The choice has always been yours.

Part IV

Crime Investigation in a Changing World

Digital Tracking of Corruption

The website Bribespot (bribespot.com) is devoted to citizens from around the world who complain that state authorities have demanded bribes to overlook infractions of the law or as an additional, informal condition to receiving a benefit or service. Corruption can occur around the edges of a political system or may have developed as a central part of the culture.

As I write this in August 2013, here's a recent example of a posting from Thailand by a motorist who paid two hundred baht (five dollars) to the police:

> 3 Lane Rama IV Road, near Bangkok University, direction Theptarin Hospital.
>
> They: 6-8 Police, most likely from Tha Rua Station were waving "all" motorbikes to stop. 2 were blocking left + middle lane.
>
> Officer: You were not driving as req on the left lane but in the middle lane & showed me a plastic home-made-menu-pricelist [laminated] sheet with a list of all offenses & their prices. On the list: Driving in Middle Lane = 400thb
>
> Me: But how can I be on the left lane, if u guys are blocking it and I need to swap to the

right lane to make a U-turn? Shall I fly over?

Officer: Give me 400thb or u go police station & this take long time.

Me: opening the purse and taking out 200 thb and telling him I not pay more than 200thb (had a meeting and was in rush).

Officer: literally pulling my 200thb out of the purse and saying: Now you go!

Q: Is it illegal to drive in the middle lane to change lanes? Only in Thailand. Police Officers I guess, they fly over the middle lane.

It is useful to start with an understanding of what "corruption" means. The word derives from the Latin *corruptus* meaning to abuse or destroy. Corruption manifests on several scales:

1) *petite scale*—when bribery in the form of small gifts and personal favors is tolerated within the larger normative values of the community;

2) *grand scale*—found in regimes run by a narrow circle of plutocrats or tyrants, where the political, social, and economic institutions are subverted for the gain of the tyrants and their cronies;

3) *institutional scale*—where process and institutions are weak and exist within a culture of impunity, where state authorities have little or no fear in exacting personal benefits. The weak institutions indeed may feed and indirectly encourage corruption by paying low salaries to employees and turning a blind eye when they supplement their salaries through bribes.

Wikipedia has this definition of corruption in the context of policing:

Police corruption is a specific form of police misconduct designed to obtain financial benefits, other personal gain, and/or career advancement for a police officer or officers in exchange for not pursuing, or selectively pursuing, an investigation or arrest. One common form of police corruption is soliciting and/or accepting bribes in exchange for not reporting organized drug or prostitution rings or other illegal activities. Another example is police officers flouting the police code of conduct in order to secure convictions of suspects—for example, through the use of falsified evidence. More rarely, police officers may deliberately and systematically participate in organized crime themselves.

At some stage we will have big data from sites like Bribespot, with which to see patterns in the behavior of state officials. It may be that the data will confirm that at the end and start of each month, and near major holidays, bribe taking increases as officials are under pressure to pay rents and school fees or buy gifts. What Bribespot relies on is self-reporting. It is difficult to assess how representative of the problem are the cases that people choose to report. The process takes effort. I suspect that most people can't be bothered to self-report.

The other problem with corruption reporting is that corruption, by its very nature secretive and non-transparent, is difficult to prove. The motorist says the cop asked for a bribe, the cop says that is a lie. "He said, she said" is an eternal loop, and the law mostly favors the police in the case of doubt. People aren't stupid. They know that without concrete evidence, they are wasting their time to complain. And if they complain, police who are corrupt are more likely to intimidate a whistleblower than non-corrupt police. As the theory goes, once the cops break one pillar of the law, it is much easier to knock out other pillars to protect themselves against the law.

The *Bangkok Post* on August 21, 2013, ran an editorial titled "Corruption Is a Two-Way Street," blaming both the corrupt official and the person paying the bribe. The editorial concludes that to stop corruption, action must be taken against both the state official and the person paying the bribe. This proposed formula to solve the problem of corruption is in my opinion fundamentally flawed and fails to address the underlying causes. It treats both sides of bribery at the same level—one corrupt state official, one citizen paying the bribe. The illegal gambling casinos run by state authorities are an example of how corruption is often a one-way street. In some systems the corruption is closer to an expressway rather than a two-way street, with eight lanes filled with traffic. That is the problem with thinking of political solutions in terms of metaphors. They quickly fall apart when the metaphor is expanded to expose the scope of the problem. The approach championed by the editorial would be as effective as asking people to drop suggestions into an anti-corruption box.

As we've seen in the categories above, bribery falls into a number of distinct categories, each of which has special issues and problems that should be addressed. In the second category, the grand scale, treating the bribe payer as equal to state officials is missing the larger issue when the system is run by tyrants who act as *rentiers* and extractors of wealth and resources. Corruption in such a system is the nature of how power is allocated. It is a symptom of a much more fundamental political issue. To focus on the bribe payer is a distraction, irrelevant to finding an overall solution.

The same analysis applies to the third category, the institutional scale, where the justice system operates with weak, highly flawed law enforcement institutions. In such a context state officials act with impunity. To suggest that the bribe payer is an equal bargaining partner with such an official neglects the power and authority that can be effectively employed to compel a target by placing them under duress, through means such as torture, imprisonment, or heavy penalties, unless a bribe is paid. To call this a two-way street requires a radically different view of how streets, rules, and traffic are interconnected.

Thailand falls into the first and third category. It is a gift-giving culture, and bribery is the slippery slope that gift givers use to glide out of a legal jam or to obtain a state concession or benefit. Many Thais don't view the giving of small gifts to officials as bribery. The attitude is reflected in the Thai phrase *sin namjai*—something like "gifts from the heart." It is part of being kind and generous; the gifts give both the gift-giver and gift-receiver face, with the benefit of oiling the social wheels and keeping them moving. Such a gift-giving tradition comes from a system of ancient attitudes that worked in a small-scale agriculture-based society (which most of Thailand remains).

The problem is that the attitudes are difficult to fit with law enforcement in the large cities where more and more people live. In places like Bangkok the cop isn't someone the bribe payer knows and has a long connection to through family, as he would be in a village. They are strangers. The giving of the money isn't an act of kindness and generosity; it is an act of desperation, made out of fear and anxiety. The institutions of justice are weak as protection isn't sought within an institutional framework but within a network of connections where a patron provides protection. The state officials are selective in enforcement of laws depending on the rank and status of the person they ask for money. If the potential briber is an important/influential person, then it is unlikely that a low-ranking state official will even ask for a bribe.

The same principle extends to protect the wives, children, relatives, and immediate households of people of power and status. It is not just state officials acting with impunity that is a sign of weak justice system institutions; one also needs to look at the elites and ask whether they can act with impunity. Sometimes the answer is the police and the powerful are both immune, but others must comply with the law. Being in that immune position, the privileged have no incentive to create a strong criminal justice as that would make the powerful vulnerable. Weak institutions, which they control directly or through proxy, can be more easily controlled. The tacit promise of a political system to keep the elites strong and the institutions weak delivers: I'll scratch your back, if you scratch mine. And all this back-scratching will occur behind closed doors. It isn't enough to say "don't pay the bribe" as that fails to address the imbalance of the power relationships and the nature of how impunity is distributed in a political/economic/social system.

Corruption shouldn't be viewed only through the lens of cops taking bribes. It involves tea money for parents to pay to get into a school, or money paid for medical services or for the installation of water, sewer, or electricity. Whenever there is a government service to be provided, the question is whether the officials administering the system seek additional payments before authorizing or approving the benefit. If the answer is yes, it likely follows that the officials inside that organization are corrupt, and the institution that employs them is weak and can do nothing to counter the culture of corruption.

Corruption continues to work because we still live in a small data world. In a few years after the methods of surveillance have advanced another technological leap and become unstoppable, then it will be difficult for state authorities to maintain the essential secrecy that is the lifeblood of corruption. In the big data political system (BDPS)—the next stage of political evolution—we can expect an advanced computerized system to monitor the behavior and conduct of its human agents and actors as well as the rest of us.

Our older, simpler world of free choice is slipping away. Our future world may greet us any morning now. It may start with a news report: "A large majority of people agree with the urgent need for preventive detentions and secret interrogations as a necessary precaution to support our government's goal to protect all citizens against terrorism and corruption." The announcement will emphasize nouns and minimize verbs. Actions will be downplayed, potential acts played up.

That morning may come sooner than we imagine. We will kick ourselves for not suspecting that corruption, like terrorism, while real, was a great cover for an invisible government to scale up its own culture, priorities, and institutions. Systematic monitoring may be sold and bought on the promise of ending corruption. But before you sign on, be careful for what you wish for. You might be trading one old problem for ten new ones. The BDPS coming soon to your country may extract a very high price in terms of liberty and freedom. We may find that we are substituting one culture of impunity for another. And we may long for the days when we paid two hundred baht to a Thai cop who demanded it even though we had committed no traffic infraction.

Citizen Detectives: An Online World of Investigations

Inside the world of crime fiction, a story starts with a murder. People have murdered one another since ancient days; what has changed in modern times is how our society investigates a murder. While the ancients incorporated the supernatural or other irrational factors into their explanation of a murder, from the time of the Enlightenment in the seventeenth and eighteenth centuries, reason, logic, and scientific proof have been enshrined as the basis for detection. From that cognitive thread emerged the modern detective narrative, with "all of the central characteristics and formal elements of the detective story, including a mystery surrounding a murder, a closed circle of suspects, and the gradual uncovering of a hidden past" (John Scaggs, *Crime Fiction*). More than two centuries after the Enlightenment, building upon the thought processes constructed then, technology has provided a wide range of detective tools. Just as significant as their invention is that access to such tools has passed from the hands of government officials and professional investigators and into the hands of intelligent, interested, and knowledgeable amateurs.

There is great political power in maintaining a monopoly over the narrative flow that detects and solves crimes in general and murder in particular. An essential part of the social contract between citizens and their government is the trust that the government's narrative is truthful. When a government lies about a murder or a disappearance, they close the door to truth. A closed door to truth is a good definition of distrust. In times of civil unrest, street protests, and demonstrations, the intensity of emotional rage threatens to return us to the pre-Enlightenment era, when gossip, speculation, the supernatural, biases, and radical beliefs evolved narratives to solve the mystery surrounding a murder.

Our ancestors consumed a diet rich in official narratives slanted to suit the interests of the powerful. The tension between power and authority and truth and justice is the rope pull contest, which in the past the authorities, with the police, armies, and guns on their side, mostly won. As we start 2014, in circumstances of political turmoil here in Thailand, it looks like we are going to see far more citizens going over the heads of government officials, investigative experts, and mob leaders who are less interested in solving a murder than spinning a narrative that advances their interest.

Thailand's political troubles produced murder victims in 1976, 1992, 2008, 2009, 2010, and 2013. The probabilities are there will be more murder victims in 2014 arising from the political activities in Bangkok streets and upcountry venues where demonstrations occur. It is human nature that both sides will blame the other for a murder that occurs amid such conflict. Whether the victim was one of their own or on the opposite side, the standard trope is the other side pulled the trigger. In Thailand, however, there is a popular tradition of both sides blaming a "third hand." A third hand is an anonymous player, usually in a tight band or group, with powerful friends and allies, who seeks to gain advantage through violence. In Thailand in recent times they are called the Black Shirts. The murky third hand, dressed in their black shirts, plays the role of the supernatural in the ancient narratives. In this anti-Enlightenment, anti-evidential narrative, secretive phantoms, like characters in a good ghost or superhero story, are cast as the real villains.

On the surface this convenient explanation appears plausible. The third hand is also a good excuse for the authorities to limit their investigation or to sidetrack it on a wild goose chase. Like a supernatural story the third hand player acts as a wonderful piece of distraction. After a while people forget about the person who was murdered as everyone is baying for the third hand to be revealed.

That house of cards is about to fall. There are several reasons for this kind of stonewalling and distraction to become increasingly more difficult to work in the near term.

First, the visual evidence is often overwhelming, graphic, and damning. Powerful video evidence can be harvested from a rainforest of CCTV cameras overhanging every street and alley, government and private, and the hand-held devices everyone carries. With the emergence of drone technology, you can expect another layer of visual surveillance to capture the moment a murder is committed.

You've likely seen on YouTube and elsewhere citizen video footage uploaded from the scenes of demonstrations from around the world. Acts of political violence are also on the increase, an upswing that correlates with the rise of video images of brutal acts of politically motivated violence. A case in point was the horrific murder and attempted beheading of Lee Rigby, a British soldier, while off duty in the streets of London in May 2013. In court the concern was raised that showing video footage of the incident would mix hatred and disgust into the volatile cocktail of moral outrage, prejudicing the jury. There is no little irony that the most advanced products of our technology are causing a flashback to pre-Enlightenment-style irrational reaction to images of actions perpetrated by other pre-Enlightenment actors.

It isn't just juries or those inside a courtroom who respond emotionally to visual acts of graphic violence. The ripple effect swiftly flows through the larger community. After the Rigby murder there was a surge of anti-Muslim hate crimes in England.

The second reason that things have changed is that official deniability is now curtailed with visual records that suddenly go viral, and within minutes of the occurrence of an act of violence, people around the world are seeing it with their own eyes. The jury is no longer confined to a courtroom. Each jury for a high-profile case now numbers in the millions and is convened twenty-four hours a day. There are many YouTube videos showing authorities' abuses of power.

On New Year's Day, 2014, the *Bangkok Post* reported that a video of a policeman slapping a Russian tourist across the face had come to light, leaving little room for the old standby: that it was all just a misunderstanding. Constable Nop, you see, was swatting a mosquito when the Russian woman rushed in front of the insect at the last moment to rescue it from death. The incident doesn't do much for Thailand's official position on tourists, that they are welcome to come and enjoy themselves, and no doubt damage control will spring into action. Someone will be dispatched to give the Russian woman flowers, a basket of cookies, and free tickets to the crocodile farm. She might want to think twice about using the tickets.

The third reason things are different now is the emergence of online versions of Sherlock Holmes, who gather and analyze the forensic evidence that can be acquired by searching Google Maps, using a knowledge of firearms and ammunition and combing through eyewitness accounts from the ground. If you have a reasonable level of online research skills, you can apply them to a murder.

A good example of such an online investigation was a blog post by an anonymous person that asked the question, who shot and killed the Thai policeman on December 26, 2013, near Gate 3 of the Japanese Stadium at Din Daeng? Anti-government protesters were at the stadium to block and disrupt registration of political parties for the February 2 elections. Those on the side of the protesters pointed the finger at the government as the killer, saying the fatal shot came from the top of a government building.

The modern Philip Marlowe who conducted the online murder investigation explained his motivation: "I write this not to answer wider questions about the rights and wrongs but to try to clarify a narrower question of whether a policeman was killed by mysterious gunmen stationed on top of the Labour Ministry, which is—obviously—under the control of the government. The protesters claim that these men were most likely hired by Thaksin to shoot both protesters and police alike in order to paint the protesters as violent. To my knowledge, the government have yet to clarify who these men were, but have accused two protesters of firing down at police from nearby flats."

In the fog of street demonstrations and violence, there are bound to be multiple perspectives, and not everyone will agree that the evidence presented supports the conclusion offered. Some media and citizen journalists reported, for example, that black-clad men were on top of the Labour Ministry (the police confirmed that the men in black on top of the Labour Ministry building were policemen), and that police attacked a protester's vehicle, smashing the windows. In the heat of street battles the roles of attacker and victim often shift, causing confusion. Reports emerging from the confusion are bound to be conflicting.

Our online detective provides a detailed investigation into the gunman's location, the height from which the shot was made, and the distance from the shooter to the spot where Police Senior Sergeant Major Narong Pitisit was killed. He presents his case to us, the jury, to decide—given the trajectory of the entry and exit wounds, the position of the body, and reports of the direction of other gunfire at the same time—whether the killer, whoever he or she was, had fired the shot from the top of the Labour Ministry.

The chaos of violence in a street demonstration makes detection of a precise killer more difficult. With multiple gunmen firing shots from various locations, and masses of people in and around the turmoil, it is often easier to conclude who couldn't have fired a fatal shot than to pinpoint the actual gunman.

The private citizen investigation into the murder of police officer Narong, by exploiting online resources, has shaped a credible scenario that eliminates the rooftop of the Labour Ministry as the location of the gunman. Of course, just because a theory is credible and plausible doesn't mean it is true or the final word, but such an investigation does put pressure on the authorities to either confirm or repudiate the scenario from the evidence they've gathered.

The result of such efforts is the creation of a new kind of courtroom for the digital age. Courtrooms and judges, prosecutors, police, and witnesses are evolving into something new. Like the monopoly of information, the monopoly of justice is being disrupted by new technology.

The fourth reason for the house of cards to fall is that millions of people worldwide are now aware that the instruments of our political, economic, and social life are being disrupted. These hugely powerful institutions appear vulnerable and weak. Like high-rise buildings following a powerful earthquake, the question is whether they can be repaired before they collapse. The elites with the most to lose take to the streets to demand governing systems that leave them in control. They wage conflict against those they fear will demolish what has given them privilege and power. Murders committed inside this landscape have significance as the identity of the gunmen will affect the legitimacy and credibility of either the government or the anti-government forces. Each side wants the other side to have pulled the trigger.

The citizen detective, armed with modern investigative skills, is entering a hotly contested political realm where murder is the collateral damage. Or it may be that murder is part of a theatre of the absurd to discredit and topple the opposition. In other words, pinpointing the killer is driven less by a need to know the truth about the murder than by the anticipated political fallout from arresting a person associated with one of the political sides. Political killings appear on the surface to be like all crimes of passion, but the reality is that a cold-blooded calculation has been made about the merits of violence to achieve political ends. That is the classic definition of war.

We head forward with new and powerful tools of detection, and with skilled and dedicated online detectives, but none of this changes the fundamentally irrational nature of man. We are predictable in our capacity for unpredictability, driven by deep-seated forces of language, culture, indoctrination, and biases. In reality there is no evidence that at this stage of modern technology we can expect to overcome our biases or, more importantly, reduce the number of murders in the political arena. Lee Rigby's killers knew they were being filmed. They performed the gruesome murder in front the camera. Violent and radical political movements have discovered that technology provides them with a cheap and effective public theatre to perform their violence.

What is happening in the streets of Bangkok is mirrored in many places around the world as 2014 witnesses a continuation of a battle waged by those allied with pre-Enlightenment forces, who are pushing back hard against forces of the Enlightenment. The anti-democratic movement wants the benefit of all the technological advantages that have emerged from the Enlightenment while maintaining a medieval political structure and a belief system that sidetracks science to the margins. It is an old war that flares up in intensity as the technology accelerates social and economic change.

What is it about that philosophy of the Enlightenment that ignites the flames of political conflict? The answer takes us back to David Hume, who famously wrote "Reason is, and ought only to be the slave of the passions." Our blood lust and self-interest have traditionally trumped appeals to evidence and reason. The slave can't be allowed to use evidence and reason to control the master. As a result we are left with moral outrage, and when the elites lead a mob to jump the fence of reason, we return to a pre-Enlightenment political era. We will have to look into a deeper future before this flaw in the human software can be patched. Only then will the slave have a chance for genuine freedom. Meanwhile, we will look to the citizen detective to bring images and voice to the slave's case. The year 2014 may give birth to the online Spartacus who adopts the tools of the Enlightenment to break the chains of enslavement.

Online Commercial Sex: The Digital Age of Victimless Crimes

here do you put your police: on the streets or online? This modern question wouldn't have surfaced twenty years ago. Now it's a major issue. A huge number of crimes have turned out to have an enhanced capability of success once they are transferred online. As austerity measures worldwide continue to squeeze law enforcement budgets, policy makers are faced with a stark set of choices. Among the challenges: how do you recruit and deploy your resources to stop crime that has migrated online?

What's often confusing in this context is where "legal" ends and "criminal" begins. Some of the policing of so-called computer crimes in countries like Thailand is at least dubious in nature and amounts to nothing more than suppression of dissent. In a number of countries, including Thailand, governments have ordered officials (and recruited an army of private volunteers) to detect and report online critics of their regime. Once caught, the critics are sent off to prison. The idea is to chill certain kinds of speech. In practice, however, when thousands no longer fear the police, such tactics are counterproductive and make the authorities look out of touch, out of date, weak, and ridiculous.

Law enforcement can't be too detached from the realm of what is possible. The problem is, the online world is redefining what conduct it is possible to suppress, whether it be political speech, dissent, gambling, prostitution, or drugs. The old methods of dispatching a police cruiser, a foot patrol, or networks of paid informants are gradually being replaced with cyber-patrols of chat rooms, Twitter, Facebook, and other social media.

One category of online activity that can run afoul of local laws is the victimless crime. Over the last few years, so-called victimless criminals have migrated from the streets, back alleyways, nightclubs, bars, public parks, and massage parlors to online venues. Gambling, designer drugs, and prostitution are the best examples of the type of online commercialization that is overrunning the front lines of law enforcement.

The trend line indicates that the old battle to contain victimless crime is unlikely to be won by the authorities. When historians look back decades from now, 2008 will prove to have been a watershed year. Why 2008? That was the year Amazon began selling ebooks. In retrospect, 2008 was also the beginning of the end of traditional publishing, though few would have predicted it at the time, and the start of an entirely new way to produce, market, and sell books. And if it works for books, why wouldn't it work for other products? Some of those other products taken online happen to be illegal in many, but not all, jurisdictions. It is that diversity of morality and law that allows the opportunity to exploit an untapped, previously risky market.

The Economist, in an August 2014 article titled "More Bang for Your Buck," takes a close look at the domestic and international implications of the growing online sex trade. (This issue of *The Economist* was, according to my bookstore source, banned from distribution in Thailand based on political content not related to the sex industry story.)

Capitalism, combined with the Internet, cyber banking, and cheap airfares, has succeeded in creating a largely untapped market for the sale of sex. The commodification of sex has found in the online world a fertile, efficient environment in which to grow. Simply put, the Internet has allowed for an expansion of the customer base. In most jurisdictions either sex workers or their customers (or both) commit a criminal act by engaging in prostitution, and yet, the irony is Internet access has rapidly increased the pool of sex workers and clients.

Is there the political will to declare war on the sex trade? The chances are that won't happen. It is too late. Too many people are engaged as providers and customers for effective law enforcement. Resources are better allocated to fighting crime in other areas.

As *The Economist* observed, before the advent of the Internet, prostitutes left "tart cards" in telephone kiosks along King's Cross Road in London. It was an inefficient way to find customers and an impossible way for those who didn't venture down King's Cross Road to find a prostitute. There are now specialized apps that connect buyers and sellers as well as review sites where buyers can read reviewer comments, which represent a full range of opinions of the kind one would find in abundance for books on Amazon or hotels and restaurants on Trip Advisor.

This is the brave new world where the amateur and semi-professional can enter a market that traditionally was staffed by hardcore professionals. The expectation of being paid for sex suddenly is no longer limited to a small, isolated group. Online prostitution has expanded both the scope of the market beyond that group of professionals and the customer base that once bought their services in person.

Something similar has happened in publishing. Until very recently, the New York and London publishing houses acted as gatekeepers, and unless they opened the door for you, your typed manuscript was doomed to gather dust in the bottom of your filing cabinet drawer. In those days you were a professional writer only if you had been published by a traditional publisher. Otherwise, you might write, but it was a hobby, and you circulated your manuscripts mostly among friends and family. Then the computer and the Internet came along. With the availability of ebooks and the sudden, newly emerged market for cheap ways to format them and to find editors and cover designers, it wasn't long before a lot of people figured out that self-publishing might be the ticket for writers who for any reason couldn't break into the traditional publishing business. In a few years self-published writers had shown there was a serious amount of money in the ebook business. A few self-published writers earned millions and became publishing superstars. Their self-published ebook success stories were taken as evidence to prove that the snobby, closed world of big publishers was finished. A whole new world of writers climbed onto the ebook bandwagon. The old filters are no longer functioning to exclude authors from publishing and finding an audience for their books.

With a cheap new way to make the goods widely available firmly established, the new controversy has been over the pricing of traditional paper books—much as with traditional commercial sex—compared to their online versions. From an economics point of view the fact that publishing is legal and commercial sex is generally not, isn't relevant. What is noteworthy here is how old markets have been, or are in the process of being, destroyed, and how the configuration of providers and users has mushroomed. The commercial sex market—its location, pricing, players, and participants— has been significantly altered, and that has implications for publishing.

What the ebook market and online commercial sex market have both shown is that in economic hard times, people who aren't professionals will seek ways to earn extra income utilizing the Internet. The online world has ushered in the part-time worker, the amateur, and the semi-professional, and on your screen it is difficult to determine how far their performance will be from the professional one you expect.

Writing and self-publishing a book isn't a crime, although reading a poorly written book may make you feel as though you've been mugged. The point is, online commerce is disrupting the old methods of screening, filtering, and limiting access between providers and their customers. Pimps and brothels are being disrupted in the commercial sex world. Likewise, publishing houses like Hachette, which is in a very public dispute with Amazon over the pricing of ebooks, are finding their business model disrupted by online powerhouses. Once the middlemen (and women) get out of the way, then all someone needs to sell sex online are some basic computer skills and marketing savvy. The resulting activities are very difficult to police. A number of people will point out that prostitution has a core problem that cannot be trivialized—human trafficking makes voluntary participation by the prostitute questionable and ultimately unverifiable. This is a problem worthy of a separate discussion.

The major problem facing sex workers and customers until the online age has been one of information. The Internet is exactly the place to allow large data banks of information to grow. Sex workers can create a "brand" like the ones created for any other commodity or celebrity. Photographs, descriptions, and details of service and price start to take on the appearance of any other commercial menu. The amount and scope of information and the reach of "broadcast" dwarf the old "tart card" paradigm. As a consequence, women from the poorer Eastern European countries have migrated to England, Germany, and the Netherlands to seek out opportunities in the sex trade, driving down the local price. Another reason for the price suppression is the number of part-time sex workers. Professional sex workers now compete with housewives, students, and regularly employed persons supplementing their income with part-time sex work.

Bars, nightclubs, escort services, and entertainment complexes from Amsterdam to Bangkok are likely to find their marketing advantage eroded. It is also likely, as *The Economist* concludes, that the number of customers for sexual services will increase as paid-for sex becomes more prevalent and more discreetly arranged.

If the future brings an increase in commercial sex, how will law enforcement officials respond? Some websites may be shut down and their webmasters charged with a crime. That approach is whack-a-mole as the website is likely to reopen in some other country outside the reach of local law enforcement agencies. As online commercial sex grows, attitudes about procreation, fidelity, marriage, children, and family may begin to change too. Remember AltaVista and WebCrawler in the pre-Google days? There were many such search engines. We remain at the AltaVista stage with online sex services. Will there be the equivalent of a Google and Amazon moment? Will we reach a time when the online commercial sex market is controlled by one large corporation? That would be interesting politically, as a new group of lobbyists would have all kinds of incentives to secure favorable legislation from lawmakers.

Gambling, drugs, and commercial sex are usually identified as permissive, antisocial activities to be repressed. When the dealings took place on the street, the police had means of containment. Once the customers go online by the hundreds of millions worldwide, their numbers will send a message to law enforcement: the jails and prisons will never be sufficient to hold them all. These services will have been absorbed into the capitalist model, which loves a market where demand continues to grow and the prices continue to fall. Moore's law may apply as well—the doubling of capacity every eighteen months. The digital world is serving notice that the analog world of law enforcement has passed it expiry date. Some "Trick Advisor" on the horizon may go into the dustbin like AltaVista, or it may become the next hot IPO, soon thereafter to be bought in a bidding war between Google and Amazon. And so it goes, from the traditional notion that certain aspects of our humanity such as sex are priceless and thus outside the realm of commerce, to the new reality that the old TV show *The Price Is Right* was way ahead of its time.

The Online Sleuths and the Cold Case

For the most part, the front line of criminal justice has been assigned to law enforcement authorities. There have always been some exceptions, where outsiders supplement the public officials' task in apprehending lawbreakers.

Three such private actors come to mind: vigilantes, bounty hunters, and private sleuths. For centuries members of these three groups have patrolled the darker paths that remain largely invisible to the ordinary, law-abiding citizen. From Jack the Ripper to the Boston Marathon bombers, private citizens have sought to assist in uncovering and apprehending killers. Traditionally, in the old, analog world, the private actors put in plenty of time on the street, using up shoe leather talking to people in neighborhood haunts, taking in oral information and following it up, until they had enough data to close the case. While their working methods were roughly similar, their motives differed. And revealing a person's motives is usually a good way to tell a story that people can understand and relate to.

Vigilantes, motivated to bring a criminal to justice by personal or ideological reasons, are emotionally driven. They are more likely to go along with street justice and dispense with due process. Bounty hunters, in contrast, have a more straightforward motivator: money. They deliver criminals to law enforcement officers in return for cash rewards, and what the authorities do with the criminals is no concern of the bounty hunters as they walk away, counting their cash.

Professional or licensed private investigators or sleuths undertake cases on behalf of clients who might, for instance, wish a wayward bank teller to be caught with his or her hand in the till. Their motivation in going after wrongdoers doesn't stem from any sense of moral outrage. Such jobs often involve not only hard work but real danger, and most sleuths seek to steer clear of exposing themselves to possible harm unless they can see the cash up front.

Today's online cousins of the PIs are the amateur digital sleuths, who work online to solve crimes that law enforcement officials have let fall between the cracks. This is a new category of sleuths, one whose characteristics also make it strangely akin to gaming or support groups. It is hard to peg all of the sleuths in this category as it is still evolving and taking in members from the traditional brigade of privateers who work the edges of the criminal justice system.

Vigilantes, for the most part, tend to be amateurs fired up by anger and hatred. That fuels the emotional rocket only for a while, though a true believer can burn up a lot of nuclear fuel before exploding into a white dwarf. Bounty hunters and traditional sleuths may have the cool and cerebral appeal of Sherlock Holmes types, who through deliberative, deductive reasoning solve the mystery that leads to the wrongdoer. Amateur digital sleuths, on the other hand, have an irrational, emotional side that belies their rational Mr. Spock persona, a side that sometimes leads them to engage in online feuds and flame wars. However, empathy for the families of the victim can be another motivator, as has been suggested in a recent CBC News report on online sleuthing, titled "Madeleine McCann to Jeffery Boucher: Web Sleuths Quest for the Missing."

A few days ago (in late June 2014) Laura Miller, writing for *Salon*, reviewed Deborah Halber's recently published book *The Skeleton Crew: How Amateur Sleuths are Solving America's Coldest Cases*. Among online sleuths there is, in Miller's words, "a methodological schism over how to interact with law enforcement and the families of the lost. Halber divides the two groups into the 'mavericks,' who prefer to proceed swiftly and as they deem fit, and the 'trust builders,' who insist on deliberating as a group before approaching officials or the bereaved."

Apparently the book is a series of anecdotes that illustrate the ordeals, successes, and drama of online investigations—in other words, reports from the lives of actual investigators as opposed to big-data analysis to see what patterns emerge from the activities of this community. The book's premise is intriguing, but I am not at all certain *The Skeleton Crew* is for me. Anecdotes, no matter how entertaining, revealing, and persuasive, are not evidence. They are a story about a story. The end.

Miller's review got me started thinking about the implications of the three traditional categories I've addressed being ultimately disrupted by a digital community that wouldn't have existed ten years ago. Halber's book has arrived at a very good time. Others are discussing the growth, meaning, and use of the online sleuthing community. If Wikipedia can find hundreds of thousands of experts to work for free to patrol the factual accuracy of information, there must be many thousands of people with a lifetime of crime movies, TV, and novels behind them, enjoining them that by sleuthing themselves, a) they can have fun; b) they can meet other people who share their interests; c) they can benefit the public; and d) they can obtain status in the eyes of others by solving cases that have stumped the police.

If you want to become a digital sleuth, tracking a murderer or kidnapper as you sit with coffee in hand in the comfort of your home, where should you start? In the beginning you are likely going to be looking to solve a "cold case." That's an old, unsolved case that the police, at least in the public's perception, have abandoned.

A number of online sleuthing websites already exist, such as Websleuths, the Doe Network, the Reddit Bureau of Investigation, the US government's National Missing and Unidentified Persons System (NamUs), and the web counterpart of the television program *Unsolved Mysteries*. Inside these websites you'll discover digital communities of people who devote much time and effort to sharing information that might help solve kidnappings and murders. The CBC article mentioned above is alive to the dangers of vigilante justice in such situations, citing the Boston bombing case, during which online detectives suggested the involvement of someone who turned out to be innocent.

What do the professionals say about this latest development in sleuthing? Journalist Chris Baraniuk, in his article "The Amateur Detectives Tackling Murders and Kidnaps" (available on BBC.com), quotes Professor David Wall of Durham University as saying that he "believes online communities can be hugely beneficial in some cases, but the temptation to get involved in more serious crimes is a recipe for disaster." In the same report Joe Giacalone, a retired NYPD detective sergeant, expresses worry about the public getting involved in old, unsolved cases. "As an investigator," he says, "where you're dealing with evidentiary issues and things, you don't want to have people poking into the case." He adds: "You gotta remember, you have anonymous people sitting behind keyboards, you don't know exactly—

you could have somebody with an axe to grind." The article reports that he has never seen a missing persons case solved by someone working through one of the online sleuthing communities.

These skeptics are joined by Nic Groombridge, a senior sociology lecturer at St. Mary's University in London, England, who told CBC News, "During the Jack the Ripper case, one of the problems the police had wasn't a lack of leads—it was too many leads."

Britain's Association of Chief Police Officers takes a slightly different view: "With regard to members of the public conducting their own research into cold cases, providing that their actions are lawful and conducted appropriately, their findings will always be considered by the officers and staff who have ownership of the relevant case" (BBC.com). There are a fair number of lawyer's demarcations as to the boundaries that private sleuths must recognize. To borrow from property law concepts, one might define the police as the owners of a criminal case. The police are alerting outsiders that trespass is something to avoid. The case belongs to them. Be careful or you might find yourself in trouble with the police, and saying you were only trying to help won't likely get you off the hook.

One law-enforcement constituency that does appear to welcome these outside communities is medical examiners, who can find themselves in possession of skeletal remains without any clue to their identity. In this area online sleuths have provided some breakthroughs.

A larger question looms over the near future of online sleuthing: is it just a passing fashion? The world of big data is developing at a speed that is difficult to assess without metadata to help assess it. (You may start to see a pattern not unlike one of M.C. Escher's recursive birds or frogs.) Solving crimes turns on the amount, quality, and provenance of data, and it is my best guess that it's only a matter of time before the amateurs will be way outside the information silos where big data is stored and analyzed.

Will the idea of police ownership of criminal cases gain more support as police forces hire experts who develop specialized algorithms to search through vast amounts of data for clues? The probable answer is the police monopoly over cases will increase over time. And a monopoly is a property owner's best friend.

Meanwhile, there are scheduled online meet-ups and book clubs for digital amateur sleuths. You'll need to do a bit of sleuthing to find a meet-up near where you live.

"Taser-Like" Cuffs for the Twenty-first Century

From prehistoric times we have been slapping handcuffs on intruders, strangers, criminal suspects, violent lunatics, and sometimes people we simply dislike. The idea of handcuffs is not to kill, but to restrain a person by limiting the movement of his or her arms and hands. From the beginning of our kind we've handcuffed each other in one way or another, using such materials as vines, reeds, and animal hides. As our technology in the Iron and Bronze ages evolved through Greek and Roman times, our handcuffs also evolved, allowing us to securely bind felons and prisoners of war with fetters, chains, and irons.

The big technological breakthrough in the field came in the nineteenth century with W.V. Adams's invention of the ratcheting mechanism. The Adams-designed handcuff became the standard of police forces around the world. Since then we've witnessed only incremental changes to the technology, including disposable plastic cuffs.

Handcuffs used by law enforcement officers and soldiers have until recently been distinguished primarily by whether the dual wrist-enveloping feature is secured by a chain, fixed, or in the form of a solid bar. Whatever their design, handcuffs have been standard issue for police and soldiers for many years and are still used to restrain and limit the movement of criminals and suspected criminals, as well as arrested demonstrators and protesters. They have also been used on prisoners of war and those captured in civil conflicts.

In our time, high-tech has caught up with the world of handcuffs. The latest invention to scale up an arresting officer's ability to restrain and control a prisoner is the Scottsdale cuffs, as described by David Szondy in *Gizmag*, December 14, 2012. What does the state of the art bring to this established technology? Built into these handcuffs are wireless controls and sensors. The theory draws from those dog collars where you want to train a dog not to chew on your new shoes. Each time the dog puts his snout on a shoe, you give him a mild shock through his collar until the dog is able to register that getting close to your shoe will cause him pain. The dog learns to avoid your shoes.

Our history as a species demonstrates that we are inclined to use violence against those of our own kind who put their noses anywhere near what we might define as our shoe zone. According to Szondy, the new cuffs have the capacity to deliver a "Taser-like" high-voltage charge. Not only is the person handcuffed, but by the touch of a remote control, the authorities can also disrupt his or her nervous system.

The implications for the future of freedom are enormous. If you don't follow an instruction, the shock runs through your body. You don't walk fast enough, more shock; or too fast, here it comes again. The cuffs can also be programmed so that they shock at five-minute intervals. Of course, the program can be overwritten, if only you will co-operate. The cuffs have sensors that restrict the prisoner to a certain predetermined area, beyond which a large electric jolt will run through the prisoner's body. The restricted area might be the back of a police van, or a room, or a house.

If that isn't enough to give you nightmares, here is what high-tech handcuffs that are already patented have in store for your encounter with the police. Future handcuffs will come with built-in timers, needles, gas dispensing capability, and gauges to monitor vital signs, emotions, and movements. They will be used for arrests, the escort of suspects to court appearances, the restraint of certain classes of prisoners in mental wards... and perhaps to adjust the attitude of political detainees.

"In addition to radio proximity sensors," writes Szondy, "the cuffs could include an accelerometer, inclinometer, potentiometer, location sensing device, microphone, camera, a biometric sensor or a combination of devices. These could not only allow guards to keep track of prisoners, but also allow the cuffs to automatically deliver a shock if they detect violent or aggressive movements or even if the detainee shouts." The cuffs of the near future will track prisoner movement and behavior, keeping useful stats on prisoner-cuff interaction all the while. On the bright side, Szondy notes, the design will include a safety cutout to forestall serious or fatal injuries. But more darkly, he continues, "In a truly Orwellian twist, the cuffs could also release gases, liquids, dyes and even inject the prisoner with sedative drugs."

Think of the countries on the US State Department's list of the eight least-free places for the practice of religion (as reported in the *Huffington Post*). These are societies where exercising near complete control over their citizens' actions, opinions, and attitudes is viewed as a paramount goal. The listed states are Burma (Myanmar), China, Eritrea, Iran, North Korea, Saudi Arabia, Sudan, and Uzbekistan. The franchise owners of the Scottsdale cuffs in these places may stand to make a small fortune. There might be a viable market for such handcuffs in Thailand too, to deal with unhappy critics of the military government, who are viewed as threatening the goal of universal harmony and unity.

Our high-tech future promises many exciting innovations to improve our lives, health, education, workplaces, and the environment. It also has the capacity to erode our freedom and dignity, and to transfer more power over our lives to those in authority. If the future of the handcuff is to achieve total submission to a police officer or a soldier, whatever convenience and comfort high-tech innovations have provided us won't be sufficient to compensate for the loss of our most basic human rights.

Not even Orwell could have imagined a world of the handcuffed underclass whose members obey like well-trained dogs. Those holding the remote control to the electronic cuffs will follow the orders of the elite few who decide whose shoes are protected.

They say you should walk a mile in other people's shoes before judging them. In a world where most will be barefoot, that old rule of thumb may no longer apply. It's more likely that you will never get a chance to put on such shoes, or if you did, you wouldn't have to walk far to know that in the not too distant future those with the shoes will have created a world where there is nowhere to run and nowhere to hide.

Chimeras in the Forensic Lab

It seems that every week scientific discoveries are upsetting conventional wisdom about our understanding of reality. The scientific shakeup of beliefs cascades through all aspects of the culture, including (and especially) the arts. The latest example concerns our understanding of DNA and genomes. Remember the race to be the first to transcribe a human genome, the blueprint of the DNA code for a human body? That was ten to twenty years ago and came at a cost of several billion dollars.

As it turns out, the first genome to be completely sequenced is more like a stick-figure drawn by four-year-olds. Recent research indicates the real picture of the genome(s) is more like Georges Seurat's pointillist painting *A Sunday Afternoon on the Island of La Grande Jatte.*

We used to think that the human genetic code was like a mystery novel, and the genome would be the one to unravel the story and fit the pieces together. Only it has turned out that many people possess not a single genome but multiple genomes. Apparently, we aren't just a single volume of instructions from one egg and one sperm, at least not all of us. There are other possibilities. The genetic story sequenced inside your body may have authors other than your parents.

The Greeks had a myth about the chimera, a female and male creature that was part lion, snake, and goat. Theirs was a world of imagination where hybrid monsters could come into being. Were the ancient Greeks onto something? There is evidence that indeed a large number of human beings are in fact hybrids or chimeras. This doesn't mean they are part goat, snake, or donkey—unless they happen to be politicians. The human chimera is a person whose genetic makeup is drawn from more than one genome.

As Carl Zimmer wrote this week for the *New York Times* (September 16, 2013), the latest scientific work in genetics is saying there is evidence that supports the theory that we are each the product of multitude of genomes. We each have a potential multi-volume of blueprints within us, and scientists are now seeing evidence of the resulting structural diversity in many areas. Rare diseases may be understood in the context of the genome complexity of the carrier. For instance, a single person may have both type O blood and type A blood.

The genome puzzle is more complex for women. If you think you've seen and heard everything under the sun, see if the following information doesn't bring something new. Zimmer's article tells the story of one woman who at age fifty-two learned she was a chimera, that is, a hybrid that results when more than one genome present in a single individual shapes his or her genetic outcome: "In need of a kidney transplant, she was tested so that she might find a match. The results indicated that she was not the mother of two of her three biological children. It turned out that she had originated from two genomes. One genome gave rise to her blood and some of her eggs; other eggs carried a separate genome."

That story seems to be highly unusual. What is apparently far more common is that when a woman is pregnant, some fetal cells are left behind inside the mother's body, from where they travel to various other organs to perform repair work at the cellular level. Scientists are finding neurons with Y (male) chromosomes, left over from the cells of male fetuses, inside women's brain and breast tissue.

Medical science and technology have an impact not just on health but on law enforcement and criminal justice, as indeed they do on crime fiction. The recent studies about multi-genomes will upset the way the authorities go about conducting forensic investigations and how conclusions can be drawn from such investigations. For example, in the case of a sexual assault, the police may take saliva from a suspect and seek to match it to DNA in the sperm found in the victim's body. If the two samples don't match, then the suspect is released. He's vindicated by the fact that his saliva DNA does not match the sperm DNA taken from the victim. Given these recent developments, the suspect's saliva and the assailant's sperm may not provide a DNA match, but that might not mean the suspect hasn't committed the crime. It is possible that the two DNA samples, though not matching, are from the same person.

In the case of a murder where DNA constitutes all of the circumstantial evidence available to identify the killer, the multi-genomes world makes it difficult, despite non-matching DNA, to assume that the suspect is in the free and clear. The studies may also raise problems with ongoing efforts to exonerate someone convicted of a serious crime such as murder or rape based on inconsistencies in DNA evidence used by the prosecution. The Innocence Project has documented many cases where convictions in the United States have been overturned based on conflicting DNA evidence.

We can no longer predict with certainty from a blood or saliva sample (or any other sampled site) what the DNA will be outside that locale. These are early days in genome discovery, exploring networks, interfaces, and combinations, and seeking to understand what is a highly complex system. From now on, the opinions of doctors, researchers, and scientists on DNA samples must take into account the possibility of different genomes.

Look for this mismatch of DNA samples to appear soon in crime fiction. Novels are often the canary in the mineshaft, carrying the message to the public that the old mine is poison. In this case, our certainty that each of us is the product of a single genome has been refuted. We can expect prosecutors and defense counsels to start calling upon genetic experts in criminal trials. The defense will be seeking to sow seeds of doubt about the DNA results that point to the accused's commission of a crime, while prosecutors will call upon scientists and genetic researchers to estimate the high probability that one of the genomes found at the crime scene belongs to the accused. It won't be surprising to find judges and juries scratching their heads as they try to reach a decision on guilt.

Forensic Trends to Watch

L aw enforcement authorities have come a long way from the days of Sherlock Holmes, when the powers of deduction and observation were the essential requirements to solve the mystery of a crime. Forensic investigations cover a range of activities, including the determinations of time and cause of death, and the analysis of blood, hair, fingerprints, and DNA samples to identify the person(s) at the crime scene.

Crime writers also draw upon forensic techniques in solving a mystery. Part of the craft of good crime writing is skillful integration of the story's scientific elements into the writing. Long technical passages about the science behind the techniques are boring for most readers, who are more interested in the human element.

It would be a mistake not to take into account up-to-date forensic techniques in a crime novel set in contemporary times. Such attention to detail indicates the writer has done his or her research. In the last few years, new scientific developments have equipped forensic officials with more powerful tools to extract and analyze evidence found at a crime scene. Modern forensic techniques allow the police and prosecutors a more detailed, accurate, and reliable basis to connect a suspect with a crime.

First, lipstick. Let's say there are a couple of lipstick smudges found at a crime scene. The lipstick is red. It could have come from any number of brands. It's like finding a boiled egg and knowing that it could have been laid by any number of hens. Narrowing down the field of possible red lipsticks might be helpful in an investigation. One way of isolating the shade is to establish its brand. Once the brand can be established, this information is helpful in identification issues when a victim and suspect have had physical contact. The suspect says the lipstick found on a cigarette in his home is his girlfriend's or wife's, but the lipstick on the victim's lips is the same brand.

In England forensic experts have devised a technique called Raman spectroscopy. The device uses a laser light to establish the brand. Apparently each brand has a vibrational fingerprint that can establish its identity. Lipsticks fall along what is called a Raman spectrum, and each type and brand falls at some point on that spectrum. The crime scene sample might be from any number of items such as a drinking glass, a napkin, a shirt collar, or a piece of wadded tissue. One of the advantages of the new lab techniques is the lipstick sample isn't destroyed in the process to determine the brand. Indeed, Raman spectroscopy allows the lipstick sample to remain in the sealed crime scene evidence bag. On the forensic horizon, look for a similar technique to identify the brands of eyeliners, skin creams, and powders.

Another area of change is fingerprints. Identifying fingerprints from a crime scene has been common for nearly a century. Today we have in our mind TV images of forensic teams arriving at a crime scene to gather clues. Sherlock Holmes would have studied the fingerprint with a large magnifying glass to see if the ridges, loops, and whorls matched those of the victim or suspect. In our time the analysis involves running the fingerprints through a large national database. If there is a match, the investigators know the identity of their suspect.

Courts require a high degree of certainty before fingerprints can be introduced as evidence in a criminal case. The issue arises when there is a partial print, a smudged print, or a print that has been degraded by weather, fire, heat, water, or a chemical agent. If the authorities discover a complete fingerprint at a crime scene, they have a powerful piece of evidence. According to *Science Daily* (July 2, 2013), "The odds of two individuals having identical fingerprints are 64 billion to 1, making them an ideal tool for identification in criminal investigations."

Fingerprints that don't find a database match remain a problem, however. How do the authorities identify such a person? Or the forensic team may have found a "latent" print at the crime scene and need a method to match it to a suspect. Also, fingerprints from some sources such as paper money have been difficult to extract.

We are entering a time when crime scene fingerprints will tell a more complete story than that of the ridges and whorls. In England researchers have been able to analyze more than just the patterns of fingerprints, extracting evidence of recreational drugs, prescription medicine, and diet. In other words, the lab can create a picture of the suspect's lifestyle. Information like this may narrow down the range of possible suspects. The more comprehensive and complete the story behind a fingerprint becomes, the higher is the probability that it can reliably identify the accused. Science of this kind reduces the scope of uncertainty, allowing courts to be more easily persuaded to admit fingerprint evidence.

Keep an eye on fingerprint analysis over the next few years. It is likely that scientists will soon be able to extract a great deal of biomedical data from a fingerprint. Those running national fingerprint databases may reorganize their categories to take into account specific data "points," and that may allow authorities to draw correlations between the presence of certain drugs or dietary practices that increase the probability of criminal conduct. As computer software becomes faster and big data analysis (assuming arrangements are made to share fingerprint databases across multiple jurisdictions) more common, it is likely the reliability of matching will become much higher.

The problem of lifting fingerprints from paper money has also been solved by new methods. As *Science Daily* has reported (November 6, 2012), a team from the Hebrew University of Jerusalem's Institute of Chemistry "uses an innovative chemical process to produce a negative of the fingerprint image rather than the positive image produced under current methods."

In the case of a sex crime (again according to *Science Daily*, January 19, 2011), investigative technical advances allow investigators to determine whether the fingerprint came from someone who wore a condom. The absence of the suspect's DNA in the body of the victim creates a reasonable doubt. However, if the suspect's fingerprints reveal lubricant from a condom, this fact becomes evidence to explain the absence of DNA.

Collecting and analyzing crime scene evidence is on course for a major transition as testing techniques and databases increase in quality and reliability. Along with the ever-present CCTV cameras and facial recognition software, the capacity for identifying suspects in a criminal case will continue to improve. The future may see a shift in investigatory emphasis from "who done it" to why: motivators that can help explain the crime. Self-defense, drugs, alcohol, and genetic factors beyond the control of the suspect are likely to surface as legal justifications of actions or at least mitigations of intentionality.

Predicting Future Crime with Big Data

New York Times correspondent Sandra Blakeslee reminded us earlier this month, in her article "Computing Crime and Punishment" (June 16, 2014), that not so long ago the law didn't distinguish between non-violent criminals and violent ones. For instance, in 1765 in England, a man named John Ward was hanged merely for stealing a watch and a hat.

Historical records reveal a world of criminals and law enforcers that differs greatly from today's. But despite the differences, up to now our world and theirs have shared a basic principle: the enforcers' response to crime has been reactive. They've had to wait until a crime has been reported before springing into action. Catching someone who has violated the law has meant rounding up witnesses and gathering the evidence that implicates the wrongdoer.

The old policing model had very little to say about the future. It functioned on what was known in the present. A victim lodged a report. It also rested on the hunches or intuition of the police. Experienced police had personal knowledge of the neighborhoods they patrolled, though that information, in the large scheme of things, was bound to be incomplete and tainted by bias. Until recently the literature of crime followed the Sherlock Holmes model of a logical, clever, and objective detective who through these attributes outsmarted the villain.

We now inhabit a very different world. Most countries no longer hang watch and hat stealers, and in many of them the police don't necessarily wait for a crime to happen before springing into action. Instead they use big data to predict places and times where crimes are likeliest to occur, and they use that information to step up patrols. We have entered the machine age of law enforcement. The old model is in the process of a radical revamping as big data arms the police with predictive models that will take us into a future where enforcement can precede crime.

According to big data consultant Mark van Rijmenam of Datafloq, Los Angeles police have managed to reduce burglaries (33%), violent crimes (21%), and property crimes (12%) by adapting software developed to predict earthquakes and aftershocks. Eighty years of crime history detailing 13 million criminal acts were fed into a mathematical model designed to predict the areas of the city where crime is most likely to occur. It seems the model has yielded good results. New crimes are constantly added to the database, and LAPD officers who were at first resistant to taking orders from a mathematical model have since become true believers.

As Matt Stroud reported in the technology and culture zine *The Verge* ("The Minority Report," February 19, 2014), Chicago police have gone beyond identifying hot spots to using big data to target people most likely to commit a crime in the future. Having established the big data mapping of criminal activity in the city, the local administration decided that the mapping of social networks was the logical extension. Commander Steven Caluris, quoted in Stroud's article, defends the new approach succinctly: "If you end up on that list, there's a reason you're there." In the future, the map of your social network may be used by law enforcement agencies to assign you a probability statistic for your future criminal activity. As with a travel ban list for airlines, you may never know what is behind the inclusion of your name on a hot list. Florida, as Neal Ungerleider has discussed on his technology blog *Fast Company*, is going down the same road.

Professors at the Rutgers School of Criminal Justice tell us they have received grants to develop software called the Risk Terrain Modeling Diagnostics Utility. Here's a glimpse of the future of big data in policing, in the words of the Rutgers Office of Research and Economic Development:

> The National Institute of Justice recently awarded two grants, totaling nearly $1 million, to conduct RTM research in seven U.S. cities: Newark; New York City; Chicago; Arlington, Texas; Colorado Springs, Colo.; Glendale, Ariz.; and Kansas City, Mo. Researchers from Rutgers' School of Criminal Justice and John Jay College of Criminal Justice at the City University of New York are conducting the studies using the RTMDx Utility. The Rutgers software is currently being used in the top four U.S. markets: New York, Los Angeles, Chicago and Miami. It is being adopted by industry and law enforcement offices in many countries, such as Australia and Canada, and major foreign cities such as Paris and Milan.

According to the news website *Business Insider Australia* (May 13, 2014), the Australian Crime Commission has also funded a big data project. The goal is "to trawl through data sets looking for patterns and potentially predicting emerging crime issues and trends across the country."

The promise of such efforts is that patterns emerging from the big data will allow the police to consolidate resources and maximize efficiency. Like Wall Street brokers, the police have entered the world of big data with the goal of assessing risks and looking for trends. For a broker the challenge is getting in and out of a stock in timely fashion so as to make a profit. For the police the idea is to predict what types of crime are on the increase or decrease for any given geographical area. And like brokers, the police, having identified a trend, can allocate necessary resources to deal with it.

Science journalist Susan Watts, reporting last year (April 3, 2013) for BBC News on the use of big data in crime prevention, has noted that the prediction of crime trends requires masses of data about an area. Mining data about individuals' international social contacts and crimes committed around the world can lead to the unraveling of complex criminal networks. The BBC report shows how far we've come since the hanging of John Ward in 1765, not just in the public sphere but the private one too. Big data allows a corporation to detect who on the inside is communicating with someone on the outside, and to look for patterns that suggest an employee may be leaking information. Big data analysis also allows the military tactical advantages in the field as new data is constantly fed into analytical models to update positions, movements, and communications on the ground.

Philip K. Dick predicted in his 1956 short story "The Minority Report" that the state would evolve a system to predict and prevent crimes before they are carried out. The authorities in Dick's future world use methods remarkably similar to those we've just discussed. Note to the wise: in the future, before you buy that house or condo, you might want to ask the real estate agent whether the property lies within a crime hot spot.

It's still early days for the collection and mining of big data. The dynamics of technological change have made predictions of the far future and even the medium future—especially the technological future—nearly impossible. The reality is that we are headed down a road to a new kind of criminal justice system, and we don't know yet where it will lead us. We only have best guesses and cognitive biases such as best-case scenarios. We run the real risk of arriving at an information infrastructure and a criminal justice system to which we will surrender our free will and liberty.

In the future some descendant of John Ward may be hanged before he steals the watch and hat, doomed by big data analysis that assigns a 98% probability of future criminal conduct. That may sound like something no free society would ever accept, but if the same man had a 98% probability of becoming a serial killer, would you agree that he should be imprisoned? On the big data road map, such decisions are waypoints ahead of us. We have set out on a long journey, and along the way we are losing much of what we value as individuals, so that a class of elites with the most to gain can create a new culture based on total security.

Part V

Space, Time, Technology & Cultural Gravity

Disruptions

Part of the role of fiction is to document the range of emotional reaction that occurs during periods of disruption. When a culture goes into a phase transition, there is a sense of excitement, uncertainty, and fear. My first novel, *His Lordship's Arsenal*, was a story about how the invention of the submachine gun changed not just warfare but the military class system. The Vincent Calvino series is mainly about the cultural changes in Southeast Asia over the last twenty-five years.

In *Comfort Zone* the postwar lifting of the American embargo in Vietnam was the pivotal event causing societal disruptions in the story. In *Zero Hour in Phnom Penh* the appearance of the United Nations Transitional Authority in Cambodia (UNTAC) on that nation's road from civil war to peace was an opportunity to examine how people were reacting to those changes. *Missing in Rangoon*, 13th in the series, peered into the Burma (a.k.a. Myanmar) of our time to survey a society slowly emerging from half a century of isolation. In almost every one of the Calvino books, the reader finds an old elite defending wealth gathered with an earlier day's technology. When a new technology threatens to make the old methods and ways obsolete, tensions inside the culture arise as those who stand to lose readjust the rules and beliefs to their benefit. Literature is a portal into that tug of war between conservative forces and the creative, innovative forces working to replace them.

In my novels set in Cambodia, Vietnam, Burma, and Thailand, I've explored what happens to people once a big disruption lessens the force of the existing culture's gravity. I spent time in Burma in January 2012 researching that fast-changing land for *Missing in Rangoon*. I'd been there many times, starting in 1993. This time was different. The country was opening up; a political decision had been made to engage the world. In 2012 I was struck by how many people were smiling happily, as if they were already floating free from the old constraints.

Communication between cultures in the pre-digital past was often conducted through the media of books, magazines, radio, and television, though in many places access by and to "other" cultures was at best limited. Look at an American bestseller list like the fiction list in the *New York Times*. You could say that most of the authors found there benefit from wearing cultural gravity boots, that anchors them in the world of local readers, who read in their stories shadows and reflections from their own lives, fears, and dreams.

The nativist, the racist, and the nationalist share a common front against an open, tolerant, and diverse approach to the world of ideas and beliefs. Such people patrol the boundaries of their cultures for intruders, defectors, and dissenters. The old slogan "Love it or leave it" is stenciled on their cultural gravity boots. Their predominant goal is to prevent change and preserve the past. These are technological consumers who hate paying the price that new technology brings.

Sometimes a disruption may be isolated inside one culture. Immigration is a good example of a type of disruption in the patterns of daily life that causes anxiety, distrust, and suspicion among those who fear the presence of the "other" will change their way of life. Immigrants enter a space where the locals wear cultural gravity boots manufactured by immediate family and neighbors through teachers, preachers, friends, relatives, TV, movies, radio, and books. The immigrant is the "other"; he or she is not one of us. The belief system is a shared social construct that is assumed to be real and not just an idea that someone can choose to accept or reject. It often takes an outsider to point out the network of lies, deception, and illusions that underlies such attitudes. You would think that such enlightenment would make the locals happy, but life doesn't work that way, and they become hostile, defensive, and angry. Kicking a drug addiction is a minor challenge compared with freeing oneself of the easy slogans and half-truths embedded in a social construct.

For those who regard it as sacred, the social construct can seem so real that defense of it can lead to violence. A classic example of such nationalism is the anxiety (as I write this in late October 2013) surrounding the forthcoming decision of the International Court of Justice on whether the Preah Vihear Temple lies in Cambodia or Thailand. A small strip of land has somehow become inflated with two nations' identity, purpose, and meaning. As always in such cases, it is difficult to control the emotions once they go through a phase transition inside the nuclear reactor of nationalism.

What has changed over the course of my writing career is the rate or velocity of change that causes disruption. In the past there was time for people to adjust their lives to the disruptions caused by technology. Political institutions had ways of incorporating such changes into the existing culture, adjusting the cultural landscape both to minimize casualties and to preserve their own power and authority. Those days are gone. The current rate of disruption through computer software and hardware is bringing fundamental global changes in medicine, health, marketing, security systems, and information gathering, storage, and evaluation. No individual culture is weathering this storm well enough to completely understand, communicate, or absorb the rapid changes taking place.

You can witness the full force of cultural gravity on a population when a national sports team wins a gold medal at the Olympics, a local beauty is crowned Miss Universe, or local scientists or scholars take home a Nobel Prize. National air carriers, flags, colors, and uniforms are part of the cultural gravity wardrobe. Then there are the annual indexes on corruption, governance, longevity, human rights, and education, to name a few, which can reveal the dark sole of the cultural gravity boot. To prevent a break in the gravitational cultural force, the negative reports are usually buried in the back pages of a newspaper.

No longer can we rely on existing cultural institutions from the political or social elite to address pressing issues with clarity, precision, and absence of bias. This failing will make fiction and non-fiction all the more essential as people wish to understand the source, nature, and dangers of the disruptive changes and prepare themselves for the future. With such help we will become more aware that our cognitive biases have a cultural contour. Being guided by our biases, cognitive and cultural, is like wearing blinders on a dark road, driving at night without headlights.

The old order in most cultures is reactive and seeks to control the rate of the disruptions caused by the new technology and the fast-changing social structure. That approach is less effective than in the past as the old order no can longer monopolize the communications, products, and services demanded by its citizens. It's not just the elites with a large stake in wealth preservation who push back, but a significant minority of ordinary citizens who form alliances with these elites. Check the footwear. Both groups are wearing the same gravity boots.

Others are discovering that the old cultural gravity boots no longer keep them grounded in the neighborhood. They find themselves free-floating in a larger world. Witness the fear, the doubts, and the heightened emotions on today's political and social fronts. Communities are splitting into smaller units. The old beliefs and systems lack the comfort and security of earlier times. People lose faith first in their political institutions, which can't control the scale and rate of technological disruptions, blaming politicians for events that few fully understand and all have limited ability to influence. For many, the appeal of soft totalitarianism is growing as slower, messier, and less efficient democratic institutions seem less able to manage disruption and as subcommunities within them no longer accept electoral mandates.

The role of thinkers and writers amid these whirlwinds of disruption is to provide context and meaning to these forces and reveal how they are shaping modern choices about life. But to thrive, writers need a democratic culture to work in. In totalitarian ones they atrophy. The totalitarian political class is skillful in sticking to the cultural gravity talking points that avoid dealing with the hard choices ahead. No one wants to hear that the old boots no longer fit. In a less democratic society we focus less on difficult issues. The void is filled with hundreds of daily data streams that promise fun and thrills, bringing us news and photos of everything from cute cats and dogs to twerking, and the latest breaking story about a celebrity. By amplifying such mental fast food, the new technology is disrupting the thinking process, too. The entertainment tidbit is read, shared, and discussed more avidly than the thought-provoking essay. It was Alejandro Jodorowsky who observed,"Birds born in a cage think flying is an illness."

As we enter a new Dark Age, it won't seem dark. The bright colors, the seductive graphics, the flash programs mask the emptiness of the message—buy something. Laugh and everything will be better. "Don't think too much," the old bar girl piece of advice, has gone viral.

Writers need to push back against these disruptions not by becoming Luddites but by laying out the implications of the choices now confronting us, the cost we will pay, and what such change may mean for our relationships. We are at the beginning of a global project of restructuring human culture. It's a scary time for many because the direction of change isn't clear. What is clear is that no culture will remain untouched by these changes. New, resilient global communities will kick off their gravity boots and find a way not only to survive but to thrive in the new environment. Others will join them. But they will also find that there's a lot of kick left in the old gravity boot brigade, who won't go quietly into the long night.

In this essay Newtonian principles have been adapted to look at the effect of culture. Newton's theory of gravity is flawless for most everyday purposes. On a larger, cosmological scale, there are problems. In my next essay I ask whether Einstein's theories of relativity might be similarly adapted to reveal a deeper understanding of culture and lead to an idea of "cultural relativity."

Discontinuity

One assumption most people share is that the past and the present are causally linked. Like children with Lego blocks, we build the present out of the building materials we've received from the past. Disruptions break that causal link and throw out the old building components and ways of thinking. How we think about literature, technology, politics, history, or culture is circumscribed by our existing knowledge, imagination, and processing ability. We draw meaning from this connection. Break that link and we are cut adrift, scrambling to find alternatives to substitute for meaning. The technological disruption we are beginning to experience is so vast that our cultural gravity can't survive it. Like a collapsing star, such a disruption creates a black hole in a culture. Nothing can escape the pull of such a disruptive black hole. The old cultural gravity becomes null and void.

Discontinuity happens at the personal level. If you've left your home culture and return after twenty years away, you will discover a wide gap between what you remember about that place's cultural life and what it is today. You will find it hard to pick up the thread because so much of it has been woven into a new suit of clothes. Your family and friends who never left wear those new clothes. They look different;

they are different. Your memory has kept the culture static and eternally the same for you, but they have moved on. They have discarded much of the world you remember, and you can no longer predict their views and behavior. You are missing too much relevant information.

On a small scale this kind of discontinuity has existed almost continually for many generations. It isn't new. What is much rarer is the very real possibility of the sort of large-scale discontinuity that follows major technological disruptions. In the event of such a disruption, the rules of the game inevitably change. Such a disruption is an act of violence; it is mass murder of a whole industry, economic system, or culture. As they try to carry on, those affected see that a bridge has been destroyed behind them, leaving the past irrelevant and disconnected to the future. A disruption at that high level washes away the assumptions people have relied on to create their identity and the institutions that have served and protected their collective selves. With change this radical we know the rules of society's game will change radically too, but until the moment arrives we won't know how.

Sitting here at my desk in late 2013, I can't see exactly what that disruption will be any more than someone in 1900 could have confidently foreseen the technology of cars, airplanes, and television and their disruptions of existing transportation and communications systems, the resulting growth of urban centers, and the political and economic shifts that followed. It is, in other words, impossible to analyze what you don't know. It is also impossible to predict outcomes by projecting what technology might look like based on our current knowledge. But there are two places to start an inquiry into the source of discontinuity: intelligence and space.

Memory Storage and Information Processing Capacity

Very intelligent people, like very tall people, are rare. In a way they are freaks. Yet the qualifier "very" is misleading. A man who is 2.51 meters (8 feet, 3 inches) in height, like the Kurdish-Turkish farmer Sultan Kösen, is indeed very tall. But there is no man who is twice the average height. A similar limitation is found in human intelligence. If your IQ is a mere 30 points or more above average, you have a lifelong built-in advantage at school and work and with regard to recognition and status. According to the AnyTen blog, the list of Top 10 IQs in human history includes world chess champion Garry Kasparov, Sir Isaac Newton, François-Marie Arouet (Voltaire), and the philosopher Ludwig Wittgenstein, each with an IQ of 190. A high IQ is no guarantee of works of genius, however. American actor James Woods isn't far behind with an IQ of 180, and yet the Oscar eludes him. An American purported to have an IQ of 195, Christopher Michael Langan, worked for more than twenty years as a bouncer, though he has since developed something he calls the "Cognitive-Theoretical Model of the Universe."

To put all this in perspective, persons with the highest IQs are roughly twice as "intelligent" as the average person. Twice as smart is as impressive as twice as fast or strong. We admire and shower attention, prizes, and glory on such individuals. The status of genius is an individual prize. That is a common cultural artifact, though any scientist will tell you that the collective minds of many people have been responsible for most of our modern scientific breakthroughs. The reality is we listen to and supply money through private and public sources to very smart people with the idea that such intelligence can increase our own competitive advantage.

We are also intimidated by the knowledge that such very smart people can run circles around the rest of us. We fear what we admire. The abilities that define these high IQ individuals are their mental processing abilities and memory storage. They can process new information at a much faster rate and remember more of it than the rest of us. We also look to these people, especially in the arts and sciences, to provide a hint of any coming disruptions that will ripple through the cultural gravity that binds us to our communities and communal institutions.

So far no one who is twice as intelligent as the average person has used that gift to cause a major discontinuity. While those with high IQ are very smart and clever, they remain recognizably human, with most of the same flaws and limitations as the rest of us. The big "what if" question is what happens if a higher intelligence comes along that isn't double the human average but ten times, a hundred times, or a million times the average. We can't predict the meaning, use, and intentions of such intelligence, should it appear.

Intuitively, we assume that an intelligence a hundred thousand times greater than the average human would likely cause a major discontinuity between humanity's future and its past. The potential of AI, or artificial intelligence, lies on the other side of one of those bridges that will crumble to dust behind us. In 1997 Garry Kasparov was defeated at chess by an IBM computer called Deep Blue. While Deep Blue couldn't "think" in metaphors, write poetry, or cook a pizza, it could calculate the implications of possible moves on the chess board (there are only so many fixed moves) and come up with a probability of outcome. Deep Blue's speed of calculation far exceeded that of Kasparov. It was a humiliation for our species when a machine could beat one of our most experienced and intelligent members. We can minimize the psychological blow from Deep Blue by taking the position that the computer software was indeed intelligent but only in a highly narrow way and resorted to "brute force" (which works well in a limited context, especially when dialed up to high-speed rates of processing in a computer) rather than reason to justify each move on its way to victory over Kasparov.

This may be a glimpse of the beginning of a machine intelligence that cannot be beaten by the intelligence of any living human being. There are debates inside the AI community about how and when an intelligence that is a qualitative and quantitative magnitude beyond us will emerge, and there is no consensus. We don't know enough about how to define "intelligence" to have a good handle on the underlying issues that need to be understood before theory and engineering can advance. It might be ten years or it might be one or two hundred years before such true AI appears. Significant developments in our understanding of quantum physics, neuroscience, biology, and chemistry must be achieved first before we can have a workable definition of "intelligence."

Once we reach that stage, an important question will arise: how will we know when an intelligence a million times faster than any human being comes into being in our midst? If it is a gradual process, a system progressively getting smarter, we can prepare ourselves. But there is the possibility that an AI system could, through self-learning and rewriting the rules of AI itself (recursive systems), spring into existence in a week. In the latter case there would be no warning and perhaps no evidence either. An intelligence of that kind might be able to conceal itself. Even if the raw information of its presence stood before us, we might fail to comprehend its scope and scale. Its very nature may exist behind a veil that can't be pierced, much as a honey bee flying over an expressway between fields of flowers doesn't comprehend the traffic below.

Recursive artificial intelligence, once it emerges, will be disruptive across the board and will likely cause a level of discontinuity that calls into question a host of existential questions about the place and role of our species. For example, human cognition, perception, and behavior are largely shaped by culture, which defines how we perceive space, time, beauty, respect, and fear, how we read the intentions of others, and how we create meaning of self. Culture and cognition, like space and time, are knitted together. It is difficult to imagine what equivalent role, if any, our idea of culture will play in a super-intelligent agent. Or the role of emotions, which make us laugh, dance, cry and sing.

AI of this kind will not be using brute force; it will grow through something very much like the associative learning of a human being. Everything grounded and understood in the context of the present world, from jobs and finance to governance, warfare, secrecy, and consumption, could be flipped into a strangely incoherent world in a week. That's maximal disruption, and it could bring systemic discontinuity. This isn't evolution, a revolution is the only way to describe this kind of possible changes at warp speed, without taking any of the baby steps through which change normally arrives. All parts of the existing human system, the interrelationships and interdependencies, could become unstable and no longer function. If such an even happens, it will change the stories we tell about ourselves. It will change how we perceive ourselves and others. It will change our views about coercion, incentives, morality, and arguments.

Spatial Connections

Historically (that is, pre-Internet), our interhuman relationships have been defined by three-dimensional space. Your immediate neighbors, if you live in a condo, are those who live people above you, below you, and beside you. We humans have lived most of our existence inside such spatially limited boxes, whether of concrete, wood, farming land, or hunting grounds. When I arrived in Thailand twenty-five years ago, the Thais I encountered there from upcountry came from villages and towns where they had never seen a *farang*. Many of them had never seen a Thai-Chinese from Bangkok either. Throughout human history, isolation and ignorance of other people and cultures have been by-products of our limited, physically defined spatial reality.

Like the natural cap on human intelligence, the cap on how we experience space, despite other technological developments, has maintained our continuity with the perceptions of those who lived before us. Strangers lived in physical spaces at some distance from ours. To move their bio-masses to our village, they had to make a physical effort. At most people had a social relationship with a hundred or so people. The "Dunbar number" (see "Grooming 150 Friends" above) arises from that spatial limitation. According to anthropologist Robin Dunbar's theory, you can have a social relationship with up to 150 people, knowing these people individually to some degree, but after you exceed that number, you and those you know need bureaucracy to communicate or the relationship structure breaks down.

Within the "low-dimensional" space of the Earth's surface, I can find anyone so long as I have two fixed points of reference: their latitude and longitude. Give me those numbers and I'll locate the person in that space. The vast reaches of the universe, however, lie well beyond the gridwork of our earthly maps, with the result that we are mostly spatially illiterate. Douglas Adams in *The Hitchhiker's Guide to the Galaxy* wrote that space is "vastly hugely mindbogglingly big." An article in last week's *Economist* (October 26, 2013), which references Adams, gives an example of how big it really is:

> During the cold war America spent several years and much treasure (peaking in 1966 at 4.4% of government spending) to send two dozen astronauts to the Moon and back. But on astronomical scales, a trip to the Moon is nothing. If Earth—which is 12,742km, or 7,918 miles, across—were shrunk to the size of a sand grain and placed on the desk of *The Economist*'s science correspondent, the Moon would be a smaller sand grain about 3cm away. The sun would be a larger ball nearly 12 metres down the hall. And Alpha Centauri B would be around 3,200km distant, somewhere near Volgograd, in Russia.

Our current technology might get us to our interstellar "nextdoor neighbor" Alpha Centauri B, a star system 4.4 light years away, in about 75,000 years. Multiply those numbers by a billion and you're starting to imagine the length and duration of a single voyage across the currently known universe. Adams was right about space being big. Our brains don't explore cosmological space except perhaps momentarily before dinner, when we want a thought experiment to take us away from being hungry. Normally our thoughts occupy a social relationship space. The people we are going to have dinner with have infinitely more pull on our choices, desires, and actions than Alpha Centauri B. It's true that, should we ever overcome the energy requirements to travel through cosmological space, the discontinuity would be immense. But then, we don't need to leave the planet to find a significant disruption of our sense of space.

In his book *Time Reborn*, theoretical physicist Lee Smolin discusses our "low-dimensional" world before modern technology expanded the dimensions we live within beyond anything that anyone living in 1900 could have imagined. Who could have conceived that a villager in rural Thailand, Burma, India, or China with the purchase of an inexpensive device, a cell phone, would gain the possibility of more than two billion possible same-time connections to people all over the world? And that's just the telephone. Smolin notes that with the Internet we have created a high-dimensional space, and many people are migrating to and living their lives inside this digital locale. The physical space we once met in, the place where we once shared our stories in face to face meetings, has been technologically demolished and replaced with non-physical communication.

In the early 1990s I wrote a novel titled *The Big Weird*, in which I explored how a Bangkok sex worker used an online avatar to expand her trolling waters beyond the dimensions of a physical bar. The space in which people meet and interact today bears little resemblance to that of our grandparents' generation.

Smolin writes, "In a high-dimensional world with unlimited potential for connection, you're faced with many more choices than in the physical three dimensions." The next logical progression in thinking would seem to be that physical space is an "illusion," masking a deeper reality of networks. Since our sense of space is our way of understanding our connections to one another, and connections can be open or closed, it's easy to imagine a world where people occupy different, perhaps discrete spatial frames simultaneously.

Importing latitude and longitude from the low-dimensional world into the new one is no longer useful. The global intelligence community may have been among the first to recognize that tracking people inside networks no longer fully corresponds with low-dimensional space tracking. When someone leaves low-dimensional space and "disappears" into a network, who are they sharing that space with, and what information and resources are involved? What is the scope of privacy and secrecy inside networks in this new high-dimensional space? We are beginning to ask these questions and to realize that the broader community ought to be engaged in deciding how government and private enterprise patrol the new space.

Governments are having difficulty grasping the implications of a high-dimensional place to store and publish stories. During their Edward Snowden investigation members of the British intelligence service arrived at the offices of the *Guardian* and demanded that the staff produce a computer that could be destroyed, even though they knew that the nature of the actual "space" where Snowden's documents were stored made the act an empty gesture. Their commandeering of the computer had a whiff of the brute intimidation of medieval times rather than a modern coming to terms with the issue of multiple copies strewn through digital space. It seems even governments can't understand, adjust, or control the spatial disruptions that in large part they are responsible for funding. Their agents look a bit like the Keystone Cops, running around as if latitude and longitude still ruled the spatial dimension that they have themselves have helped to destroy, leaving an interesting contradiction for us to contemplate. The expansion into high-dimensional space calls into question where journalists will fit or if they can survive as a profession. Journalism is a good example of a casualty of disruption, currently waiting in ER with no doctor able to determine the extent of the injury.

The duality of spatial sensibility creates discontinuity. Those who live in a pre-Internet world occupy a different space than those who are connected digitally to billions of others. The old test to divide the haves from the have-nots was formulated to look at living standards and wealth disparity. The political, social, and economic influences of the old distinction have been the stuff of literature for millennia. This gap has existed long enough to shape our thinking about social relationships, culture, history, and ideals such as social justice and fairness. But when a high-dimensional space becomes accessible to the vast majority of people, what will happen to social, political, and economic disparity?

We need a new literature that will examine this process of spatial evolution into huge networks and what that means for individual opportunity, identity, and relationships—and what meaning is still attributed to your position in physical space. Until now culture has depended on low-dimensional space, a concept that is shared among all cultures. When that concept gradually comes to be seen as an illusion, the result will be a weakening of the cultural gravity that has traditionally been the natural force holding communities together. When space dissolves in meaning and networks become the login to reality, we can expect major discontinuity.

Think of the larger "space" in which you watch, listen to, or read news, or in which you buy books or anything else. Then ask yourself how that space differs from the one you navigated ten or twenty years ago. Count all of those new network connections you didn't have back then. You have broken out of the low-dimensional space in which you were born.

In many countries today one can find authorities passing laws to censor the new multi-dimensional space and to criminalize certain interactions inside that space. That is gravity of the cultural type seeking to increase its force, seeking to reclaim the physical space inside digital space. It is the last gasp by authorities who fully understand that by allowing people to roam inside the vast world of networks, they run the risk of the old spatially bound narratives coming under attack and falling apart.

It is a real worry. People and institutions alike are anxious because we can't look to the past as a guide to how to react to this new idea about space. Sometimes the result of this anxiety is repression, to make people fearful about their interactions in digital space. Authorities patrol the new networks, but the means of monitoring high-dimensional space effectively will remain inaccessible to them for the foreseeable future.

Humanity has no guarantee of safe passage into the future. But I suspect that books will evolve to examine our potential to live inside high-dimensional space with super-intelligent beings. That will take time. By the time we have adjusted our visions, expectations, dreams, and desires to life inside a higher spatial dimension, we may discover we are sharing it with an artificial intelligence that, to our human sensibilities, performs cognition in a way that appears like magic. How friendly will we find this AI? How will a super-intelligent agent shape our experience of high-dimensional space? Civilization is based on an idea that our security is bought with freedom as the universal social currency. The more people are fearful, the more likely they will pay down their freedom surplus in gain protection against the worst aspects of ourselves—*Homo homini lupus* (man is wolf to man). Soon there may be a new, more dangerous wolf to worry about, and our idea of civilization may not be able to cage that new animal. Who will bell that wolf?

Duration

Time is etched in our culture. Our language reflects this fact; "losing time," "wasting time," and "saving time," for example, are all essential phrases. When people break the law, we punish them by confining them for periods of time, sometimes for life. Lawyers, to choose just one profession, bill their clients according to minutes spent, an indication that time and money are interwoven. You can go out in a blaze of glory like Miles Davis, John Coltrane, and Jim Morrison—"no one gets out of here alive"—or you can live a long, flat, and anonymous life that doesn't leave a ripple, either way, your life is still measured by calendar years. A meaningful life may be more than the sum total of years lived—one that leaves a legacy beyond immediate family and friends—but when we examine such lives we can't help thinking how brief they were.

We all have this in common: an expiry date like the one on that bottle of aspirin above the bathroom basin. Take out the bottle and look at it, and you'll know when to throw it away. But when it comes to your life, that information is withheld from you, unless you face execution or suicide. In the great Hindu legends time passes through very long cycles. One day of Brahma equals 4.32 billion years in our realm. Ancient Egyptian mythology was also based on cycles of time. The Western culture of time is expressed in this passage from Ecclesiastes 3:

> For everything there is a season, a time for every activity under heaven. A time to be born and a time to die. A time to plant and a time to harvest. A time to kill and a time to heal. A time to tear down and a time to build up. A time to cry and a time to laugh. A time to grieve and a time to dance. A time to scatter stones and a time to gather stones. A time to embrace and a time to turn away. A time to search and a time to quit searching. A time to keep and a time to throw away. A time to tear and a time to mend. A time to be quiet and a time to speak. A time to love and a time to hate. A time for war and a time for peace.

We are born into a culture that wires our perception to time. No culture can overlook the universal fate of all people whose duration—short, medium, or long—comes to an end. A great deal of literature and crime fiction revolves around the unfolding of the present, linking it to the past as something important to determining our future fate. Poets, playwrights, novelists, and songwriters can compress or expand time or reverse its direction, distorting it for dramatic effect. Homer's epic poems the *Iliad* and the *Odyssey*, for instance, are epic journeys through time cycles.

Our endless fascination with time is reflected in the movies. As we watch a movie that lasts about two hours, a number of lifetimes can unfold before our eyes. Sometimes cinematic time moves in a backward direction, as in *The Curious Case of Benjamin Button* and *Memento*, and sometimes time is on auto-repeat, with each day the same as the day before, as in *Groundhog Day*. Movies can fulfill a longing to go physically back in time, as in *Field of Dreams*, *Back to the Future*, and *A Connecticut Yankee in King Arthur's Court*. Movies can also transport the characters, and us along with them, to a distant future, as in *Planet of the Apes* and *The Time Machine*. These movies indicate that we just can't get enough entertainment that transports us to time ports that reality denies us.

Once you close a book or leave the cinema, you are back to our temporal reality, where the end of your time hovers like a drone with a sealed order to strike, and you are the target. You live in the crosshairs, waiting. That's pretty morbid, you may say, and you'd be right. We avoid thinking about that time for that very reason: it gives us an uneasy feeling. Our lives are lived in time. In the scheme of things the time of any mortal life is short. When you think about four-letter words, "time" ought to be at the top of your list. An insult or obscenity may hurt our sensibility, but time, in the end, destroys sensibility and the body housing it.

People escape in all kinds of ways—into booze, religion, sex, rock 'n' roll, books, opera, dance, and travel. Whether you are a billionaire or pauper, time doesn't care, no more than it cares whether you are famous, popular, loved, adored, or have made the planet a better place. You still are axed. With time there is no escape. At some point in your life you reconcile yourself to the reality that time existed before you were born and will continue to exist after your death. In between those bookends of time is where you are. Now. At this minute. Reading these words. Where we are sharing time in the land of thoughts.

Time and destiny are tightly woven into our lives. In the previous two essays I've discussed the ideas of disruption and discontinuity. Duration fits within this context as both of these earlier concepts assume the passage of time. Time is also part of the equation that includes space.

It seems that each week new exoplanets (planets outside our solar system) are discovered. In all there are perhaps 40 billion potentially habitable planets in our universe, data from NASA's Kepler spacecraft are currently suggesting. The problem is one of time; it takes huge amounts of it to travel in space. As I mentioned in the previous essay, with our current space travel capability, even the voyage to the nearest exoplanet would take something like a thousand lifetimes.

The human life span has so far not evolved to live on the scale of the time required for space exploration, barring the intervention of a time-bending new technology. Not that it stops us from dreaming of the possibility or reading science fiction premised on such technology. Still the universe remains unimaginably big (and dark too; galaxies and other matter are just the five-percent icing spread on a ninety-five-percent dark cake).

Each time I start planning a new novel, I must decide when it starts. Without a time anchor the suspense of a crime novel would fall to pieces. The same applies to each novel's mystery elements, which evolve through time. These puzzle pieces are time envelopes I leave for the reader to open to better understand the characters' past and their present reactions, clues to what will follow next. In *The Marriage Tree*, the latest Calvino novel, the time setting is around the Songkran festival, which falls in April each year. If you know something about Thai culture, weather, history, and language, this piece of information is valuable. It immediately gives you a mental image of Bangkok around this time. The novel may confirm your own experience of how people move in and out of the city during this important Thai holiday. For those who have experienced

April and Songkran as a cultural-temporal unity, the novel will have added meaning.

We are drawn to narratives in which time "flows." In a flashback the author takes us back in time. A lot of readers don't like flashbacks. Literary time travel is counterintuitive. We are stuck in the moment, and each moment succeeds the next. In life there is no returning to a past moment except as a matter of memory. That past is time in our heads or, if you will, "time in a bottle," as it is recalled or imagined rather than experienced in the reality of the moment.

Some novels offer expansive time frames; others keep time on a very short leash. The narrative may occur over centuries, years, weeks, or mere days. Or in the case of *Ulysses*, for instance, an entire novel may be confined to a single twenty-four-hour period. Crime fiction usually sticks to a time frame of months or weeks, whereas science fiction can take on multiple-century sagas, as in Issac Asimov's *Foundation* trilogy.

You and I are time contemporaries. Our lives overlap in time. The fact that we share the same time is significant. We think about Socrates or Plato in a quite different way, much as we regard someone we imagine will live two hundred years from now. People who exist outside our time are more alien and foreign to us than any isolated Amazon tribe of hunter-gatherers living now.

We know people who choose to live in the past. For them the past is a gilded cage containing a legacy mentality, a thought process that glorifies the achievements, wisdom, civility, and morality of the past. Such myth-making is inevitably backward looking to a fault. Its obvious emotional attraction is the promise of a comfortingly stable boat on which to ride out the chaotic and ambiguous present. Conversely, those who discount the present to live in a future of their own imagining drift on a sea of speculation.

Many of us are tempted to wonder about the fate and state of humanity in the deep future, a time we will never see, and we make up stories to satisfy this urge. All of these time-based emotions are fueled by the existential anxiety we all share. Personal extinction is about as personal as it gets.

We can't stop time. The reality is we exist moment to moment. Our attempts to escape into the past or the future are futile. Our best remaining option for making life's span satisfying is to find ways to slow down our sense of time's passage.

What makes time speed up or slow down? When we are young, time seems to move slowly. The endless summer days of youth are fondly remembered when, by middle age, that slow boat to China becomes a Japanese bullet train with our remaining days flying past the window. One theory is that novelty slows down our perception of the flow of time. The more we encounter that is new, the more we slow down. For a child everything is new, revealing a vivid color, sound, smell, or taste. By the time we reach middle age, most of our senses are functioning on automatic pilot. Our minds no longer need to sort out the world around us. We are convinced we know it well. We are experts at our work, and nothing surprises us. We've seen it all before.

Losing one's sense of novelty is like stomping on the time accelerator. Before you know it, you're old and time is racing away. Science is beginning to understand that our time perception is a product of the human brain's natural development, as British author Robert Twigger has written for *Aeon* ("Master of Many Trades"):

> Between birth and the age of ten or eleven, the nucleus [basalis] is permanently 'switched on'. It contains an abundance of the neurotransmitter acetylcholine, and this means new connections

are being made all the time. Typically this means that a child will be learning almost all the time—if they see or hear something once they remember it. But as we progress towards the later teenage years the brain becomes more selective. From research into the way stroke victims recover lost skills it has been observed that the nucleus basalis only switches on when one of three conditions occur: a novel situation, a shock, or intense focus, maintained through repetition or continuous application.

If you want to slow down time, do something new and novel. Learn a new language or musical instrument, or expand your reading to a number of different fiction and non-fiction areas. Improvisation should be a lifelong habit. It increases acetylcholine levels, and those are chemical actors that recreate that inner child who started out improvising with a totally unknown world. Don't let yourself slip into automatic pilot, simply repeating patterns or cycles in your work, life, and community of friends. You have a choice about how you experience time by yourself and with others. You can make it slow down, drink it in, and prolong it with novelty and wonder. We can choose to occupy a time to love or a time to hate, a time to cry or a time to laugh. And if enough of us find the time to embrace and the time to search, our passing through time has the possibility of rewarding us with hope.

Part VI

Information and Theory of Mind

Where Do You Get Your Information?

Time is etched in our culture. Our language reflects here has never been a time with more sources of information available at little or no cost to so many people. A mere Internet connection can launch you into a sea of information that your grandfather would have found astounding. But there is also a dark side to the information revolution: misinformation, lies, fraud, and deception, deposited like cuckoo eggs throughout the information nest. The same can be said about the dissemination of opinion masquerading as fact. It is no surprise that opinion, information, facts, and evidence can be interfused like a rugby scrum on a muddy playing field. Often you can't tell one player from another.

The first question to ask someone who makes a supposedly factual statement should be about the source upon which it rests. Take a statement such as: "Vitamins are good for you. They will help you live longer." Is this information reliable, supported by scientific research, and accurate without qualification? As a matter of fact, recent studies indicate that vitamin taking correlates with a higher rate of mortality.

If someone is getting most of their news from the TV or a local newspaper, and accepting this "information" as factual, reliable, and tested, chances are they are forming opinions based not on actual knowledge and reality but on the biases that the news sources wish others to share. A useful exercise regarding bias is to take any news story and run a background check on it. Make yourself into a habitual reality checker, a sort of detective who regards each news story as a suspect with a questionable relationship to the truth.

Not only must the truth seeker of today weather a tsunami of information, but also risk being drown by a flood of misinformation. The high-stakes games of profit making and political power retention present an abundance of reasons to propagate falsehoods. In the struggle for the minds of the public, facts and information incur high casualty rates. Foundations, institutes, and TV stations draw large audiences with lies, half-truths, and mere opinion disguised as fact.

True ignorance is allowing oneself to be trapped in a narrow information zone, which is easy because this brew of views and ideology has a strong emotional appeal. Cults are built on faith. Information within a cult flows from faith, loyalty, and authority and is to be defended against any contrary information. The bad blood in many countries today, including Thailand, is caused by failures of information access, processing, discussion, and evaluation.

Freedom of expression includes the right to consider all information and facts. In restricted political expression systems, censorship and the threat of imprisonment are used to confine and narrow the sources of information. Open access to all information is threatening to entrenched elites who have or seek to have a monopoly over information channels and content. In many parts of the world it is only with the globalization of information channels, and the people's access to them from their offices and homes, that the possibility of challenging the old information monopolies has arisen.

But for many people access isn't enough. Lazy thinkers are content to let others "bake that pie." They're happy enough to eat what they're served, without asking too many questions about ingredients or whose kitchen it was prepared in, let alone the goal of the baker. The Hume distinction between "ought" and "is" makes their eyes glaze over. Pass the popcorn. The idea that information requires intellectual work on the part of all citizens is not popular. For many, so long as the news is ideologically consistent with their worldview and/or is entertaining, that is sufficient to believe it is true. There is no independent background check.

Education means teaching students that "what you see is all there is" is a bias. One must always ask what is missing or absent from any study, survey, or opinion. It also means teaching students that information is messy by its very nature. Most of the time we can't remove all uncertainty or doubt about agency and causation. Nor can we predict outcomes in the future. We can only come up with probabilities of outcomes, understanding that "dark" horses sometimes win a race.

Consumer society has been a great success because of its ability to create a vast population of docile, passive, and status-seeking consumers. Huxley's *Brave New World* warned in 1932, long before the advent of computers and the Internet, that these characteristics of the new human would allow state-sponsored repression of the truth to go unnoticed and unchallenged. Soma: the mental state of artificial well-being that covers lies and deceit.

We live much of our lives online, where bit by bit we give up for free information about our social networks, private thoughts, medical history, doubts, political positions, the books we read, and the TV shows and films we watch. This information is shoveled into the great maw of surveillance systems to track those with deviant connections, thoughts, or ideas, to create better soma to lull consumers into a deeper sleep. In this brave new world, information independence becomes a crime. Those who dig too deep can find that they are digging their own graves.

The Global Language of Bias:
What Do We Use Language For?

Isn't one of the goals of a university education the exposure of students to a wide range of ideas, cultures, histories, and theories, as an introduction to the complicated reality of the world? The world is often in conflict over ideas, events, personalities, and history. If you read *Slaughterhouse Five* by Kurt Vonnegut, who found himself at ground level during the Allied firebombing of Dresden in 1945, you will discover one way of processing such a traumatic event. Every great book ever written triggers an unsettling emotion, upsets values, threatens orthodox views, and, yes, makes you appreciate that we have always lived in an uncertain, contentious, messy, dangerous world, where people are injured, "disappeared," killed, tortured, and abused. Shouldn't university students be busy acquiring a deeper, more diversely sourced, more complex understanding of the ways in which reality is fashioned in our world?

Apparently that is a minority view within the American trend for bringing in a system of "trigger warnings" for student readers because, as a recent *New York Times* article (May 17, 2014) signaled with its title, "Warning: The Literary Canon Could Make Students Squirm." Is it far-fetched to wonder whether such warnings, if popularized, might be a further step toward creating a state of near total control? If I were one of the oligarchs, I think I'd very much

225

support and fund such a trend. The reality is that anything that might threaten the oligarchs' social construct of reality is widely deemed a threat to all. But the trigger warning is itself a warning about who has a finger on the trigger and where the barrel of that gun is pointed. Among those it is pointed at might be some writers once thought safe for young minds. "Among the suggestions for books that would benefit from trigger warnings," the *Times* article suggests, perhaps disingenuously, "are Shakespeare's 'The Merchant of Venice' (contains anti-Semitism) and Virginia Woolf's 'Mrs. Dalloway' (addresses suicide)."

The purpose of higher education has narrowed considerably as universities have gone into the mass education business. Trigger warnings look set to become a strut in the new infrastructure of reality, to reinforce the prevailing view that university is a place to learn job skills.

Our biases ensure that we are hardwired to believe things that are not true, though as *New Yorker* writer Maria Konnikova found in a survey of current research on the subject ("I Don't Want to Be Right," May 16, 2014), there may still be some hope of correcting false beliefs: "The theory, pioneered by Claude Steele, suggests that, when people feel their sense of self threatened by the outside world, they are strongly motivated to correct the misperception, be it by reasoning away the inconsistency or by modifying their behavior." The key to unlocking a false belief, Steele's research suggests, may lie in setting challenging ideas on a table of self-affirmation. Konnikova writes, "Could recalling a time when you felt good about yourself make you more broad-minded about highly politicized issues, like the Iraq surge or global warming? As it turns out, it would."

Recent research such as Steele's has shown that most people live in a "fact-free zone," and debunking lies and deceptions draws a backfire effect, like ack-ack guns firing at the incoming facts until the barrels melt. Most people, it appears, seek protection from the blitz of images, facts, and opinions that challenge their reality operating systems. Having internalized the message, the herd becomes self-censoring. The elites react negatively and intervene when an individual or group attempts to divert the masses from their auto-pilot setting—perhaps when someone asks a dangerous question, such as: Is wealth equitably distributed by unregulated capitalism?

America is, in other words, trending toward the Chinese model of higher education. Intellectual and emotional controls are only a step beyond eliminating the awkwardness that may get in the way of learning how to build a bridge or a computer program. If a professor must live under the shadow of the trigger warning, the temptation will be to avoid any literature that might present such a trigger, for fear that his warning will prove to have been too little, too late, and he will be open to a lawsuit for failure to make a full and informed disclosure. Every professor in such an environment would need to retain a lawyer with expertise in what constitutes an actionable trigger and how to give preemptive warnings. Does society really want to go down that path? It seems there are many in America who do.

Some academics wish to cocoon students in an assigned, manufactured reality where disturbing, disruptive, or destabilizing images, scenes, or characters are taken care of for them. An Oberlin College behavior guideline is specific: "Be aware of racism, classism, sexism, heterosexism, cissexism, ableism, and other issues of privilege and oppression. Realize that all forms of violence are traumatic, and that your students have lives before and outside your classroom, experiences you may or may not expect or understand."

Unfiltered, ugly, twisted, confusing, and threatening reality is an enemy to those in power. Most people are willing to hand over their liberty and privacy to escape that reality. Oligarchs know this about the human condition, and they exploit this design defect to their and their heirs' enduring advantage.

We tend to think of the techniques of control as either the outright repression of Orwell's *1984* or the soma of Huxley's *Brave New World*. We are learning through experience that this is a false choice. In many countries the oligarchs use a combination of both techniques to quell rebellion and to dampen fears of the disturbing, inconvenient truths of most people's lives. In freer societies, issues of "privilege and oppression" are starting to be seen as triggering events, and professors may soon be forced to protect students from cognitive dissonance.

Not all messages are allowed equal passage along the pipeline of information. The medium has more than one way to deliver a message and more than one message. The most powerful symbol of blocking the herd from seeing what the caretakers wish them not to know about their plans, policies, and self-dealing is ▨▨▨▨▨▨▨▨▨. When an unauthorized person wishes to send a public message over the heads of the caretakers to alert the herd of a danger, a misdeed, or an abuse, the message is blocked behind a wall of ink: ▨▨▨▨▨▨▨▨▨. Analog or digital, the traffic of ideas, information, and theories is under constant surveillance. Censors patrol all public spaces, searching for the words and images that challenge authority's version of reality. We can follow their trail. Our overlords leave behind the historical signature of disapproval, ▨▨▨▨▨▨▨▨▨, erected like a tombstone over the grave of a murdered thought.

Trigger warnings are a sign of a desire to restrict and ultimately to abolish cognitive dissonance. No one should be surprised by this desire. Thais often say that thinking too much gives them a headache. That complaint, as it turns out, may have gone viral.

Deliberate calculation, skepticism, doubt, and calls for falsifiable theories are slow and time-consuming thinking in a world where change is ever-accelerating and people are afraid of being left behind. The sheep keep dogs as house pets, not quite seeing the terrible irony of that relationship, not seeing that what has happened to the wolf over evolutionary time has happened to them.

Marshall McLuhan in *The Gutenberg Galaxy* saw more than fifty years ago what we are experiencing now: "Homogenization of men and materials will become the great program of the Gutenberg era, the source of wealth and power unknown to any other time or technology."

Trigger warnings are another example of the hyperreality that maintains an environment for the herd. In dense concentrations in modern cities, the members of this herd, individually and collectively, remain calm, content, and undisturbed as they study, work, eat, love, pray, and shop. The gates leading from one enclosure to the next give the appearance of freedom. People feel the need to believe they glide along one seamless path where they are warned in advance against any thoughts or images that might disturb them. Guidelines are issued to carefully control their ideas and to monitor their psychological states, insulating them from what are seen to be degrading and horrible experiences, injustices, and arbitrary actions, as if these were dangerous injection drugs. The best of literature is indeed dangerous, as it shows that manufactured reality is a drug enabling the worst kind of oppression.

The future is a fight against a model of reality that is a monopoly, controlled by the powerful and formidably defended against dissent. We are already far down the road to a place where our reality is one manufactured under close supervision, blending entertainment, status, prestige, and pride. In recent weeks the non-corporate media have noticed how the big corporate media have been relatively quiet in reporting on a study by Martin Gilens and Benjamin I. Page of Princeton and Northwestern universities, respectively, that revealed the considerable power to influence government policy held by the economic elite (as Steve Rendall wrote in "Study Confirms US Is Ruled by Rich, Corporate News Ignores It," *Truthout*, May 17, 2014). Information is currently thoroughly filtered by big corporate media; the question now is how long before non-corporate online players make the old filters irrelevant? When that happens, the information dam will blow. People will know who has what and where they've stashed it. In fact, it seems that chase has already started.

I try to imagine how this will work out. The economic elites still operate the main feed line of what you experience every day. Every object around you connects you to a product that comes off the feed line. Personal emotional attachment and engagement become detached from day-to-day reality. We are attached to what isn't real, and reality, which we no longer engage with, seems less and less real. Disneyland is the prevailing metaphor; we live in a 3-D cartoon world. The artificial environment becomes the new real. The Eiffel Tower displayed by Disney World in Orlando becomes as real to the visitor as the one in Paris. People can no longer distinguish one from the other. A copy becomes as valid an experience as the original. It is inside this blended reality that students feel they need to be shielded against an earlier world of experience and reality where bad things happened to good people.

The best writing will continue to explore the sharp edges of reality, the hypocrisy of power, the abuses of authority, the inequities and injustices of those behind the veil. At this point it may be a rearguard action, as those who use truth to challenge power will discover that those holding the reins deflect their efforts under the guise of protecting youth from the harmful consequences of truths they need not know. We have advanced technologically beyond what our ancestors could have imagined, while emotionally we run on the same treadmill that Socrates pointed to in the public square. And that cup of hemlock takes a new form as we escape deeper into the world of sheep, forgetting the history of dogs.

Marshall McLuhan wrote in *The Gutenberg Galaxy*: "We now live in the early part of an age for which the meaning of print culture is becoming as alien as the meaning of manuscript culture was to the eighteenth century. 'We are the primitives of a new culture.'" We enter this new culture with our bias guns fully loaded and blazing away.

The Illusion of Understanding

O nce any argument settles into a battle over who is right and who is wrong, people become uncompromising. Everyone wishes to be right. Arguing that your opponent is wrong only redoubles their faith in their beliefs (the "backfire effect") and ensures that you will be banished from their list of people who know the difference between right from wrong. Everyone in Thailand and elsewhere is arguing over their positions, preferences, values, and beliefs—husbands and wives, neighbours, friends, colleagues, and strangers. We live in an angry, emotional time. And I am trying to get a handle on why this is.

Public debate in this country seems (as I write this on June 6, 2014) to have reached an intellectual dead end. To comprehend the forces that have driven us there, one approach is to ask a few basic questions:

(1) What do we really understand about an issue or policy?

(2) What knowledge of it do we have, and where did it come from?

(3) How complete and up to date is our information?

(4) What are the limits to our understanding of the underlying complexities of the system from which the issue has emerged (or within which the policy must be implemented)?

Researchers have suggested that one reason we end up at loggerheads so easily is that we suffer from the illusion of understanding how things work. Consider a flush toilet or an air-conditioning unit. These are familiar objects in our daily lives. Because they are familiar, we believe we understand how they work. But unless you are a plumber or an air-conditioning engineer, that is probably an illusion. The illusion of understanding also applies in the political realm to policies on immigration, transportation infrastructure, health care, energy, climate change, and so on. Given where I live and write, I am interested in the politics of change.

We may read newspapers (fewer of us do it each year), but mostly we just scan the headlines. Most of our opinions on policy issues have a headline depth. It's a pool that's a mile wide and inch deep. We believe, though, that we know all there is to know about a preference or position because we've read, at most, an 800-word story. If pressed, we would begrudgingly admit there are a few minor details we could still look up if need be, but we are pretty confident that our knowledge is solid and relevant. Our 800-word world of knowledge has prepared us for a policy debate, and we enter the battle over right and wrong with a brittle, dull blade and no shield. But we are confident that our weapons of knowledge will allow us to prevail and emerge in victory, and that they, fools and charlatans that they are, will see their defenses turned to ashes.

That's pretty much our world of political debate. We dive headfirst into that pool that's an inch deep and seek to shut down the counterarguments made by people whom we take for ignorant, know-nothing troublemakers. We feel a powerful need to convert them to the right side.

In a utopia people would come to their senses and realize that they lack an in-depth understanding of a policy position. In the real world, "humans have a tendency to take mental short cuts when making decisions or assessments," explains the BBC's Tom Stafford ("The Best Way to Win an Argument"), making us what social psychologists call "cognitive misers."

Our cognitive vulnerability flows from two sources. First, we are lazy thinkers and would rather know just enough to lay down an emotional platform of support that plugs us into our community of like-minded believers. Second, our headline knowledge gives us a feeling of familiarity with the greater policy debate, whether the issue at hand is gun restrictions or the rescue of kidnapped Nigerian schoolgirls or a coup in Thailand. Whatever the particular application, a throng of true believers will emerge with slogans and similar talking points. Abbreviated arguments of that kind create a comfortable sense of real knowledge.

An extremist position for or against a policy is almost always drawn from a slogan, a talking point, or a headline grab that passes as reason or justification for a position. This leads to conflict between people on opposite sides of any issue. They hurl reasons at one another and sneer at the reasons of their opponents. Deadlock ensues, positions harden, and violence sometimes starts to rear its ugly head.

But there is a third reason for our cognitive miserliness: our mental processing of patterns, knowledge, and values passes through cultural filters. These biases are presistent and difficult to overcome; they are our setting, channels, frequencies over which information is sent and received.

Red flashing lights should come on to warn us when we unquestioningly accept that our understanding is sufficient to support high confidence in our position. That's why "the illusion of understanding" is an illusion. We deceive ourselves into believing that our simple understanding is an accurate summary of how a complex system functions, when actually the system's complexity eludes us.

Researchers have shown that politically polarized positions rest on superficial understandings of the complexity of how policies work. When pressed, we can't explain how any given policy functions within such complexity. We don't have the information or breadth of knowledge needed to connect policy, policy outcomes, and the system in which policy sinks or swims. The problem with requiring someone with a polarized position to give such an explanation is that it threatens the black-and-white thinking most of us cherish. The mark of an extremist is the refusal to undertake such an inquiry.

We need diverse information about systems, and that can only come from people who see and experience the system in diverse ways. But a diversity of explanations can be viewed as mere challenges or criticism. If you had true power, you'd close down those explanations that didn't support your policy or actions. Here's an example from my week: an email that I received from the Foreign Correspondents' Club of Thailand (FCCT) about an event.

POSTPONED:
A Week in Military Detention
An account of life as a 'guest' of Thailand's new
military rulers by Pravit Rojanaphruk

6.30 pm, Tuesday June 3, 2014
(Please see pricing and reservation
procedure below)

This event has been postponed until further notice.

Please come along to the FCCT on Tuesday to hear veteran journalist Pravit Rojanaphruk recount his experiences under military detention in the first week after the 22 May coup.

Under the conditions of his release Pravit has had to sign an agreement not to encourage opposite to military rule, but he says he is determined to try to tell us as much as he can about his unusual week in an army camp – one of his campmates was firebrand PAD leader Sonthi Limtongkul – and his impressons of how the military is doing in its attempt to estabilish its authority over Thailand and to reshape the country's political landscape.

With absolute power, you can shut down all public voices that probe for a deeper knowledge and a broader explanation of the mechanism working inside the system. Just asking a question can be viewed as an act of aggression. While a coup would be an unusual step in most countries, the impulse to control policy making by steering citizens away from the deep waters of knowledge that may cause "confusion" or "undermine authority" is nearly universal.

In a recent study by professors from four American universities, titled "Political Extremism Is Supported by an Illusion of Understanding," the authors (Philip M. Fernbach, Todd Rogers, Craig R. Fox, and Steven A. Sloman) started with the hypothesis "that extreme policy preferences often rely on people's overestimation of their mechanistic understanding of complex systems those policies are intended to influence."

Our comprehension of policies remains stuck at the abstract, headline level of reality. That understanding is disconnected from any inquiry into how policies function inside the day-to-day system. The takeaway from the "Political Extremism" research is the conclusion that when people discover their illusion of explanatory depth, they moderate their opinions. They become less confident in supporting an extreme position.

How do we discover whether an illusion of explanatory depth has warped a person's understanding? When asking someone about a policy, the trick is to refrain from asking them to give a list of their reasons to support their preference or position. Why not listen to their reasons? Because the probability is their reasons are degraded products built from inferior materials such as vaguely understood values, third-hand reports, or talking points by leaders, opinion-makers, celebrities, or pundits they trust or admire. Or they may just be fabricated from the stardust of generalities that don't require any depth of knowledge.

Current policies of airport security are a good example of an issue that inspires polarized positions. The government claims its security and inspection policies are essential tools to fight terrorism. This is their reason for what we go through at airports when we travel—young, old, quadriplegic, it doesn't matter. The possibility of a terrorist boarding a plane with a potential weapon is the headline reason that in a given year nearly a billion airline passengers must remove their shoes, belts, watches, keys, and coins; produce their iPads, laptops, Kindles, and other electronic devices; and leave at home any liquid more than 50 ml in quantity.

Remember while you're putting your shoes back on, and gathering up all the bits and pieces from the plastic tray, that in many countries, officials don't bother to check boarding passengers' passports against a database of stolen passports. In a story about stolen and false passports in Thailand, *The Guardian* (March 10, 2014) noted:

> Created after the September 11, 2001 terror attack ... [Interpol's database of Lost and Stolen Travel Documents (LSTD)] now has some 40m entries.

> The inter-governmental police cooperation organisation says this weekend it is searched more than 800m times a year, mainly by the US, which accessed it 250m times, the UK (120m) and the UAE (50m).
>
> Authorities in many other countries, however, appear to search the database far less often, or not at all.
>
> "Last year," the agency said, "passengers were able to board planes more than a billion times without having their passports screened against Interpol's databases ...

On the ill-fated Malaysian Airlines flight that vanished without a trace in March 2014 (remember that?), two passengers boarded with dodgy passports. If we think incidents like that suggest that current security procedures aren't working, we might demand that authorities who support the current airport inspection regime give their reasons for what they do. We would likely do better, though, to ask them for a mechanistic explanation of the effects of the procedures, how those procedures were designed, how they have been subject to quality control, how system operators have been trained, how their skills are updated, what disruptions occur inside airport processing systems, and how the policy accounts for those disruptions. These aren't questions to elicit a defense of a polarized position; they are designed to start an explanatory discussion of how inspection works; who works in that system; who supervises, updates, manages, and is accountable in the system; the cost of the system (direct and indirect); and what outcomes the policy has produced.

Certain problems can only be resolved by a military solution, that is, the use of force to remove an obstacle to the state's interest and neutralize the threat of the obstacle being reinstalled. Most problems, however, are political in nature, and a military solution is ill-suited to serve as a substitute for a political process that is inherently civilian, where the military is only a component in the overall scheme of governance.

In our time, taking off your shoes at an airport and executing a military coup to overthrow a government are both justified on the basis of providing public security. Can one discover a rational link between these two very different situations in which security is invoked? We seek explanations to a set of questions: why these policies are applied, how they are implemented, and how the targets are detected and deterred. All policies, including ones connected with security, ultimately must pass the test of whether the operational filters reduce security threats. Are we, in other words, detaining the people who threaten security or are we just detaining them because we can?

People can argue all day about the use of military means to resolve societal conflict and never persuade the other side to change its view. Pro-intervention supporters would reason that the military could be trusted as a last resort, when politicians prove themselves to be evil and corrupt. Anti-intervention supporters would reason that a democratic system by its very nature cannot emerge from a military dictatorship. And the two parties would go round and round, each emerging from the debate feeling more confident that they've been right all along and the other side is insane.

Might there be another, more promising approach, one that might defuse each opposing party's fixed position, based on the idea of the illusion of understanding? There is. And it works like this. You do not ask the other person for his reasons to support his position on resource allocation or climate change, for instance; instead you ask him to explain step by step how the side of the argument he supports would define its policy and the goal or outcome it seeks to achieve. The cognitive miser theory kicks in at this point. It is likely to expose that the person's fixed knowledge of how something works—along with what it takes to make it work, how it breaks down, and other limitations—is very shallow.

Finding a middle ground means that people learn to abandon their dependence on hearsay, knee jerk responses, and headline knowledge. The breakthrough comes with the realization that these elements promise the illusion of an ocean of truth but deliver a tiny, muddy pond. Rather than attack their policy (that won't be productive), ask them to explain how the policy they support will bring about the outcome they claim will happen. Ask them to give you the specifics of how the policy is connected to and integrated with the larger system, and how that system will be modified, altered, and updated, and how someone can measure whether it has achieved the intended outcome.

Remember that this approach to defusing political extremism is a two-way street. No one thinks they hold extreme views; this is a label that we use to stigmatize others. If you ask another person to take you along an explanatory tour of how the policy he or she supports integrates with the larger system and produces the outcome claimed, he or she may well ask you to do the same. Your explanation may also stall or fail. In that case you may recognize that the illusion of understanding doesn't only reside within your opponent; it lives inside you, too. That's when both sides of a policy debate realize that they need to revise their understanding about the meaning, design, and purpose of a policy, that their grasp of the matter wasn't as absolute and perfect as they thought, and a compromise becomes possible.

Debating the influence of an illusion of understanding is an interesting idea. Unfortunately it can't be seriously proposed until the possibility of an illusion is acknowledged. That acknowledgment is difficult to come by, and that is the core of the problem. Many people are frustrated because their minds are tuned (perhaps "imprisoned" is a better metaphor) to the easy ride they are accustomed to through the lazy mental landscape of illusions. Suggesting they are illusions is to touch a nerve, and the patient may jump a mile high out of his armchair. Anger and hate are the preferred anesthetics in dealing with cognitive dissonance.

For now the discussion between those holding conflicting policy views and the steps that will be needed before we can go on that explanatory journey have been put on ice. But I write from the tropics, where the ice, sooner or later, melts under the noonday sun.

Spotlights and Flashlights

Life is messy. So are the component parts of life: our politics, the environment, the economy, and social relationships. History teaches a valuable lesson that there is something inherently unstable about our world, and we are forever seeking ways to achieve an equilibrium that seems to elude us. The utopian view of this struggle is that there is an ultimate solution to fixing all the world's mess. Others argue there is no global fix out there, and that we must learn to adjust and live according to the limitations of what we know and can know.

This messiness of life causes widespread anxiety. We're like viewers of a PGA golf tournament, when the professional who is on the green but twenty feet from the hole sends the ball on its way. We hold our breath. Is the putt on target? Is it too soft or too hard? We must simply watch and wait with everyone else.

In politics, the person holding the putter claims the ball will drop. Even when it misses the hole entirely, the political golfer is likely to claim the putt has been expertly sunk. Ambiguity trails political life like a shadow. It's not like real golf, where we can rely on our own eyes to gauge success. With politicians there will always be doubt about whether they are using the right club, lining up correctly over the ball, and accurately reporting the trajectory of their shot in relation to the hole. Whether the ball has thereby landed in the hole or not becomes a matter of faith.

We live in a world where a large number of people exchange their doubt and anxiety for the promise of a more certain, stable, ordered, and predictable world than the one we actually live in. That is costly, as politicians must rely on various illusory devices and tricks to conjure up this illusion with enough credibility to create their alternative reality.

We are willing to pay a relatively high price in the reality stakes for answers that allow us, individually and collectively, to believe that what we are told is true. The illusion of understanding (see the preceding essay) is thereby easier to maintain, and the tacit conspiracy to pretend that the illusion is real allows us to move on from vexing issues and spend our cognitive resources elsewhere.

There is a constant wrestling over who owns the official story—struggle within groups and between them. The groups may be a circles of friends, relatives, or colleagues, sports teams, religious or secular organizations, or political parties. We draw much comfort from shared, collective beliefs, and we draw our identity from our group associations. Mostly we place group solitary and group-derived identity as higher priorities than understanding complexities where the truth is difficult to detect with certainty. Our group, returning to the golf metaphor, always makes a hole in one, while those in rival groups are lost in the tall grass, looking for their ball as night closes in.

How do we resolve this dilemma that arises as we move between the conflicting goals of group grooming and truth-finding? We have two basic models to work with, which suggest the answer is either insubordination or challenge. Each model offers its own means of working through the messy realities that confront us. Sometimes these two very different systems work in harmony, side by side, with each delegated a role; sometimes one model is ascendant and marginalizes the other.

The Spotlight Culture

The first model that controls how we perceive reality rests on a system of subordination. Officials inside an institution such as an orchestra or movie crew work along a chain of command. Orders are passed down the chain. The orders are to be obeyed and not to be challenged by subordinates. The film director (who has a producer breathing down his neck) or conductor (who has a wealthy patron breathing down her neck) is in charge. Despite certain limitations, the director's or the conductor's word is the law when it comes to what the final product will be.

The essential job for the men and women in these positions is to avoid chaos. So long as everyone involved follows their lead, the director or conductor can deliver a certain quality of performance. The price of a subordination system is the voluntary submission of all involved to a disciplined hierarchy. Each person's role within this hierarchy is clearly defined, and those giving the orders possess the rank to require that their subordinates act without question.

Officers in the military expect their subordinates in the chain of command to follow their orders, and they themselves expect to follow the orders of those officers who rank above them. This arrangement is fundamental to the culture of the military. Subordination systems of all stripes share values such as authority, loyalty, honor, respect, and continuity. Whether it is a military division, a police force, a court system, a sports team, a factory assembly line, a film crew, or an orchestra, subordination values exist to co-ordinate work within a group of people.

An orchestra in which the first chair violinist stops the performance and challenges the conductor's interpretation of a movement would change our experience of music. Whatever the private feelings of the individual violinist or cello player may be, they are not expressed in the workplace, and the conductor's authority remains unchallenged as the orchestra performs.

In other words, criticism and dissent give way to the rules of subordination. Otherwise, the performance by the orchestra collapses, a lower court overrules an appellate court, the quarterback's call is overridden by the right tackle, and a sergeant decides against his officer's command to advance on an enemy position. All of these reversals happen now and again, and when they do, the person who makes such a challenge is guilty of insubordination. Treason, betrayal, faithlessness, and disloyalty are elements of the stigma commonly attached to such insubordination.

In the world we currently live in, at least, subordination does have its limits. If the conductor had absolute power, he or she might seek to expand his or her authority to encompass a level of central control with unchallenged certitude. That is unlikely to happen. There are too many different visions, tastes, and traditions, and too much messiness in any collective enterprise, for any one person to assume absolute control. Within the arts any attempt at such a command and control system would drive artists underground. In the arts, as in science, we assume that experimenting and limit testing are healthy practices to be encouraged. Note that some experiments will lead to dead ends and prove valueless both to the artist and to society, but that is only discovered by allowing the experimenter the space to fail.

The spotlight culture—culture where only one person or one elite group command the undivided attention of the many—is a place where truth is manufactured and then distributed to consumers in top-down fashion. The finished product is officially deemed to be complete, reliable, and ready for immediate, unquestioning consumption. No alternatives are allowed to challenge the truth in the spotlight culture.

Flashlight Culture

In contrast, the flashlight model is based on the individual's right to criticize, challenge, or question authority and the authority's policies, motives, efficiency, or outcomes. Journalists, scholars, NG0s, whistleblowers, and outside experts are obvious players in the flashlight culture. The flashlight has also become a symbol in protests and demonstrations, as recent news photos from Ukraine illustrate. People have a huge desire to see the hidden and buried story. Those who seek information about activities occurring behind the scenes of power rely on the flashlight. These lights are pointed into the dark areas well outside the spotlight and act to keep government officials honest and transparent. In the case of someone like Edward Snowden, the flashlight is on the magnitude of a supernova. Flashlight advocates all the way back to Socrates have urged people to to ignore the facile answers found in the spotlight and ask questions as a way of shining a light into darkness.

A flashlight culture assumes we all share similar, flawed knowledge and the same cognitive biases that will distort reality unless they are corrected. At the micro level, the individual challenges the group leader because the leader is one of us and knows no more than anyone else about the complex network of information. At a much higher level, Western parliamentary-style political systems rest on the idea of opposition, an embedded challenge to the government of the day to explain and justify its decisions.

Unlike an orchestra conductor, the prime minister answers his or her critics with explanations rather than threats or suppression. The role of the opposition is to make the government account for its choices. The purpose of shining a light on evidence that is contrary to the government's narrative is to expose weaknesses of policy or its execution. The motives of flashlight holders may not be pure. They may be exposing facts only for political gain at the expense of the government, but such exposure works to the favor of the general population, which benefits from a correction in policy or a change in personnel to carry out the policy.

The institutionalized encouragement of challenges to authority is what has given us a robust scientific method. The most junior member of a research team is not disqualified from overturning the theory of the most respected member of the scientific community. The theory, in other words, is separate from the personality supporting it. It's true that, as emotional beings, we have difficulty distinguishing attacks on theory from attacks on the person who supports the theory. The question in science isn't, what does this critic have against the person who supports any given theory, but rather what evidence does he or she have to refute the theory? In non-scientific areas such as politics, we are still a long way from isolating policy for critical analysis from the personality, background, and reputation of the person who has proposed it.

We can also accept that the challenge-the-authority paradigm isn't always appropriate in all circumstances. An orchestra, a military division, a police force, and a football team, to name a few examples, all depend on subordination to work effectively as cohesive units. The question is how is it decided, and who does the deciding about, what are the right places for one system to operate and claim legitimacy over and above the other?

The flashlight culture exposes flaws and defects in the spotlight culture's truth products. Flashlight illumination exposes dangers, risks, omissions, and distortions. Truth becomes stripped of illusions in the process.

Fitting Spotlights and Flashlights into a Unified Lighting System

Every culture has a different interpretation of how to fit these pieces together, and who gets the job of deciding, and how those with power are selected, controlled and discharged. How best to light the political stage is a question every country answers in its own way. The reality is we need to find the right combination of subordination and challenge. Let's take a look at the BBC's Top Ten list of the largest employers in the world in 2012:

(1) US Department of Defense

(2) People's Liberation Army (China)

(3) Walmart

(4) McDonald's

(5) National Health Service (UK)

(6) China National Petroleum Corporation

(7) State Grid Corporation of China

(8) Indian Railways

(9) Indian Armed Forces

(10) Hon Hai Precision Industry (Taiwan)

From the American Defense Department to the Chinese People's Liberation Army, the ability to scale huge operations relies on implementing an effective subordination system. The utilization of a "soft" subordination system accounts for the presence of Walmart and McDonald's on the same list. Co-ordination at the huge end of the scale is impossible without some sort of order-and-command structure, in which insubordination is punished.

The question is whether a spotlight (subordination) system in which flashlights are confiscated and the people's use of them is criminalized can operate effectively at the political and government level. Can a government be run along the lines of an orchestra, with a single conductor choosing the music and every detail of performance? We're talking about the sort of orchestra that precludes any other orchestra from performing a note, the kind that jails any music critic who claims the cello player made several mistakes or the piano needed tuning.

As I look around the world in June 2014, from Thailand to Egypt, Syria, Ukraine, and beyond, I see that the old consensus about the right mix of spotlight and flashlight has broken down in many nations around the world. Instability, the messiness of life, leads to fear, and to banish fear, many embrace subordination. There is a belief that salvation rests in choosing the right conductor and letting him run everything. Challengers to this vision are seen as enhancing fear and instability. They are the first violinist who rises and objects to the conductor's interpretation. In times of fear the pendulum swings to subordination. But the nature of pendulums is to swing back, too. In time the flirtation with expanding the subordination model into the political realm will reinforce a historical lesson about the nature of governing.

Because the world's flashlight culture has migrated online, shutting it down is becoming ever more difficult. The digital flashlight exposes hypocrisy, deception, half-truths, and cover-ups in a very public way. This is inconvenient and embarrassing for those who seek to banish flashlights and wish to return the people's attention back to the spotlight.

Throwing your opposition in jail or sending them fleeing into the mountains or jungle or exile may work in the short term, and you can then control the performance for a while. But in the long term, people who tune in only to classical music will understand that they need to leave room for those who love jazz, hip-hop, pop, and Broadway show tunes, and even those repulsive noise traps called rap, country, and Korean boy bands. Politics is a noisy place. When there is only one conductor and he or she plays only one tune, you can be sure people will sooner or later find a way to switch the channel. To return to our lighting metaphor, the amount of repression required to neutralize or co-opt flashlight holders entirely will eventually turn the world against those standing in the spotlight.

The Twilight of Prophecy Cultures

News stories in Thailand frequently have a supernatural or superstition angle. Two examples this week (in mid–October 2013) illustrate the point. First, Pemmika Veerachatraksit received a four-and-a-half-year prison sentence following a fraud conviction for her role in deceiving a famous applied physics tutor named Prakitpao Tomtitchong to give her nine million baht (over a quarter million dollars) in cash and gifts. She had convinced him that they'd been a couple in a past life and he had abused her at that time. In the second case, in Songkhla in the South of Thailand, a sixteen-year-old Thai died in an exorcism ceremony after drinking eighteen liters of water. The ritual was supposed to release a tiger ghost from the boy's body. In the same week on the same planet, physicists François Englert of Belgium and Peter Higgs of Britain won the Nobel Prize in physics for their discovery of a theory of the Higgs boson particle, popularly known as the "God particle."

We live in two worlds at once: that of the duped physics tutor in Thailand and that of the physics geniuses in Britain and Belgium. One world consists of people who believe an exorcism can banish a tiger ghost, and another world produces scientists who believe a tiny particle causes the fundamental units of nature to stick together to form atoms—you and me, planets, stars, and moon cakes. Thailand is a good place to explore the psychological and cultural gap that separates these two ways of understanding reality.

Part of the challenge of writing a crime fiction series set in Thailand is understanding the cultural mindset that comes into play. Solving a crime doesn't happen in a cultural void. To understand how police, judges, prosecutors, prison wardens, private eyes, and others assess criminal behavior, search for law breakers, and provide for victims, the cultural mindset needs to be addressed. What constitutes a crime and who gets punished and how—these are artifacts from a much deeper cultural well.

An author from the West is more likely to have a mindset based on scientific probabilities, facts, and evidence. It isn't that Thais are oblivious to facts. They aren't. But the role of facts and evidence in their lives is filtered through a different way of understanding and reacting to the world around them. In places like the United States there are millions of people who live inside a prophecy culture and butt heads with the scientific community at the political level, over education policy, medical care, and other issues such as abortion and gun control. I have lived the last twenty-five years in Thailand inside a culture where a large number of people of all classes and ranks believe that certain monks, ex-monks, or astrologers (they can be found on TV, behind charge-by-the-minute phone numbers, and in newspapers and magazines) can predict a future outcome. There are tensions inside Thai culture, but disagreement over the role of prophecy isn't one of the hot button issues. Most Thais seem indifferent to the fact that these prophecies have an accuracy rate equal to that of a coin toss or random chance. The failure of predictions isn't generally seen as a bug in the system. It's like horse racing; there's always the next race to bet on.

There is a large market in Bangkok for personal predictions. The customers pay for the usual things people long to hear about the future—you will find wealth or a kind, loving partner, or rise to a high position in your company, or become famous. Prophecy comes in a package with other values, like multi-colored feathers on a peacock's tail. You need to believe not only that certain human beings have a deep insight about the world, but that they can accurately forecast what will occur next week, month, or year.

If you think of everyone from politicians to civil servants and on to soldiers, sailors, police officers, schoolteachers, and students, you still haven't begun to imagine the breadth of the shared belief in the supernatural and superstition in this country. Far more public attention is focused here on prophecy makers and their predictions than on mathematicians who rely on complex algorithms for their predictions, expressed as probabilities. Uncertainty is built into the scientific system, which analyzes patterns by attempting to draw inferences about the patterns' meaning and determining the likelihood that any given pattern will repeat itself. Will it rain tomorrow? A 70% chance of rain means there is a 30% chance it won't. So do I take an umbrella or not?

The large, modern city that I live in contains another, unmodern world—one of omens, spirit houses, spiritual mediums, magical tattoos, amulets, astrologers, feng shui masters, palm readers, and various other gurus. The undercurrents that drive this magical realm in Bangkok and elsewhere in Thailand are found in Hindu myths, animism, and a particular vision of Buddhism. No one is excluded from participation. Everyone has roughly an equal understanding and belief that invisible forces are at work in their lives.

What makes prophecy so seductive is that the prophets don't hedge their bets with mathematically expressed probabilities. The prophet's authority doesn't spring from anything measurable by science but from an invisible spiritual connection with a higher celestial being. The prophet's direct pipeline to the gods isn't a fact. There is no evidence to support such a claim. It has to be taken on pure faith. The prophet is a messenger, but unlike your FedEx delivery guy, this kind of messenger is conferred with a halo. The prophet claims, basically, that a god told him that such and such will happen to so and so.

Often what is predicted by such prophets isn't the garden variety of future—for example, that a red traffic light at Asoke and Sukhumvit Road will in three minutes transition to yellow and then green. Prophets, like novelists, are lovers of high drama. Predictions spring from the same well of belief as the biblical apocalypse with its messy, inky-dark non-future. Prophets announce prophecies. Abrahamic religions were founded upon the writings of prophets. Humans have a long tradition of masses of people believing that prophets were the output pipe fitted to an input pipe of a higher being who wrote a holy book without the aid of a computer. Once you are on that slippery slope, all you can do is enjoy the ride into the waiting jaws of the apocalypse.

The worldview of Peter Higgs and his God particle and that of the exorcist in Songkhla have been on a collision course since the dawn of the Enlightenment. The core insight of the Enlightenment was that superstition and prophecy are poor ways to work out an understanding of the fundamental nature of reality. That battle continues to be fought three hundred years later, although, sitting before our computer screens, we may seem very far removed from the reality of billions of people whose identity is tribal or clan-based. Prophecy functions as a belief in a transcendent realm that protects a tribe or clan and its members from harm. It is also part of the "religious" justification for the tribal leaders' decisions and the basis of their legitimacy as rulers. In Peter Higgs's world there is no transcendent realm where prophecies are handed down to local prophets; there is only a material reality that is subject to investigation, testing, evaluation, and analysis. No politician will use the Higgs boson as a justification for punishing an opponent or to support his or her authority to govern.

A prophecy culture is hostile to people like Peter Higgs, François Englert, Christopher Hitchens, Richard Dawkins, or Jon Stewart. The writer of noir crime fiction isn't safe there either. Over an epic scale of time there have been a great many wars between people claiming their prophet's predictions were the absolute and universal true word of God. That sort of thinking can't brook doubt, evidence, irony, or satire, and sooner or later the conflict is bound to come to blows. Even when one of the vague predictions of such a prophet turns out to be clearly false, there is little fallout; rarely does a dent appear in the credulity of those who believe.

Can these two seemingly incompatible worldviews co-exist peacefully? A case can be made that they will remain in conflict and even at war with one another. Modern technology is being used to disassemble the tribal world and reconfigure it as part of the global system. Essential to that task is changing the way tribal people are bound by their own "Higgs boson" of prophecy and superstition. The process is to make prophecy a commodity and prophets just another set of system providers, motivated by profit and expanding markets.

Tribal and clan leaders have long benefited from a prophecy culture that exists outside time, markets, and dissent. The American military drone program provides an example of a high-tech device that seems to have the capacity to dismantle the tribal-warlord system. The idea is that superstitious people will fear the armed drones that hover overhead twenty-four hours a day. Drones will force the inflexible tribal leaders to leave their villages for the safety of caves and mountains. Drones and their power of destruction show that the tribe's local gods can't protect them, and there is a new god on the block who can kill them in an instant, so they'd be wise to abandon their old leaders, ways, and beliefs and become absorbed into the modern high-tech world. But the unintended consequence so far has been to increase loyalty to the prophecy culture, strengthen tribal ties, and allow extremists with strong traditional values to assume leadership roles.

It's not exactly that I have a problem with people who believe in prophecy and subscribe to the idea that someone among them is connected to a higher voice that communicates an event before it happens. This is the way they process the reality of the world. What usually goes hand in hand with this view, though, is the belief that there is nothing anyone can do but accept the prediction. If you have power, suppressing dissent is always a goal, and if you can shelter behind the veil of predictions from a divine source, you can crack a lot of heads, eat most of the buffet, and claim these outcomes are ordained. Things are changing, though. These days you don't have to look far in the world to see that a lot people are having second thoughts about the prophecy business and how it drives social, political, and economic choices in ways that serve the prophets and their best clients.

When a modern, globally wired society tries to communicate with a culture of prophecy, it becomes apparent that the two worlds don't have a common vocabulary. The globally wired society of fiber optics, computer chips, nanotechnology, and waste treatment plants is with us because science and mathematics banished prophecy from the way we understand the world. In its place came theories that could be tested through experiment. That's how human knowledge has accumulated to bring the modern world to where it is today. That accumulation continues to accelerate. As new evidence arises, old theories are thrown out. I recently read that in 1920 most people, scientists included, thought that Earth's surface was fixed and immovable. The discovery of shifting geological plates launched the new science of tectonics, which destroyed the old belief. Science doesn't deal in absolutes; it deals in the probability of outcomes.

The implications of this one vital difference between the old world and the new drive the worldviews and behavior of people. You won't get the engineering required to put a space station into orbit from a prophecy-guided guru. The guru and the rocket scientist live in two different worlds. When a prophecy culture imports the engineering and technical know-how to build dams, bridges, roads, trains, and planes, they seem to have achieved the best of both worlds. You get to use the modern transport, appliances, weapons, and means of communication without giving up your belief that Wednesday is a bad day for a haircut or that a lucky lottery number came to you in a dream.

A brand new, fully automated rail system appears to be like a young adult at his physical peak, but it is actually more like a newborn that needs constant attention. Not surprisingly, in a prophecy culture the technical knowhow may be accessible, but the mindset of many of those in the system stems from luck or chance and blessing ceremonies. This year Thailand has had 114 train derailments. Every other day a train seems to fall off the track. Many explanations for this have been given, including a lack of sufficient funding for the national rail system. But not funding the system makes perfect sense if you believe in prophecy. The civil servants in charge of the rail system recently decided it was a damaged painting in the HQ that had caused the spirits to become angry and have ordered the artwork's repair. When the Thai army invested heavily in GT200s, mine-detecting gadgets quickly revealed to be fraudulent, they insisted, once the scientific evidence showed them to be less reliable than pure chance in locating mines, that they still had "faith" in the devices.

The twin of prophecy is the belief in the world of spirits, angels, demons, and forest fairies. No one needs to waste years acquiring a Ph.D. in mathematics, physics, chemistry, or engineering to join the club that makes a living from the prophecy business.

Here is my horoscope for October 8, 2013:

> This is just the kind of day you like, intense and supercharged, just like you! It seems there's a deadline coming up, or a time-sensitive project. You'll have a lot to do and not a lot of time in which to do it. Just remember to drink plenty of water and eat. Lucky Color Dark Red. Lucky No. 5.

As a harmless form of entertainment, astrology has a place on *The Daily Show, Not the Nation*, and *The Onion*. But the limitations of prophecy cultures with respect to the operation of highly complex systems from scientific cultures are apparent.

Scientific development progresses as scientists and mathematicians gain new insights into fundamental reality. Those insights can be tested. The insights of a prophet are of a different order. You can't build a safer nuclear reactor or cure cancer based on a guru's prophecy. Scientists will explain to you that predicting future outcomes is extremely hard. They'll tell you that too many variables are in play, and their connection, lack of connection, or random shifts influence outcomes in ways that can't be predicted in advance. Prophets don't process reality with this kind of humility, either with regard to their limitations or the limits of the laws of physics.

It's not uncommon to climb into a Bangkok taxi and find amulets hanging from the rearview mirror, or to witness the driver touching them as he races through a red light. Amulets in this way of thinking somehow neutralize the laws of physics, allowing the believer a safe passage through danger.

In a science culture the devil is *in* the details, in a prophecy culture the devil *is* the details. Prophecy is an example of a deception used by rulers in the past to keep themselves in power. With prophets on the payroll they could claim a pipeline to the divine themselves. The unfortunate thing with prophecy is the lack of an audit trail through which a thoughtful person could break down a prediction after the fact into a series of steps, to determine where it went wrong. That is one reason why accountability is difficult to graft onto a prophecy culture. No prophet could withstand an audit. Nor could any prophet be held accountable, as he's just the input pipe, and the output pipe, being divine, is beyond accountability.

In the end a culture decides as a collective intelligence how it knows things and how to explain what it knows. If the culture is based on prophecy, that way of knowing about the world will produce a certain kind of society. In a culture where science is allowed to flourish, evolving insights lead to better and improved precision measurement instruments, and those lead in turn to more advanced technology.

In the West the scientifically minded believe that the stories that science tells derive their power from the fact that other scientists can verify them through repeated investigations, that is, experimental results are reproducible. Thailand is in transition from a prophecy culture to a scientific one. This is a long process, and during the transition one is bound to see contradictions. The more connected Thailand becomes to the outside world, the more its prophecy culture will lose its force. In far less developed countries in the Middle East, the fog of conflict masks the rate of any such transition. Military drones are the response of a science-based technology, and tribal cultures haven't shown an inclination to give up their transcendental beliefs in the supernatural world to embrace the material world. Meanwhile, at the front line of this conflict, we have panic, irrational claims, terrorism, and violence—as the world of the prophets lashes out against the world of science.

It is the struggle of our times. One thing to consider: in the world of prophecy the general populace are equally at the mercy of the gods, and that creates a degree of solidarity. Meaningful immersion in the new science culture requires a deep knowledge of difficult concepts. The level of understanding required to tackle Peter Higgs's theory and the like excludes the average person from participation except as a consumer. The new culture may lead to a temple of awe for some and a shopping mall for the rest.

Crunching Big Numbers, Understanding Short Lists

Give a writer some facts, numbers, or basic information and ask him to use it to tell a story. See what happens. What kind of story does the writer tell? Is it plausible? Is it true?

Most of the time writers unearth information from personal experience and observation, but sometimes we stumble upon information sent by others that stimulates our imagination. A friend★ sent me a link to a Top Ten list of the world's largest employers. I immediately saw a story, one told in numbers. As the repercussions of big data filter into our daily lives, you can expect more story-tellers to mine these huge information warehouses for stories. Let me explain the kind of story to expect in the future.

Mathematics conceals all kinds of interesting stories about how societies, economies, and governments are entangled. The language of numbers opens doors to understanding the complexity of these relations. When we examine the numbers, we can draw conclusions about the dynamic relationships between private and public sectors within cultures and across cultural boundaries. This is an essay about economic and political structures, allocation of power, concentration of resources, and how power is projected inside a political system. It is also an essay about how Top Ten lists influence our view of reality.

★ Thank you, John Murphy.

I've become suspicious of all the lists: Top Ten, Top Fifty, Top 500, and so on. One reason for that is that all of these lists share an implicit promise of completeness. The promise of a list is, like a map, it will be a coherent and reliable guide to make a judgement or form an opinion. It is as if a list has a roundness of knowledge that deflects our lack of understanding, knowledge, or awareness. At their best lists create an illusion of knowledge. At their worst they promote a lie or deception that tells us that doubt has been addressed and answered. The main danger of lists is that they seduce us not only by the false promise of completeness by also by the allure of their simplicity. A list obscures the higher level of complexity that it eclipses. Using any list as a reality manual is like playing chess in a dark room where you can't clearly see the board or the pieces; you know there are thirty-two pieces and sixty-four squares, but that's hard to grasp visually. The average Top Ten list you read is addictive because you are playing in the dark like the rest of us and want the edge of knowing the right ten moves to win the game. In the final part of the essay, I have a look at how difficult it is to play chess in the dark using lists as your cheat sheets.

A List: The Top Ten Largest Employers in the World

Work is an essential component of any economy, whether based on capitalism, socialism, or any other ideology designed to govern the business of extracting resources and energy, and distributing and allocating products and services. An employee's work is carried out under the authority and supervision of an employer. The employer may be the government or it may be a private company. One way to understand any national system is to ask who are its largest employers. Identifying a country's major employers and the enterprises it controls tells a great deal about the country's values, politics, beliefs, and policies.

If you were to draw up a Top Ten list of the world's largest employers, including public and private, what would you expect to find on that list? In 2012 the BBC produced such a list (you'll find it in "Spotlights and Flashlights" above). Among the information it shows is that in 2012, 30% of the world's largest employers came from the private enterprise sector; the other 70% were state enterprises or government workers. (Although we don't often think of soldiers as government workers, that is indeed what they are.) Leaving aside what the figures suggest about India, where the Indian state railway has more employees than the Indian army, my attention is on the big employers in the United States and China. These two countries, with three employers each in the Top Ten, comprise 60% of the big employer list for 2012.

Military Employees

Take the US Department of Defense. According to Wikipedia's article on the department, there are "2.13 million active duty soldiers, sailors, marines, airmen, and civilian workers, and over 1.1 million National Guardsmen and members of the Army, Navy, Air Force, and Marine Reserves. The grand total is just over 3.2 million servicemen, servicewomen, and civilians." Private contractors working for the department are no longer a niche but viewed as part of the total military force (source: www.fas.org/sgp/crs/natsec/R43074.pdf). It is difficult to source the role of private contractors in China's People's Liberation Army. It is enough to note that the two top positions on the list are military organizations (the American and Chinese armies), organized, equipped, maintained, and deployed by governments, with, at least on the American side, a healthy percentage of private contractors being part of the enterprise as suppliers.

According to Statista, the US population in 2012 was 314 million people (for China it was 1.35 billion). That means that more than 1% of Americans were employed by the US military in that year.

In contrast, the military footprint in China works out to less than a fifth of 1%. Thus in rough population terms there is a huge disparity between the two countries in the relative size of the military. Based on the BBC statistics, we can see that in sheer numbers the US military was about 39% larger than the Chinese in 2012. According to Marketplace. org, roughly 143 million Americans were thus employed that year (an interesting graphic showing the growth of the US military can be found at www.marketplace.org/ topics/economy/visual-history-us-workforce-1970-2012), which works out to 2.24% of the total US work force being Department of Defense employees. In 2012 (according to Statista) China's workforce reached 764.2 million, and its military personnel constituted 0.3% of that number. In terms of comparing overall employment numbers between the two countries, the disparity between those employed by the military indicates that the US military is more than seven times the size of the Chinese military as a percentage of the total work force.

The statistics reveal something about the presence of the military employment footprint within the general population and workforce of each country. Size matters for a lot of reasons, including politics and economics, not to mention the social impact of having a large number of people in uniform. The military has a particular culture based on rank, duty, discipline, honor, and authority. Profitability doesn't appear as part of this culture. Its primary purpose (some may disagree) is to project power in order to instill fear, which will cause adversaries to bend to the will of the political establishment in charge of the military.

What may come as a surprise is that Walmart, owned by one family, employs almost as many people as China's People's Liberation Army. And if Walmart and MacDonald's were to form an alliance, their combined employees would outnumber the entire American military with a significant number of employees left to take over part of the Chinese military as well.

In other words, the world's two largest private sector employers have under their umbrella more employees than the world's largest military. When you start to register the power employers have to influence the attitudes and values of their employees (retail has boot camp for new recruits too), the political influence of such employers' wealth would attract the attention of politicians and their campaign staff. Beyond this obvious risk of system policy being wealth-driven, there are other, deeper implications to consider.

Private Enterprise Employers

Walmart and McDonald's share, in a manner of speaking, certain similarities with military culture: there are no unions; recruits are assigned largely routine, front-line jobs that take stamina and discipline; and they have uniforms, codes of behavior, and little prospect of mobility up the chain of command. They are cannon fodder for the elite. They are also paid less than soldiers.

Walmart is a dystopian vision of what a peacetime military might look like if it had different uniforms and grunts were assigned to patrol aisles of merchandise with the mission of maintaining order and security. McDonald's, like the US military, has bases established all over the world, siphoning money to shareholders in return for distributing dubious foodstuffs with a questionable health value and a tendency to make regular diners obese. According to the website Making Change at Walmart, the average Walmart grunt earns $15,576 per year, or 13% less than is paid to a US military private.

These two huge US employment giants weren't created by acts of God, and they didn't evolve from nature. Their corporate growth and success came largely through good luck, which in retrospect has been attributed to brilliant leadership. Myths are created to support the conclusion that these companies' rise was inevitable. The myth of American exceptionalism has its private-enterprise counterpart. Walmart and McDonald's were never destined to become the third and fourth largest employers in the world by 2012. In fact, each company emerged in the domestic US market as a result of an ecological system comprised of culture, history, values, and laws. Had the variables changed, everything might have turned out quite differently. And their corporate success can be attributed, in part, to the protective umbrella of the US military, funded by all American taxpayers (including Walmart and McDonald's employees).

This private army of soldiers serving the domestic consumer appetite for food, gadgets, and aisles stocked fire-ladder high with consumer goods is itself protected against intruders from abroad and can enforce its presence in the intruders' backyards by using the military. Guns protect existing markets and open new ones. That's why the military is so important for a country on an economic march, whether it's a matter of grabbing resources or opening new consumer markets.

Compensation Disparity

The Top Ten list of the world's largest employers presents an opportunity to compare compensation paid to those at the top of management with that of their counterparts in other sectors, and and to consider the disparity between the top manager with the medium pay of a worker employed by that employer. If you want to know why Thomas Piketty's *Capital in the Twenty-First Century*, with its evidence of huge income and wealth disparity, has struck a chord, a good place to start is an examination of the US military and Walmart pay.

Income: The salary of the chairman of the Joint Chiefs of Staff is $20,263.50 a month, and that of a private in the army is $1,468.00 per month (source: Military-Ranks.org). The chairman makes roughly fourteen times as much as an army private. That's right. Fourteen times is what separates the top soldier from the one pulling the trigger on the frontline. The army pay range from top to bottom is closer to a Denmark or Norway than to the big employers inside the world of private enterprise in the US.

Not only is the Walmart grunt paid 13% less than a private in the army, the CEO of Walmart is paid 1,034 times the median salary of a Walmart worker (*Huffington Post*, March 29, 2013). The CEO of McDonald's is paid 434 times the median salary of a MacDonald's worker. In the rankings of the highest disparities between CEO pay and medium worker pay in the company, Walmart is number one, but MacDonald's falls to number five. Three companies pay their CEO at the following multiples of one medium worker: Target (number two) at 597:1, Disney (number three) at 557:1, and Honeywell (number four) at 439:1.

If you applied the Walmart ratio of 1,034:1, using the bottom pay (note this is likely lower than the medium pay of all soldiers), which is that of a private, the chairman of the Joint Chiefs of Staff would be paid $21 million a month, or $8.8 million a month if applying the McDonald's 434:1 ratio. One person is in charge of the defense of an entire country; the other is in charge of selling consumer goods and services inside the same country.

It seems that in the scheme of things someone is vastly underpaid or overpaid in the military, if the values of the private enterprise system are applied to the military. The system that generates muscles has a wholly different compensation arrangement from the underlying profit-generating system it is designed to protect. One way to accomplish that goal is to underpay the hugely numerous military personnel, especially those at the higher leadership ranks.

Capital: The generals in the US military don't own the tanks, forts, jet fighters, submarines, aircraft carriers, cannons, rifles, and flame throwers they deploy. More importantly, the sons and daughters of the generals don't inherit their father's rank and step into the old man's shoes upon death as owners. While the generals stand in as leaders of the enterprise, they don't own it.

The top Walmart leadership is under the control of the descendants of Sam Walton. There are no congressional hearings, no public vettings, and no presidential appointments. When a family member of the Walmart dynasty dies, his or her share is inherited most likely by another member of the family. Any family that has 2.1 million people working in its business is, in effect, a kind of aristocracy. While the original meaning of aristocracy was "rule by the best," it has come to mean control over the most. In our time of democracy, aristocracy and oligarchy have risen to new altitudes of power and influence that would have been the envy of dukes and earls of the past.

The Walmart family, given the size of its private workforce and the profits generated, are a potent economic and political force. The influence of the Walmart family, as its wealth accumulates, has a likely prospect of continuing expansion over multiple generations. And the accumulation of greater wealth, power, and numbers of workers inside one family will likely persist as military generals come and go like store managers.

Complexity and Story-Telling in the Reign of Big Data

The number of employees isn't necessarily the best way to gauge who is in control of the world's wealth. You can't really understand the true lay of the pieces on the chessboard by limiting your study to the Top Ten list of the world's largest employers. The relationship of employee numbers to control of wealth is, for example, misleading when the real question is, who is in control?

"The Network of Global Corporate Control," a 2011 academic paper by Stefania Vitali, James B. Glattfelder, and Stefano Battiston, examines a database that includes 37 million companies and finds that 147 companies in the world control 40% of the world's global wealth. Walmart comes in at number fifteen on the list of the top 147.

Thomas Piketty has used big data to break the code of silence and ideology around the issue of the wealth owned by the 1%, but there is another shoe to drop. Examining the history of wealth concentration is useful, but it doesn't necessarily tell us how wealth translates into control. It is the nature of control that flows from wealth that allows us to move a step closer to understanding how economic and political power is financed and allocated and how it functions. The old adage of "follow the money" needs to be refined to read, "follow how the money is leveraged." The 2011 study on global corporate control asserts, "Network control is much more unequally distributed than wealth. In particular, the top ranked actors hold a control ten times bigger than what could be expected based on their wealth."

The underlying grid of connections is emerging from big data. As our information accumulates, the emergent patterns will likely show correlations that are predicted by dogma and lists, or from our usual inventory of cognitive biases. In the future others will look back at our "list mania" as another example of how we played chess in a dark room, without a true understanding of how the game worked, and how we compensated by simplifying it, dumbing it down to a game of checkers or draughts.

Final Thoughts

This essay has glimpsed at the Top Ten list of largest employers of the world in order to make sense of how we are governed, how we are compensated, and how we protect and exploit resources and markets. It is an essay about the perils of lists in a sea of complexity. Knowing who are the largest employers on the planet reveals an *aspect* of existing economic and political systems and the public institutions that carry out government pro-business and growth policies.

I suspect the BBC list is based on less than big data. The data it is drawn from are probably crude and limited. The time will arrive when we will have a better idea of the truth from much more complete data sets and links between data sets. The Top Ten is what we have now. Kurt Gödel's incompleteness theorems suggest that no data system will ever be complete, and that contradictions will emerge. *This sentence is false*—a sentence we can never shake off, answer, or ignore. It follows us like a black dog on a moonless night.

Meanwhile, story-tellers can practice their skills by examining the numbers. They will be important in the future; when confronted with big data, we will want plausible explanations of meaning. Also, story-tellers will highlight what is missing from the existing numbers.

For example, it would be interesting to know, in a Thomas Piketty statistical way, whether the ratio of employees working for public and private companies in the Top Ten positions has been constant over time, whether the ratio is connected with concentrations of wealth and income, and the consequences of major economic events like recessions on downsizing, wage capping, and the successes of rival economic powers and systems in taking market share.

More data will provide answers as to whether the world's largest private employers are best explained by the use of Western-style democratic systems, or whether they might have evolved in modified form from a Chinese-style system. Walmart and McDonald's might not have emerged from the chaotic American democracy without the presence of American coercive power at its back. The culture of the military, with its authoritarian command structure and democratic compensation system, may have played an essential role.

Other powerful US companies with fewer employees, such as Microsoft, Google, Facebook, Apple, Hollywood filmmakers, and war equipment manufacturers have added new members to the American aristocracy. Defense contractors might reasonably be added to the employees of the Defense Department as the separation between public and private and between civilian and military is often artificial and maintained for political purposes—thus allowing retired generals a second career to cash in on the profitable side of violence.

I leave you to consider this data: Walmart is committed to hiring 100,000 ex-military personnel by 2018 (source: http://walmartcareerswithamission.com). But they should keep in mind that grunts at Walmart start at less pay than a private. This is a story that between now and 2018 will likely be told by some writer, somewhere, wondering about the complexity of our future life, which is unfolding. Now.

Part VII

On Writing and Authors

The Graying of Word Weavers

One of the questions commonly asked of a novelist is, who is the audience for your novel? The realistic answer is, I don't know but I guess I'll find out. But you'll rarely see that answer. Every novelist believes that he can spot a huge audience on the horizon, and that with some hand waving they will notice the object he is holding, called a book, and wish to own, read, and share it. The audiences of J.K. Rowling, Dan Brown, and Stephen King are our windmills. Like Cervantes' Man of La Mancha, we charge ahead.

Novelists are dreamers. We know the lyrics to "The Impossible Dream" by heart. Big audiences are part of the dream for word weavers. Big personal libraries are as important as the air we breathe. We dream and we read, merging two activities into one, and before long we are ready to set pen to paper (in a manner of speaking). We can feel something in the wind: a Thomas Pynchon-like screaming through the sky, and then a deadly silence. The prospect of receiving a direct hit, and then crawling out of the rubble with a professional career as a novelist, is a low-odds bet.

We novelists are also old-school creators. Like weavers or potters, we have a talent to marshal creative forces to build, strand by strand, a finished work of art for readers to enjoy, learn from, discuss, and share with others. Since Cervantes' time four hundred years ago, novelists have recorded and communicated the central preoccupations, ideas, and emotions of their time and place.

This week I had lunch with an eighty-two-year-old writer who wants to find a publisher for his novels. He's written more than one. To have reached that age and still wish to enter the current publishing scene is a testament to true grit. At the same time his desire reinforces my theory that there are likely more eighty-two-year-olds writing books than there are thirty-two-year-olds, many of whom will have long since moved on to means of expression that don't include book writing.

I have been reading Facebook feeds from a recent mystery convention in the United States and looking at photos of audiences at author readings. One inconvenient truth stands out: fiction authors and readers are old. Like Don Quixote, most of us are nearing our expiry dates. We might have a debate of what age marks one as old as there is a large cultural component in that assessment. In Thailand the retirement age is sixty. Upon reaching that age, Thai police and army generals, civil servants, university professors, school teachers, and others are put out to pasture.

In the world of novelists that pasture is well stocked. In a recent *New York Times* bestseller list for hardcover fiction, we find: Sue Grafton, age seventy-three; Clive Cussler, eighty-two; Thomas Perry, sixty-six; J.A. Jance, sixty-nine; Alice McDermott, sixty; James B. Patterson, sixty-six; and Margaret Atwood, seventy-three. Other internationally famous authors include John le Carré, who is eighty-two; Martin Amis, sixty-four; and Salman Rushie, sixty-six. The youngster on the *Times* list is Gillian Flynn, age forty-two. Alice Munro and Philip Roth, both authors who are in their eighties, have announced they've retired from writing.

In contrast, Robertson Davies, Graham Greene, and Saul Bellow continued to write into their eighties, right up to the time the Grim Reaper snatched away their pen and paper. The takeaway here is that writers of fiction don't have a mandatory retirement age. If they retire, it is voluntary withdrawal.

Are old writers being read mainly by people of their generation, or does their audience include the younger generations? I don't have an empirical answer to this question, though I suspect publishers must have some idea of the demographic distribution of audiences for their bestselling authors. When I look at photographs from readings and book signings by leading authors, I see an audience that in terms of age is a mirror image of the author. The same is true of photographs from mystery writers' conventions.

It is likely that the time when authors older than sixty can maintain a mass cross-generational audience has peaked, and in the digital age such novelists will become increasingly rare. There are a couple of reasons for this trend. Younger people, as a group (of course there are always exceptions), aren't willing to pay the time-price to read a novel, or to give the undistracted attention that is required to enter the world found inside one. I am not suggesting that the novel is dead or that novels won't continue to be written and read, just as artisans who weave baskets by hand will continue to have a market, even though machine-woven baskets are much cheaper to buy. But the originality of the weaver's art becomes less meaningful as machine weavers mimic any pattern with fidelity.

The disruption of novel writing by the new technology will be another casualty as cheaper (read "free"), more efficient reading matter, with embedded video, images, music, interactive interfaces, and games, becomes the preferred way to tell and experience a story. This leaves novel writing and reading locked inside the enclave of senior citizens, in a kind of extended bingo night for old intellectuals who haven't shed their view that literature has intrinsic value.

Novelists will become a novelty from another time and place. Fiction authors will become curios like medieval scribes, whose devotion to writing a text, line by line, word by word, now seems strange, wasteful, and limited. We will join the ranks of the cave wall painters in France thirty thousand years ago. Or a few may follow Banksy's example and go into the street to find the metaphoric walls where provocative images become the medium to spread a message. The world as it is experienced and understood in terms of words is receding.

The next time you attend a reading or book signing, ask the person next to you why their children or grandchildren haven't come along. And also ask what books their offspring are reading? I'd like to hear the answers to those questions. Meanwhile, if in the new digital age competition for a publishing spot requires an author to meet the standards of beauty and youthfulness set by Gillian Flynn, 99% of writers are doomed. You will excuse me as I've spotted what looks like a windmill... Sancho, prepare my lance for that four-armed giant over there. And there's that unreachable star.

Beagle Sailing Lessons for Writing

I've been writing books for over thirty years. The other evening I explained several of my ideas about the writing process to two writers, one from the world of journalism and the other from the world of academia. This essay is for Gwen and Pavida, who asked me the question, how do you go about writing a book, and who encouraged me to put my thoughts down for other writers.

I believe all writers develop their own secret formula to describe the writing process that works for them. Mine is not that original or profound, but I will set out some of the guideposts that have served me well along the journey to writing a book. When I am asked how I go about writing a book, a closely related question that often follows is, what book on the subject would I recommend to others?

When we seek satisfactory answers to these questions, we need to address how a writer thinks about books and the writing process. We need to go deeper than the usual discussion about when an author writes, how many words he or she writes in a day, where inspiration comes from, what his or her office looks like, what time of day he or she writes, and so forth. These are the questions we are generally curious about and wish to ask an author. I will start instead with a question that I believe writers should always put to themselves: what kind of book should I write?

I start answering this question for myself, each time I write, by glancing up at two boxes on the Borges library shelf in my imagination. Each box contains an infinite number of pieces to an infinite puzzle. My first decision is which of the two boxes to take from the mental shelf and start to work.

The Fiction Box

In the first box the puzzle pieces require the author to assemble a number of complex relationships that grow and fall apart, set up conflict, ignite emotional reactions, detail involvements, and track the maturity and damage to characters who face hard decisions and life-changing choices. When I write a novel, the Fiction Box is the one I choose to pull down from the shelf, so I can start taking out the pieces and figuring out how the pattern connects.

Yes, there are novels of ideas where the characters' emotions are far in the background. This proves that the Fiction Box presents a range of possibilities. Because an intellectual novel can succeed doesn't undermine the basic premise that most novels succeed on an emotional plane, explaining the sources of our feelings, the depths of our fears and anxiety, and the tensions arising from relationships, family, schools, political systems, and religion. The author probes inside people's lives to examine their personalities and attitudes, their character and limitations, and their failures as well as their successes.

The Non-Fiction Box

The second box, the Non-Fiction Box, is also filled with infinite pieces of infinite puzzles. This is the box I open to write essays such as this one. When I open the Non-Fiction Box, my approach is to build logical arguments based on evidence, facts, and statistics. The idea is to persuade the reader that my interpretation of the evidence supports my argument, solution, or policy proposal. In this box there are few if any pieces that represent a character whose emotional reaction is central to the book.

Yes, there are highly polemical books charged with emotional calls urging others to join a cult, a political party, or a life-style. These are confirmation bias-based books that promise to confirm what you already believe to be "factually" true or consistent with your "faith," or the stories manufactured about history, culture, and language. The best non-fiction, in contrast, challenges the reader's preconceived assembly of facts and evidence and argues for a change of his or her views. The successful non-fiction book is deliberate, rational, and analytical, and emotions are seen, like a cognitive bias, as weakening a clear assessment of the evidence.

My personal role model, whether I choose the Fiction Box or the Non-Fiction Box, may come as a surprise to you. It is Charles Darwin. His *Origin of the Species*, published on November 24, 1859, not only changed science but also immediately raised a serious debate about religion and the existing social order. Darwin's creative process is instructive for any writer.

Darwin's journey resulted in a book that, over time, changed the way we perceive our world, though a significant minority remains to this date unconvinced by the evidence to support the theory of natural selection. Darwin in the 1830s signed on to an expedition of discovery. The *Beagle*, his ship, allowed him to explore the Earth with his lab in tow. Darwin went deep into the field, observing firsthand the evidence of the diversity of life. His theory of natural selection arose from the evidence that he gathered.

Every time I start a new book, I tell myself that I am signing on as a crew member to a new launching of the *Beagle*. My job while on the expedition is to observe, note, research beyond the shoreline, go deep into the interior, peering under rocks, down valleys, and up the sides of mountains, looking for patterns.

Thomas Piketty's *Capital in the Twenty-First Century* is an example of one such *Beagle* exploration. On that occasion computers and historical records combined to yield patterns of wealth and income that create a picture of the real world.

The Entanglements

What a writer is doing, whether conscious of the process or not, is finding patterns in objects, things, ideas, people, animals, language, history, and culture that are knotted up, entangled in seemingly random, chaotic ways. A writer's goal is to find patterns, correlations, and causations that give a sense of order to the mess of what is life. Quantum physics is a good place for a writer to explore the hidden reality of entanglements.

A writer needs to sign on to his own private *Beagle* and set sail. A writer needs to take time to observe, record, and search for connections. A writer needs passion because a book is a long voyage. Without a burning passion fired by curiosity, a sense of wonder, a withholding of judgment, and a love of research, the journey can become intolerable. You really must be honest how passionate you are about revealing in the entanglements a plausible story.

Ultimately what readers look for in a book is a voice that they can trust to take them beyond the complications, incoherence, and randomness of life. A charlatan earns trust through empty promises and sleight of hand; such writers never take a personal journey on the *Beagle*, though they may try to convince you that they have. Readers hunger for meaning and purpose, and a writer's task is to fulfill that desire.

Buddhism's Lessons for Writers

Buddhism offers several lessons that help me as a writer, and they may help you once you've decided to write a book. I am grateful to Professor John Paulos for drawing my attention to an interview with Jay Garfield, who discusses the key premises of Buddhism. All three lessons are stories about fear and how we deal with fear.

Non-attachment: A central theme of Buddhism is non-attachment. The writer may apply this idea to a theme, facts, emotions, a character, a plot point, a sentence, or every writer's personal base camp: the self. Many writers become frustrated and angry with a troublesome dialogue tag, setting, scene, or phrase and can't move on until they have resolved their internal conflict. My advice when you hit that impasse? Let it go. Don't get attached to your idea that this passage, sentence, or word must be perfect before you give yourself the green light to move through the intersection and continue your journey. The desire for perfection is a destroyer of creativity. When you are trying to be perfect as you write, ask yourself whom you are trying to please, the reader or just your own perfectionism?

You may think that your perfectionism is you. But most likely you've learnt the perfection habit from someone in your past. Perhaps your mother, a person who had her share of disappointments and frustrations (as many mothers have), wanted you to be perfect and to have a perfect life like the one she once imagined for herself. Or it might have been your demanding father, an uncle, a teacher, or a neighbor who passed along the idea, the one you've never allowed yourself to seriously challenge, that you must be careful, organized, perfect in every detail before you are allowed to take the next step.

When you write, you will sometimes reach a dead end. Don't panic. Find a new trail around the avalanche that has blocked the path ahead. Don't stop, in other words. Creativity is finding another path when the one you're on is closed. Fear is the roadblock that keeps you clutching onto something you can let fall away. Non-attachment is a way to defeat the fear of disappointment, regret, failure, or being less than perfect.

Unpredictability: Another important tenet of Buddhism is that reality is unpredictable and chaotic. We spend our entire lives trying to make sense of a reality that science increasingly shows makes no intrinsic sense. Most people hate and fear uncertainty and doubt, and seek refuge in illusions of certainty. The rest of us find our way by making correlations, even while knowing that the patterns we create aren't fixed or permanent. They are that temporary pontoon bridge that allows us to get from one side of a river to the next.

If your characters are too predictable, you will likely bore your readers. If they are too chaotic, readers will also abandon your book. The challenge is to build characters and stories that have real-life unpredictability, so that as your story navigates a road, a bridge, a passage in a boat or a life raft, your readers are confident that they are in good hands. Specifically this means you don't need to have a full solution to every problem. Not everything will turn out the way you thought, but then, the things that strike you as having turned out right might not last. The closer your fiction sticks to these rails of reality, the closer you will come to writing in an authentic voice that others will trust and learn from.

Predictability, like control, is an illusion. Let it go. Don't become attached to a world of certainty. Doubt is your friend, your ally, and keeps you researching, thinking, and feeling. When you feel yourself trying to be a hundred percent accurate in your choice of a word, a plot point, or a character development, you are guaranteed to get lost in one of those mental funhouses filled with mirrors.

Learn to accept ambiguity and uncertainty as the natural state of all things. This will free you up to see reality in a different way, knowing that sometimes not all the pieces of the puzzle fit. That is the paradox of the two puzzle boxes: the pieces are infinite in number, and you will never fit them all together.

Self: The last of the Buddhist lessons for a writer is the idea of identity or self. The fear of losing self is a hard one to overcome for any writer or any person. It goes to the core of how we perceive ourselves. Buddhists believe that our psychological construct of self is an illusion.

For a writer the concept of identity is the substitute for self. A writer's identity, like everyone else's, is shaped by many social forces ranging from tribe, ethnicity, and religion to place of origin and language. Our myths and memories are all rolled up into the default image we see in the mental mirror. This raises a couple of problems for writers. To write about others is to enter their network of memories and slowly reveal the factors that give them identity. As writers, if we can't get past our own identity, we can't ever truly describe an identity that is alien to us without becoming judgmental. We are also misled by our desire for a fixed, permanent self or soul. Our fear of death is on a deeper level tracks our anxiety that death erases all sense of our identity. We clutch onto our identity as if it is real and eternal and thought this might not be true makes us highly susceptible to the explanations found in religion and mysticism.

The act of writing requires an act of forgetting one's personal set of memories and substituting those of the characters. Once you are free from your self, it is much easier to enter the selves of your characters. Once you cast aside your self, your characters stop being clones of you—your thoughts, dreams, plans, fears, hopes, jealousies, and desires.

Once that happens, it is possible to create a rich, authentic character whose identity lets readers feel they are immersed in a story that has come alive. The author fades away. The author is the story-teller, not the story, and between those two positions lies a big gap. Especially for fiction, to find that sweet spot called empathy, where you enter another person's mental processes, means you need to shed your own self.

Our overwhelmingly powerful sense of self can contaminate our search to understand the interior lives of others—and without such access to the workings of a character's interior life, the characters in a novel will not be fully realized. Overcome your fear and let the self go. Detach from it. While you are writing, remember that this attachment will prevent you from exploring all you can on your *Beagle* journey into the unknown.

Darwin didn't set out on the *Beagle* to become a celebrity. He journeyed neither to write a book that would change the world nor a book about himself. He set out to explore, discover, record, and examine the world around him. His technique and process, in my view, are what make Darwin a good role model for all writers, fiction and non-fiction. Overcoming our sense of self is one of the most difficult projects we confront. Without the self, the question "Who am I?" rings as one of those trick existential questions. You can read others much better qualified than I am for a full range of opinion on this.

My point is that your sense of self is a prison you need to break out of to fully appreciate that the book doesn't have to be about you—that your sense of self may be the major obstacle to writing your book. If you are writing a book to find your sense of self or confirm your self in the world, then you will have a lot of company. There are many such books written every year. You can write one if you wish, and it might become a commercial success. With an infinite number of puzzle pieces and lots of time, all kinds of books are possible. For certain kinds of books, though, the best books, another approach is useful. The author must sign on to the *Beagle* and go exploring.

This is a look into my writing process. Other writers will have their recommendations concerning how the process works. I love the sense of the unknown and the adventure of exploration. I find an idea, a character, a theme for which I have a passion. Without passion to sustain you, it will be a long, lonely, and isolating voyage. Find a subject that you feel passionate about and then go sailing on your own personal *Beagle*.

Fictional Character Migration into the Digital World

"It's no use going back to yesterday, because I was a different person then." —Alice in Lewis Carroll's *Alice's Adventures in Wonderland*

Fictional characters, even the most memorable ones, are creatures of their place and time. Time is an inescapable aspect of character, giving it weight, dimension, and volume within a work of fiction, like a physical property. As real people are born, live their lives, and die, so it goes with their fictional counterparts. While the expiry date of literary fashion condemns most characters to the literary graveyard, a few manage to achieve a kind of immortality. This elite roll call of characters is handed on to future generations. But as election to this list is such a rare event, we should be asking how and why that happens at all. As Lewis Carroll implies in my epigraph above, people, like novels, are period pieces, who understand themselves in a way that has little relevance to their contemporary world, shaped as it is by complex and unseen forces that are in constant flux.

A cartoon I came across recently, showing adoring children at the foot of an old man, bore the caption, "Grandpa, tell us about the days when you had to buy the whole album even if you only wanted one song." As the cartoon suggests, an essential quality defining characters in a novel (as in life) is the way they are products of the technology of their time. Their technology has always shaped their view of the world and how they see themselves and others.

In vintage crime fiction the office of a private eye might contain a Remington typewriter, a hat and umbrella tree, a Bakelite rotary phone, and a couple of metal filing cabinets containing neat rows of paper folders. The private eye's secretary takes shorthand and then transcribes her boss's dictation as required. Investigations based in such offices take place in the analog world where people are watched and followed, sometimes leading to face-to-face meetings, confrontations, discussions, and arguments. We can read the classic fiction of Raymond Chandler and Dashiell Hammett with pleasure simply by imagining ourselves in a world of very different artifacts, mores, and above all, technology. This conceit works because inside that world everyone is working, living, stealing, killing, lying, and running on the same technical infrastructure. None of them have a significant technological advantage over others. It is then a combination of wits, shoe leather, discipline, and one or two lucky breaks that makes the difference in a private eye's fate.

I have described a world that predates the age of big data, computers, GPS systems, Google, Facebook, Twitter, tracking programs recording computer keystrokes and website searches, CCTV cameras, and computer forensic experts. This technology provides the context in which we now live, move, and die; it is how we perceive what is meaningful in our time. Let's take the example of a murder. If the police or a private eye of today were to discover a murder victim who had no email, Facebook, Twitter, YouTube, Pinterest, or Skype accounts, and who had no text messages or smart phone, and whose sole possessions were a black-and-white TV, a radio, and a cassette player, they might wonder if this person was a time traveler from decades past. Certainly it would seem odd; a character who chose in 2014 to divorce himself from the digital world would be a fish out of water. His murder would appear a little freakish to the new generation because he chose to find happiness in a life totally removed the digital world. That would seem incomprehensible to many young people.

It is easy for the older generation to devalue communication channels such as texting and tweeting. In an interview for the *Harvard Gazette* (May 6, 2014), Steven Pinker, Harvard psychology professor and author of many books including *How the Mind Works* and *The Better Angels of Our Nature*, has a good response to this tendency to criticize the new channels:

> ... I am wary of the 'young people suck' school of social criticism. I have no patience for the idea that because texting and tweeting force one to be brief, we're going to lose the ability to express ourselves in full sentences and paragraphs. This simply misunderstands the way that human language works. All of us command a variety of registers and speech styles, which we narrowcast to different forums. We speak differently to our loved ones than we do when we are lecturing... And so, too, we have a style that is appropriate for texting and instant messaging ...

What makes for a good character? He or she plays well across the narrow bands of class, education, and status. As readers we delight in following the lives of characters moving within fictional worlds that differ significantly from our own. Even within a world of primitive information and communication systems, strong characters and strong stories can (and will) allow a modern, plugged-in readers to enjoy the human aspect of the experience that makes the book's culture very different from theirs.

Readers now expect characters living now, however, to be affected and influenced by, and in reaction to, the things that happen in the digital world. The technological distance between 1974 and 2014 is only forty years, but in many ways the forces that shape lives have changed considerably over this brief period. Part of the fallout is that more people have vastly more information about each other. Meet someone new and want to find out who they are? In the analog world that might take a long time. Today we Google them and in a few minutes have a profile.

All of us have become private investigators with access to far more information than even totalitarian governments had at their disposal fifty years ago. The lives, possessions, and luxury life-styles of the top 0.1% are no longer secret. Inequality and the gap between those who own the system and those who work for it has created digital interest, with the online communities channeling statistics, reviewing books, and discussing causes, priorities, policies, and propaganda. A worldwide audience has created a conversation that goes on twenty-four hours a day and leaves its traces online for others to find later.

Our ideas about secrecy and privacy are shaped by the technological environment we live in. Are the old classics relevant to the new generation? And what about those who will live with even more advanced technology in the next fifty years? Will they enjoy Richard Stark's Parker novels like *The Score* or James Crumley's *The Last Good Kiss* or James M. Cain's *The Postman Always Rings Twice*?

Today Cain's title begs for a cartoon with a ten-year-old asking, "Was his email account down?" The issue isn't limited to crime fiction. The classic early '70s novel *Zen and the Art of Motorcycle Maintenance* by Robert M. Pirsig assumes a technological platform that has long since vanished. A son and father on a road trip, discussing the meaning of life, with no digital connection. For much of the novel there are just the two of them on the road and the stars above their heads at night. Hard to imagine, isn't it?

We are at a crossroads (some would argue we are always at a crossroads). There are those who read these novels, learn from them, share them with others, and increase their understanding of others (call this the empathy bonus). But there is no doubt that the characters in such books experience life in a quite different fashion from contemporary people.

We shop online. We socialize with one another over large distances, fall in love and out of love, feud, form alliances, vent anger and hate—all online, from the safety of our home, office, car, local Starbucks, or perhaps the Siam-Paragon shopping mall. Most young people spend as much time (if not substantially more) online as they do in their offline world. People hang out online the way they once did at the local pub. A character's personality, desires, motives, and goals are likely to be as much defined by his or her relationship with others online as in the analog world. We think we know others in the digital world, and they know us. But what do we really know about each other from our computer screen, iPad, or iPhone? Pinker might argue there are different styles of knowing. To some extent that is true. Even in the analog world, we all know some people much better than others.

But the medium of the new form of message, its style, is also a clue to its limitations. The digital world remains a substitute for face-to-face conversations. When you choose to rely solely on the digital medium you risk discounting the importance of the personal encounter and assume the high quality of digital information collecting and analysis is untainted by eliminating this human component. In the analog world you can see a person's facial expressions, their hands making a gesture, their posture as they sit, talk, stand, walk across a room, and their eyes during a moment of silence, when all kinds of information about mood, attention, veracity, and openness/resistance is revealed beyond the channels of formal language. Emoticons are a poor substitute. The judgments we make in the analog world are both more restrictive—what you see is all that you get—and more expansive—they include smells, sounds, bodily feelings, and tastes.

Many readers hunger for a reading experience that explores the technological impact on the lives of fictional characters. The popularity of the English TV series *Black Mirror* is an example of drama serving this need. A novel can recreate the risks, dangers, and opportunities such innovations bring, ones that disrupt like a knife blade cutting through skin and soft tissue, and ones that change the ways we think about ourselves and each other.

News feeds produce a huge volume of information about the global migration of people across geographical boundaries. The Rohingya flee Burma on old, unseaworthy boats to escape persecution and murder under the eye of local authorities. Africans escape hopeless conditions, again by boat, to look for economic opportunity in Europe. Poor Latin Americans flock across the border into America with the dream of a better life. Cambodians and Burmese come to Thailand for the same reason. We don't get a true sense of the proportions of such stories and problems in our cozy digital social networks. One justification for writing a novel is to make such people "real" and "tangible." How do such people fit into our hybrid analog–digitally divided lives? That's the question you should be asking a novelist.

The physical world continues to draw our attention, but when we read of these stories we rarely ask how much longer until the digital world distracts us completely from such analog things as the migration patterns of our species. As the locus of the real action moves into "hyperreality," blurring what is real along with what we are paying attention to, we may be losing our ability to distinguish physical migrations from digital ones.

We can easily make a list of our favorite analog world authors, where the technological perspective is pre-1982 (when IBM PC went to mass market). Crime writers like Raymond Chandler, Dashiell Hammett, Georges Simenon, James Crumley, Richard Stark, and many others who are still widely read, discussed, and admired fall into that category. The Bakelite phone generation, as a result of the scope and nature of their technology, have (to our modern eyes) severe limits on how they can find out things about other people, how they go about looking for information and where they do it, and what they do when they find what they are searching for. We see them as handicapped in a way that we are not.

The people in pre-1982 novels had no devices others than telephones to communicate with each other. Most of the interaction is face to face. How primitive, the new generation might be tempted to conclude. We expect a character from a contemporary author to mirror the reality of our times, and that expectation entails an accounting of the character's connections to the digital world. Readers presume they will find hybrid characters with a foot in each reality. In real life, these connections are essential to understanding people's identities. The separation of what they believe, know, or understand from the two worlds is blended in a way that can't be untangled. Person and device are blurred into one. The device augments, enhances the person, makes him or her feel smarter, more knowledgeable, capable, and in control. Like drugs or alcohol, in the digital world the information flow becomes an addictive river in which people wish to bathe for hours at a time. Such people start their morning and finish their day checking their timelines, email accounts, and browsing for the latest breaking news. People who have crawled deep into the digital world are readers looking for stories about how others have used this crawl space, their problems, ups and downs, and the way they handle relationships in the online and offline worlds.

The final chapter on the technological view of character remains as open-ended as technology itself. But at this point there seems to be no going back to the time of the classics, not in crime or any other literary fiction. Authors who wish to purchase a piece of future readers' fragmented attention will need a story that transcends time and technology. That's a tall order, and no one can say which stories will survive. Readers in different times have wanted the same experience: a literary mirror, a compass, a shield, and a sword to go forth and wage the battles in their daily life. They have also sought to understand the meaning of those battles, both the victories and the defeats.

Authors will need to adjust what their characters pay attention to and who pays attention to them. Those who ignore the evolution of human relationships and identity building will be writing about a lost past. It is true that there will always be a market for nostalgia and idealized fictional characters, just as there will be those who suffer from the delusion that such characters whose lives never touched the digital world are meaningful to the new generation of readers. Those of us who reached adulthood long before our world was rewired for broadband-width communication remember that earlier, off-the-grid, analog world we grew up in. We also know that this world is behind us. And the new generation of readers will expect what we expected: characters we could identify with, not characters that would judge us or look down on us and our way of life and values.

What will this new generation of readers expect from fiction authors? In my view we will enter fictional worlds where characters' emotional reactions, intentions, and preoccupations shift between analog and digital experience. Young readers will have many more people they call friends than prior generations. Most of these friends they will have never met outside a computer screen, but that won't lessen their feeling of connectedness and intimacy. Friendships in the analog world will have a different time scale and priority. Books will chart the connections between characters' lives in the two worlds. Technology disrupts not only jobs and industries, but also the nature of our identity. Authors, in the future, will discover ways to tell the stories of people whose identities are the products of information and communication linking two different realms of thought, experience, ideas, values, and relationships.

An Orwellian Look at Henry Miller

George Orwell's 1940 review of Henry Miller's *Tropic of Cancer* is worth revisiting for several reasons. Not the least of these is the critical lens that one novelist uses to examine, evaluate, and analyze another novelist's work. Reviews often reveal as much about the biases of the reviewer as they do about the book under review.

Orwell's review betrays biases about Miller's class (working class), nationality (American), art (failed, in Orwell's view), and politics (devoid of political context). Orwell's sensibilities were fashioned at Eton; Miller's, on the hardscrabble streets of Brooklyn. Orwell's sympathies were with the working class; Miller was *from* the working class, the American version. In the English world of 1940 the class distinction would have been a significant factor within the literary circles in which the Orwells of the world were expected to write meaningful books and the Millers and D.H. Lawrences were given a shovel and told to dig coal. It is important to remember the rigidity of the class divide and everything that flows from it whenever an Orwell reviews a Lawrence or a Miller.

Reading Orwell's review of Miller is at times painful when his class talons are involuntarily exposed. His review of *Tropic of Cancer* displays a conflict between the ideal of what the working class consciousness ought to be—politically attuned—and the reality of Miller's working-class absolute focus on the sensual, to the exclusion of the larger political framework.

Henry Miller and George Orwell broke free of the bonds of their culture and class by traveling and living abroad. In Orwell's case, fighting in a foreign war (the Spanish Civil War) showed a commitment to overcoming the walls of class and upbringing and revealed how very hard a road that is to travel. Orwell sought a literary life devoted to repudiating the chains of his class, but in his review of Miller it is apparent that those chains were never fully severed.

Orwell wrote *Down and Out in Paris and London* in the place where Miller set *The Tropic of Cancer*. Both books are intensely autobiographical. Orwell may have had a proprietary feeling about his Paris. This is a kind of old-hand attitude that one finds in many places, including Bangkok, where the old days were always better, more alive, more interesting and stimulating. Orwell couldn't quite figure out why Miller would bother with Paris after the golden age of the late 1920s, when "there were as many as 30,000 painters in Paris, most of them impostors." Paris was swamped with "artists, writers, students, dilettanti, sight-seers, debauchees, and plain idlers as the world has probably never seen." Orwell didn't live long enough to see a similar accumulation of people in Bangkok in the late 1980s and early 1990s. For Orwell the Paris scene that was populated by the expats of the 1920s had vanished by the time Miller arrived to find "bug-ridden rooms in working-men's hotels, ... fights, drinking bouts, cheap brothels, Russian refugees, cadging, swindling and temporary jobs."

Orwell, an old Paris hand, felt that 1930s Paris had less promising material for a novelist. Actually, this idea comes across more forcefully; he thought Paris was a waste of time, a distraction in the larger European theatre, a spent force where nothing of interest would emerge. By comparison, in Orwell's view there was vastly more interesting material to be mined in Rome, Moscow, and Berlin as Hitler and Stalin worked the military and political levers pushing toward war. The fact is, by the time of this review Orwell had the advantage of hindsight. Miller was writing in Paris in the 1930s, before the war started. To strike Miller with a cross-over punch to the jaw for not anticipating the future outcome is an easy shot because the fist is coming from an arm originating in 1940.

To ignore the European political developments, to Orwell's mind you would have to be "either a footler or a plain idiot." (Note: A footler is someone who wastes time or talks nonsense.) Orwell chose not to state which of those categories the author of *Tropic of Cancer* fell into. But it was plain to Orwell that Miller's literary credibility was on the line—or, more graphically, Orwell was driving a stake through the heart of a minor monster that no one should take seriously. He wanted to grab Miller by the throat and shout in his face, "You fool, what about Hitler? Concentration camps? Forget about bonking and look at what is happening around you as the forces of history are building to send you and the rest of the working class back to the battlefield!"

While Orwell came to the brink, he then blinked and chose to sidestep the absence of political context and the fact that Paris had become a backwater. Despite a silver literary stake driven through Miller's heart, Orwell concluded that Miller's novel was "a very remarkable book." That is a significant observation given Orwell's doubt about the value of a novel "written about American dead-beats cadging drinks in the Latin Quarter."

What brought Orwell around, despite his obvious reservations about Miller's complete lack of interest in the dark political clouds forming over Europe at the time the story, was that Miller was genuine working class. As much as Orwell fought for and wrote about the working class, he was never a member of it himself. Orwell was as much an outsider to the working class as Miller was to the French in Paris, and for comparable reasons: attitude, education, and sensibility.

What saved *Tropic of Cancer* for Orwell and made it linger in his memory was that Miller was about to "create a world of their own," not based on the strange but the familiar. Miller's genius lay in letting readers know that they were being understood. Miller's reader might say, "He knows all about me. He wrote this specially for me." There is no humbug, moralizing, trying to persuade you to understand his perspective or values. What Orwell valued was that Miller dispensed with the usual lies and simplifications and instead wrote about "recognizable experiences of human beings." Miller gave readers the feeling that the things he was writing about were happening to them.

The nature of the experience chosen by a writer mattered a great deal to Orwell. It is interesting that Orwell, who was born in India and was a colonial official in Burma (and whose first novel was *Burmese Days*), should take a negative view of expatriate life and the role of authors writing about such lives. He noted that Miller's book wasn't about "people working, marrying and bringing up children" but about people who lived and survived by their wits on the street, in cafés, brothels, and studios. Orwell believed that expatriate writers transferred their "roots into shallower soil" as a result of concentrating on these experiences.

I suspect that what the Eton-educated Orwell secretly loved about *Tropic of Cancer* was what he must have seen as Miller's interest in bringing what was common in the real life of ordinary people, with all of its callous coarseness, out into the open. Privately, he must have envied Miller's class credentials. Orwell might have lived down and out in Paris, but his self-imposed suffering could never have made him a member of the working class. Orwell fought alongside the working class in the streets of Barcelona. Henry Miller drank and fornicated in the Latin Quarter. *Tropic of Cancer* made it clear that it was one thing to make an intellectual commitment to the working class, to argue their cause, and to fight their battles, but quite another to become an authentic spokesman of their emotions and desires.

Miller laid open working-class lives through their spoken language. As Orwell wrote, "Miller is simply a hard-boiled person talking about life, an ordinary American businessman with intellectual courage and a gift for words." There is no protest about the horror and meaninglessness of contemporary life. In its place Miller wrote a book about someone whose life circumstances should have made him miserable but instead made him extremely happy. Such an epiphany must have been a slap in the face for someone committed to the struggles of the working class.

In contrast Orwell thought James Joyce was an artist who turned ordinary working-class life into art. Miller was the tabloid writer who entered the mind of the ordinary person and brought his words to the ears of those who had marched on the playing fields of Eton, bypassing the usual filters that censored language and thought.

What separated the two men transcends class, nationality, and politics. It comes down to Orwell's view of a writer, regardless of time and place, which is to resist fear, tyranny, and regimentation. When Orwell looked into *Tropic of Cancer*, what horrified him wasn't the language or the whoring, it was Miller's acceptance of "concentration camps, rubber truncheons" as well as Hitler, Stalin, machine guns, putsches, purges, gas masks, spies, provocateurs, censorship, secret prisons, and political murders. From Orwell's perspective, for a serious writer to "accept civilization as it is practically means accepting decay." Orwell makes the case that Miller's point of view was passive; in effect he lay down and with a sense of resignation let things happen to him.

On reflection, who are the characters in *Tropic of Cancer*? They aren't the ordinary factory worker or family in the suburb, but "the derelict, the déclassé, the adventurer, the American intellectual without roots and without money." And what saves *Tropic of Cancer* and gives it value is isolated by Orwell to one crucial factor: Miller "had the courage to identify with it," as he was part of this group. He didn't look down on them, didn't try to explain or justify. He reported their lives, troubles, loves, and sensual preoccupation.

Orwell was a political writer who used the form of the novel to great effect in *1984* and *Animal Farm*. He would hardly be the reader of choice for a novel preoccupied with sex among American expats in 1930s Paris. For him the sensual man was out of fashion, it was the time for the political man to take a stand on principle. Miller's *Tropic of Cancer* accepts that the world, with its endless cycles of violence, greed, aggression, inequality, and injustice, is largely unchangeable, and that the best shot anyone has for happiness is through an escape from the constraints of the madness and limitations of one's own culture to explore real emotions. Both Orwell and Miller lived in a world that was pre-global, by our standards. Literature was identified with the writer's nationality and class. This is less true in our time. To read Orwell's essay on Henry Miller is to see how far we have traveled since 1940 in terms of what readers expect of authors, and what authors expect from each other.

Miller, an American, was an escape artist, a hustler, and sensualist. Orwell, an Englishman, was a Barcelona street fighter and British colonial official. The divide between the two men could hardly have been greater in terms of personality, education, temperament, and philosophy. The gap between Eton and the working class slums of Brooklyn was (and is) huge. For all of those differences, though, Orwell saw why Miller had attracted readers—he brought them into his story, never talked down to them, and made them feel they should step inside and join him on a grand odyssey through the sensual world. His story was recognizable and real and spoke directly to their own lives.

That part of Orwell's review is as true today as it was in 1940. The social, economic, and political distance between these two types of consciousness may be even greater today. Few novelists of our time have taken up the cause of the working-class struggle. That orientation fell with the Berlin Wall, and in place of a wall there is now a growing inequality, repression, and acceptance. At the moment it seems that Miller may have won. What is important to remember is that Orwell took Miller seriously even though he was critical of Miller's failure to take a political stand on behalf of the working class. In the modern world, writers situated along this Orwell-Miller axis are receding from each other like galaxies traveling at the speed of light. They no longer review each other. They have lost contact with visions that don't mirror their own. Retreating into their coconut shells each frog hears his or her own echo. As recently reported in the *New York Times,* novelists are no longer critically reviewing each other's books. The competition for money, academic position, and literary prizes has silenced a generation of novelists, who are now too afraid and timid to speak truth, not just to authority but to each other.

Kafka the Grand Master of Noir:
A Lesson for Thailand

The *New Stateman* ran an article two weeks ago (January 16, 2014) titled "Death by Data: How Kafka's *The Trial* Prefigured the Nightmare of the Modern Surveillance State" by Kafka biographer Reiner Stach. While the familiar rallying cry against government oppression is drawn from George Orwell's *1984* or *Animal Farm* or Aldous Huxley's *Brave New World*, it is Kafka with *The Trial* who might best lay literary claim to being godfather to the modern noir fiction movement. Stach reminds us that while we don't particularly like Josef K, the doomed protagonist in *The Trial*, we can't stop ourselves from following him on his downward spiral to oblivion.

Josef K is you. He's me. He's done something along the way. What that something is remains vague, like a fog that obscures and terrifies. It is that foreboding, that sense of the gravity of terror pulling one headlong into a dystopia, that is the heart of noir fiction. Josef K is a victim. But when that victimhood is traced back to the source, Stach concludes that the victim can find the tormentor by looking into the mirror. In other words, without our personal complicity with the surveillance state, we wouldn't become its victims.

We are partners in our own victimhood. We work alongside the surveillance state, feeding it our most private thoughts, fears, and desires and confessing our transgressions. We do this in public. We post our confessions daily. No need to go to church to find a priest; our surveillance overlords are our new confessors, and they find us. We know this is happening and we do nothing to stop it. Not only do we do nothing, but we can't stop ourselves from exposing the details of our life.

This passage from Stach's article struck me as relevant to understanding something about the current political turmoil in Thailand:

> Kafka was deeply sceptical of the therapeutic promises of psychoanalysis but he was captivated by the way it described the propagation of power, which chimed with his own experiences. Someone who keeps getting told that he is incapable, inferior or guilt-ridden will have to expend a good deal of energy to resist such a self-image and not make himself guilty in his own eyes. He has to struggle not because the forces of power have violated or diminished him but rather because he has been infiltrated by those forces. The poison lodges in his own body.

The elites and their supporters in the streets of Bangkok are a minority who have pushed back against mass political power. They want to suspend elections. They view representative democracy as the enemy. To delegitimize the governing party, they demonize and belittle the common, ordinary upcountry voters who have consistently elected to parliament a political force that fails to preserve and advance their interests. They refer to the ordinary voters from the North and Northeast as uneducated, stupid, easily bought, and misguided, implying their votes ought to count less as a result. They wish to shut down Bangkok, throw out the election and the prime minister, and seize her assets.

In the last twenty-five years, the ordinary non-urban voter has carried this baggage. And everywhere he or she looks, from TV dramas, movies, and novels to magazines, newspapers, and TV news, this negative image acts to diminish and belittle. It infiltrates the mind and heart. The effect is to blunt a movement to expand civil and political rights. The mind of the diminished person, like that of Josef K, feels under constant pressure, watched and excluded, an object of suspicion.

With a broad-based message from the media, schoolrooms, the better educated, and politicians, people aren't just influenced; the operating system of their consciousness is built upon unquestioned beliefs. It is difficult to reset the mental operating system of a mass of people who are marginalized. For example, most Americans don't believe that their government's storing of metadata from their phone calls and email accounts is a problem. They have, they say, nothing to hide. Neither did Josef K. That's the way it starts: believing one is innocent—as if that will be sufficient when the shadow of authority falls over one's path. The reality is that the politicians are merely the edifice of an invisible civil service that expands ever more into the private sector, merging bureaucratic procedures in a seamless web.

Like a fly Josef K fell into an invisible web, long before there was a World Wide Web. It is what makes *The Trial* relevant and undated. We experience a personal fascination with the fly that hits the web, sticks to it, struggles, protests, and slowly resigns himself to his fate. In the end he blames himself and not the web. That is the irony of the dystopia he lives within, where the structure of the web is such that no one is responsible.

One morning people wake up and find that they are caught in the web. They panic. Who can they turn to? There is no hotline to phone for rescue. There is no possibility of escape. There are no courts or other institutions that remain impartial and work to restrain power; instead they have come to represent aspects of absolute power. Evidence is always insufficient to bring one of the overlords to justice. There is no justice. And in *The Trial*, no one hears Josef K's cry for help. His protests of innocence have no meaning once he is caught in the web. He's there because he put himself there. He's a victim, and he's to be blamed for being a victim.

The vast majority of Thai people in Bangkok and the countryside alike continue to believe in elections as the solution. Would representative democracy have saved Josef K? The answer to that question is the big issue of our time. Not just in Thailand, but elsewhere, there is evidence of growing discontent within the wide spectrum that ranges from dictatorship to democracy. The belief in government as a protector of personal safety and welfare has collapsed. The rich withdraw into gated communities with private security forces, placing their children in private schools and their wealth in offshore banks. The poor are left to fend for themselves on the scraps.

What is left is escape. Hit the road. Unplug from the grid. That is easier said than done. The hope of escaping from the grid—that is, steering clear of the web—has a few people making a run for it. They won't get far. The surveillance system will grow until ultimately there will be no place to escape to. At that point we will all be guilty of something. We will wait to plead our innocence, and we will rail against the injustice of it all, as does Josef K. But when Joseph K's end comes, he longer objects, no longer chooses to protest his innocence. He condemns himself. He is both victim and executioner. The state remains hidden, faceless, without responsibility. They no longer need to pull the trigger.

Today, similar forces have infiltrated our consciousness, installing an operating system that works on automatic pilot. Once it is in place, we are programmed to carry out their dirty work on ourselves. It's how the new governing system has been designed to work. What has changed from Josef K's time is the role of technology in making the state's goal of infiltration vastly more efficient. We file daily status reports on ourselves through social media. We are our own parole officers. It works because it all appears so benign and friendly. All these digital communities ask of you is to "like" them and to feel mistrust and guilt that you have private thoughts and feelings that they may not like. Those "likes" are harvested, stored, analyzed, and cross-referenced.

That's enough big data to clone a population who process patterns much as Josef K did. The police state broke George Winston inside Room 101, but Josef K needed no Room 101. He broke himself.

Man with a Scarf

The legacy of artists depends on their enduring ability to make succeeding generations pay attention to nature, humanity, beauty, and the dark, dangerous shadows that surround life. They make us notice things about ourselves by framing them in a universal way. Mozart, Bach, Sibelius, Shakespeare, Goya, Titian, Rembrandt, El Greco, Lucian Freud (you weren't expecting that one), Wagner, Dante, Chaucer, Dickens... the list of great artists is the length of Borges's Library of Babel.

Lucian Freud, a grandson of Sigmund Freud, was along with Francis Bacon one of the most important painters in England over the past hundred years. Both artists specialized in portraits. They observed people and painted what they saw in others. Some say they painted images of themselves reflected in others. What of those who sat for these paintings? These patient sitters, most of whom no one will remember, spent many hours in the effort. What is their story of being observed? What of their observations of the painter observing them?

Think of these painters as emergency room doctors who took the pulse of their time. Blood, bone, and flesh are preserved inside these artistic works. They embody a range of states of health and disease. They create an illusion of immortality.

In his brilliant memoir *Man with a Blue Scarf: On Sitting for a Portrait by Lucian Freud* (2014), Martin Gayford, who sat for a period of one and a half years for a portrait painted by Lucian Freud, reminds us that in 1800 there were a billion people on the planet. Each and every one one of them is now dead. Not a single survivor walks amongst us. Considering the names on my list above to discover the ethics, morality, and temperament of those we will never meet, it seems to me that our passions and emotions are no different. What moves us to tears and laughter may have changed (though *As You Like It* still makes us laugh), but the reality of tears and laughter is unaltered.

These artists have taught us how to look, what to look for, and which patterns bring understanding, joy, hope, terror, hate, anger, and despair. Mostly we don't consult this list. We dart in and out of their worlds much as we clean our teeth, and shortly thereafter we are greedily on to our next meal. But artists like these have thrown out a life preserver to someone in the middle of a sea with no horizon but the sky on all sides. We are that dot floating, waiting for rescue. In the world of noir, that rescue never arrives. We are abandoned inside our lives to a struggle to keep our heads above water. We seek not truth but allies, those who experience life as we do, and share with them a common emotional reaction to life, experience, others, and meaning.

Our looking is an experience of bias management. Like wanderers across a saltwater sea, we search for water to drink. We reject any idea that such a search is futile or that we are going about it the wrong way. Our group feels its way toward the shared goal. Nothing can persuade us that we are deluded or looking in the wrong place.

We are prisoners of these biases. No one escapes them. They are our black hole. The pull of their gravity is far stronger than reason. What we see is all there is. What we want is confirmation of what we believe and feel. Contrary evidence is misinterpreted so we can maintain our illusions. We all claim to be truth seekers. What we seek is the truth that makes us comfortable with what we believe to be true. We can't accept there might be a contradiction. Cognitive dissonance makes us angry and dangerous. Our cure is to back into our corner with our community and turn up the sounds and sights of what we know in our hearts to be right, truthful, honorable, and fair.

Our tragedy is we fail to train ourselves to pay attention to the fine details around us. We gain our identity, our selves, our information from instruments and machines, not from nature or each other. That separates us from our ancestors, their lives, burdens, and social life.

It takes endurance to pay attention, and to seek clarity and definition in what we are attending to. If there is a single reason why I continue to write books and essays, it is to continue on a journey of exploration of what is in front of me, and to express and enjoy the expression of others in words, pictures, and music of what is found along the way as we stop to take in life. Those who lived before our birth continue to dwell in our time through art. These "sitters" share our space along the river of time. We look over our shoulder and let them inside our minds. We try to see through their eyes. We seek a glimpse of ourselves in their faces. Mostly, though, I fear we suffer an illusion that we navigate on our own, that we captain our own boat, without much thought for those who lived before us.

It takes a large portion of our psychological resources to pay attention. Basically we are lazy. Putting on filters and recharging our biases is our lazy way of idling through life. We crave excitement but fear adventure and take no real risk. When we are exposed to risk, our adrenaline rush is soon over, and we lose interest quickly. We move on like junkies looking for a new fix. What all great artists teach is the discipline to keep paying attention to those small details most of us no longer see, and to keep up that concentration for weeks, months, and years. Great art results when the artist channels his or her attention over time and emerges with an artifact that makes us feel larger than ourselves, expansive and connected.

We avoid disorder, chaos, ambiguity, and uncertainty. These things are unsettling and frightening. The great art doesn't pander to this fear. Instead such art animates and discloses how our current of charged feelings passes through this invisible, unstable field. We need an artist's angle to view our own passage through life. Paintings, music, and literary texts provide psychic maps to master new landscapes of the world inside and outside us. If we allow them in, we find that they've created a bridge between our everyday "us" and the objects that surround us. We are in harmony with those objects, and those others, people and animals, when we understand the nature and scope of our connection.

Here's what Lucian Freud had to say about a visit to the Toulouse-Lautrec museum in Albi:

> It is was very interesting, very exciting. That marvelous subject of the whores sitting round a circular pouf, when you look at it you realize that the one thing he couldn't do was people together. To me, the most touching Lautrec in the museum is the one of the two girls, both whores, in a bed; you just see their heads. It's so moving. They've finally finished their work and there they are; because they actually like each other.

Toulouse-Lautrec captured the most human of all moments: mutual liking of two people, and in a setting that is commercial and not thought of as a place where people like each other. It's a fleeting moment, and it reminds us that liking, love, pain, hate, and anger are constantly shifting into and out of our lives. None of these things are stable; just the opposite, they are in constant flux. Five minutes later the two "whores" could have been at each other's throats, but that is not the moment in the painting. We choose our moments like artists. What to record, what to remember, and what to ignore. The two women in the Toulouse-Lautrec painting showed their liking. In our time they would click the "like" button on Facebook.

Gayford's lesson in sitting for Lucian Freud is that we are different every day, even every hour of every day. Our moods, the facets of our temperament, and our interests fade in and out, cancelling one another, and that leaves us with the sinking feeling of unreality. It is not possible for the artist to capture the "real" you because that person is in constant transition. Underneath the mask we wear is someone who is in flux. The idea of "persona" from the Greeks was a reference to our masks. These are the masks we put on at home, at school, at the office, inside a car, or at a restaurant—or on Skype video calls. We have a certain face for the camera and another for looking in the mirror, and others for displaying to our loved ones and to strangers.

Underneath the face all is changing moment to moment. We look at paintings, listen to music, and read books to find out what lies beneath the mask, to embrace it, to recoil from it, to recognize it inside us. It is the part of our psychology hidden from our own view. Gayford shows us how Lucian Freud, like his famous grandfather Sigmund Freud, was in the business of reading the person hidden behind the mask.

He waited until the sitter (like the patient) involuntarily revealed himself or herself. It was a process that might take hundreds of hours. Lucian Freud was a psychologist who diagnosed using paint, recording his patients' moods found deep inside their faces, much as a psychoanalyst would do through notes of each session.

All portrait artists pretty much do the same thing, treating their subjects as palimpsests to be decoded. They blend observation, memory, emotion, and imagination, and then find the right colors and shades and tones of paint to recreate these layers on a flat surface. A writer or composer does something very similar with words or musical notes. Artists see a wide range of possibilities that most of us overlook in the hurry of the day.

Gayford reminds us that we have twenty-two muscles on either side of our mouth. The muscles are attached to our skin as well as to bone. They can move like a forty-four-instrument orchestra, and the number of musical pieces that can be played is huge. Douglas Adams was off by two digits; forty-two was the number that the supercomputer called Deep Thought, in *The Hitchhiker's Guide to the Galaxy*, gave as "the answer to the Ultimate Question of Life, the Universe, and Everything." There is a near infinity of possibilities in the human face, body, attitude, mood, and disposition, and like clouds passing by overhead, none of it stable for very long. How to express the depth of that range? That's always been the unanswered question. No one knows. The answer may well lie in observation of the human face.

I also recommend Alan Lightman's *The Accidental Universe*. Lightman is an interesting author as he holds a dual position at MIT in humanities and physics, and is a novelist as well. He lives on both sides of C.P. Snow's "two cultures." Scientists and non-scientists in the humanities have long sought to understand each other's languages and premises and to establish a line of communication. This has been a divide as large as any political divide. Near the end of Lightman's book he writes about how electromagnetic fields exist across a broad spectrum and how the light we perceive represents only a very narrow range of it. We know these other ranges not from our sensory system but through our instruments. Unplug the instruments, study these elusive fields a thousand hours, and you will still see nothing. They could never be painted, like the infinite positions of the forty-four muscles around the mouth. The physicist in Lightman notes that at the upper range of the electromagnetic field there are more than 10 trillion frequencies, and in the lower ranges an excess of 100 trillion. Those are numbers beyond our imagining.

Art is carried inside our sensory range. It is what we share as we pass through time and the electromagnetic fields pass through us. Lightman leaves open the possibility of mortality as a state of perception experienced along a narrow band nestled in an infinity of possibilities that preceded and will succeed our brief experience inside the human band range. It is a comforting speculation, but it's not provable. It's a belief. So the debate will never end.

Meanwhile, Martin Gayford has left us with a testament to Lucian Freud's artistic temperament and way of being, which created portraits of the many layers within each of us. They will be studied for their expression of the range of emotions and moods and vulnerabilities a face can hold so as long as there are people to care.

Lucian Freud had a burning need to closely observe, to understand what he observed, to find paints to explore the range of observations. As Gayford concludes, though, he wasn't a man given to introspection. What an observation meant in the larger scheme of things didn't interest him that much. He lost himself in an observer's world where he was in control.

At the end of the book, Lucian Freud's own words make for a perfect closing, a way of making the debate largely irrelevant:

> The notion of the afterlife is much the same, giving people the idea that this life—your actual life—is just an hors d'oeuvre in comparison with what comes later. As far as I'm concerned, the whole idea is utterly ghastly. I'm not frightened in the slightest of death; I've had a lovely time.

This may be the most lasting of legacies, the final obit when wishing to remember a departed loved one or dear friend: "He had a lovely time."

If you observe long enough, closely enough, Lucian Freud's life suggests you will find your own key to Number 44. Time passes on this search, but the searcher lets it go without regret, knowing that the full of richness of life comes from observing the fine details. There lies enduring satisfaction. It's enough. Enough at least for a lovely time.

THE CULTURAL DETECTIVE

Heaven Lake Press (2011) ISBN 978-616-90393-8-9

For more than twenty years, Christopher G. Moore has been writing about the history, culture and politics of Southeast Asia, in particular Thailand. *The Cultural Detective* is a behind-the-scene view into Moore's writing life.

In this selection of essays, Moore discusses with the humor and insight that he has become famous for. He draws widely on anthropology, neurology, psychology, ethnography, history and recent political conflicts.

Readers new to Moore's work will find an entertaining and discerning author worth getting to know better, while fans will recognize an echo of his essayist's voice and perspective from his novels.

"It is perhaps a judge of excellence that I would pull down one book from the shelves, read it again, and thoroughly enjoy it once more? If so, then *The Cultural Detective* by Christopher G. Moore is an excellent book. Not only a good book, but for me, the best book reviewed in 2011."
—*Pattaya Mail*

FAKING IT IN BANGKOK

Heaven Lake Press (2012) ISBN 978-616-7503-13-4

The Cultural Detective established Christopher G. Moore as a writer whose essays deliver a unique perspective insight into Thai culture and contemporary political and social issues. In *Faking It in Bangkok* gangsters, gamblers, killers and other criminals are brought to life in the essays. Readers who follow Moore's crime novels will enjoy his detours through the hard-edged noir world of Thailand with whistle stops on the digital age express. Moore's signature irony and humor riffs are also not to be missed as he explores an eclectic range of subjects, from ghosts and fortunetellers to the de facto tribal seating on the BTS.

"Moore is a keen observer of 'Thai-ness.' His insights are offered in an entertaining and cheeky manner.... The truths he reveals are at times comical, endearing and cringe-worthy, but they all show a side of Thai society worth examining.... He shows a love and appreciation for a society that has its flaws and virtues."—Voranai Vanijka, *Bangkok Post*

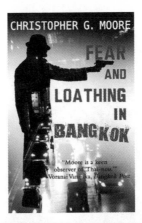

FEAR AND LOATHING IN BANGKOK
Heaven Lake Press (2013) ISBN 978-616-7503-24-0

TV images and news reports of demonstrations, deaths, demands and chaos in Thailand make Moore's essays in *Fear and Loathing in Bangkok* a timely book. These are essays to read at this vital crossroads in Thai political development. The essays will deepen your understanding of what makes Thailand a special and unique country.

In an age of anger and fear, the culture of non-confrontation and smiles is going through a rocky ride. These essays take you along the bumpy road of ghosts, criminals, illegal migrants, and false prophets. The essays on crime fiction and on writing explore noir, chance, muses, and ideas—the ingredients of Moore's successful Vincent Calvino crime novel series.

"I find the essays either make me think, have me nodding in full agreement or just totally entertained. To be quite honest it's often all three of these things. Crime and superb muses and ideas." —*The Life Design Detective*

RalfTooten © 2012

Christopher G. Moore is a Canadian novelist and essayist who lives in Bangkok. He has written 25 novels, including the award-winning Vincent Calvino series and the Land of Smiles Trilogy. The German edition of his third Vincent Calvino novel, *Zero Hour in Phnom Penh*, won the German Critics Award (Deutsche Krimi Preis) for International Crime Fiction in 2004 and the Spanish edition of the same novel won the Premier Special Director's Book Award Semana Negra (Spain) in 2007. The second Calvino novel, *Asia Hand,* won the Shamus Award for Best Original Paperback in 2011. The previous collections of his essays are *The Cultural Detective, Faking It in Bangkok* and *Fear and Loathing in Bangkok.* For more information about his books, visit his website: www.cgmoore.com.